MODERNISM, MEMOR
T. S. ELIOT AND VIR

T. S. Eliot and Virginia Woolf were almost exact contemporaries, readers and critics of each other's work, and friends for over twenty years. Their writings, though, have never been paired in a book-length study. *Modernism, Memory, and Desire* proposes that some striking correspondences exist in Eliot and Woolf's poetic, fictional, critical, and autobiographical texts, particularly in their recurring turn to the language of the body, desire, and sensuality to render memory's processes. The book includes extensive archival research on some mostly unknown bawdy poetry by T. S. Eliot while offering new readings of major work by both writers, including *The Waste Land*, "The Love Song of J. Alfred Prufrock," *Orlando*, and *To the Lighthouse.* McIntire juxtaposes Eliot and Woolf with several major modernist thinkers of memory, including Sigmund Freud, Friedrich Nietzsche, Henri Bergson, and Walter Benjamin, to offer compelling reconsiderations of the relation between textuality, remembrance, and the body in modernist literature.

GABRIELLE MCINTIRE is Assistant Professor of English at Queen's University, Kingston, Ontario.

MODERNISM, MEMORY, AND DESIRE: T. S. ELIOT AND VIRGINIA WOOLF

GABRIELLE McINTIRE

CAMBRIDGE
UNIVERSITY PRESS

CAMBRIDGE UNIVERSITY PRESS
Cambridge, New York, Melbourne, Madrid, Cape Town, Singapore,
São Paulo, Delhi, Dubai, Tokyo, Mexico City

Cambridge University Press
The Edinburgh Building, Cambridge CB2 8RU, UK

Published in the United States of America by Cambridge University Press, New York

www.cambridge.org
Information on this title: www.cambridge.org/9780521178464

First published 2008
Third printing 2009
First paperback edition 2010

A catalogue record for this publication is available from the British Library

Library of Congress Cataloguing in Publication Data

McIntire, Gabrielle.
Modernism, memory, and desire: T. S. Eliot and Virginia Woolf / Gabrielle McIntire.
p. cm.
ISBN 978 0 521 87785 5 (hardback)
1. Eliot, T. S. (Thomas Stearns), 1888–1965 – Criticism and interpretation. 2. Woolf, Virginia, 1882–1941 – Criticism and interpretation. 3. Memory in literature. 4. Desire in literature. 5. Modernism (Literature) I. Title.

PS3509.L43Z7835 2007
821.912 – dc22

ISBN 978-0-521-87785-5 Hardback
ISBN 978-0-521-17846-4 Paperback

For Mary Carolyn and Harley

Contents

Illustration

Acknowledgments

Book making is a solitary project, but one supported at each instance of its private labor by a community whose presence is felt everywhere in its pages. In a sense, my ideal community sits perched around the generation of this book. I want to thank first of all the people who have been my teachers. They have given me a gift beyond what these words can acknowledge, and have made the task of thinking *joy*: Molly Hite, Jonathan Culler, Ellis Hanson, Eric Domville, Daniel Schwarz, Linda Hutcheon, and Hortense Spillers.

Six weeks spent at Cornell's School of Criticism and Theory in the summer of 2006 prepared me for the final revisions of the text by all at once sharpening, quickening, and intensifying my lenses for reading. I am especially indebted to Dominick LaCapra for being the condition of possibility for the session, Geoffrey Hartman for his inspirational words on Blake and poetry, Ella Shohat and Robert Stam for graciously allowing me to quote from one of their lectures, and Eric Santner for attuning me to a whole new way of seeing.

In Kingston I am deeply grateful to the students and colleagues in the Department of English who make it a delight every day to be in that environment of gentle intellectual reciprocity. I want to single out especially Pat Rae, Chris Fanning, Elizabeth Hanson, Chris Bongie, Maggie Berg, and George Logan. Just down the road, a number of colleagues at the University of Toronto have also made my return to Canada especially fine, including Paul Stevens, Lynne Magnusson, Michael Cobb, and Melba Cuddy-Keane.

Eduardo Cadava has given me the gift of his mentorship and friendship for many years, and I remain profoundly moved by his example. A number of other friends and family members, often in far-flung places, have also been a part of the life-breath of this project, helping along its writing in ways they may not even realize: Tibra Ali, Anna Parkinson, Fiona Griffiths, Greg Stork, Sarah Copland, Ewa Badowska,

Stephen Clarkson, Eoin Finn, Daniel Brayton, Heather Levy, Adam Moldenhauer, Alixe Buckerfield de la Roche, Arlene McDonald, David Markus, Yehudi Lindeman, Claire Boudet, Craig Walker, Donato Santeramo, John Sutton, Rahul Sapra, and Curtis Bashaw.

This book involved significant archival research, and I am obliged to the Social Sciences and Humanities Research Council of Canada and the Principal's Advisory Fund at Queen's University for generous funding that supported the endeavor. Andrew Graham and John Jones facilitated a wonderfully productive stay at Balliol College, Oxford, and John Fraser, Elizabeth MacCallum, and Geraldine Sharpe made possible my time at Massey College in the Fall of 2006, where I completed the manuscript. The librarians at the British Library, the University of Sussex, Colindale Library, the University of Leeds, Cambridge University, Oxford University, Yale University, the Bibliothèque Nationale, and the Archives Nationale, were always patient and accommodating as I searched amidst their archives, and for this I am very appreciative. My thanks also go to Ray Ryan at Cambridge for seeing the worth of the project before it was fully elaborated, and to three anonymous readers for their thoughtful and rigorous engagements with the text. Nicole Bobbette and Tim Conley also gave very helpful criticism at various stages of the editing process. Cassandra Laity and Lawrence Rainey have kindly permitted me to include a version of chapter 1 that first appeared in *Modernism/Modernity.*

Finally, Eliot, Thomas, Matthias, Olivia, Anna, Harley, and Mary Carolyn, I thank you for sharing with me your love, your lives, and your openness to the work of memory and desire.

Introduction

WRITING TIME

> I am now & then haunted by some semi mystic very profound life of a woman, which shall all be told on one occasion; & time shall be utterly obliterated; future shall somehow blossom out of the past. One incident – say the fall of a flower – might contain it. My theory being that the actual event practically does not exist – nor time either.
>
> Virginia Woolf, *Diary*, 23 November 1926[1]

> This notion of Time embodied, of years past but not separated from us, it was now my intention to emphasize as strongly as possible in my work.
>
> Marcel Proust, *Time Regained*[2]

To write of memory, time, and desire in early twentieth-century literature is to touch the place where modernism's intense concerns with its historicity and belatedness converge with the versions of temporalities and sexualities it was articulating; it is to investigate the sustained provocation of a modernist predisposition to think of the past through the language of sensuality and eros. T. S. Eliot's now well-known lines from the opening of *The Waste Land*, "April is the cruelest month, breeding / Lilacs out of the dead land, mixing / Memory and desire, stirring / Dull roots with spring rain,"[3] capture an agonizingly raw protestation within the modernist project, offering one of those rare moments when a poetic conceit happens to express a key dilemma of the time. Eliot's terms forcefully conjoin the incommensurate temporal pulls of memory and desire while highlighting the "cruel[ty]" of such a mixing: memory is intrinsically backward looking – it casts its gaze to what is sealed off "in time," even as it insists that the rules of temporality and closure are unpredictable – while desire pushes to the future for its realization. In Eliot's poem, "April is the cruellest month" because it links what are otherwise potently disparate (birth and death, "Memory and desire," "dull roots" and "spring rain") through a sudden revolution of the earth's cycles. Fragmented psychic time meets "natural" cyclic time, and in so doing confronts the enduring enigmas of (re)birth, eros, fertility, and death. The tension in this yoking of memory and desire, I want to suggest, marks a highly charged and productive entanglement between anteriority and eros that persistently haunts modernist fiction and poetry on both sides of the Atlantic.

Modernism, Memory, and Desire focuses on the poetic, fictional, critical, and autobiographical texts of T. S. Eliot and Virginia Woolf to argue that despite political, gender, religious, and national differences, and notwithstanding critical tendencies that for decades read their work as asexual and practically disembodied, representing the past was for both a sensuous endeavor that repeatedly turned to the erotic and the corporeal for some of its most authentic elaborations. That is, I want to propose that for Eliot and Woolf memory is always already invested and intertwined with writing sexuality, the body, and desire. Undoubtedly the mixing of memory and desire is in itself not specific to the modernist age. What is deeply singular, though, are the "new" ways modernist writers rendered and returned to the (convoluted) paradox involved in this "mixing." In the modernity specific to the modernism of roughly 1890–1945,[4] avant-garde writers found themselves open to exploring a newly psychoanalytic body and psyche (replete with drives, desires, and an unconscious), in conjunction with shifting global and national politics, emancipatory (and queered) gender and sexual identifications, rapidly changing technologies, and a post-Nietzschean, post-Darwinian secularized skepticism. All of this contributed to a new aesthetic uninhibitedness, and to new registers for addressing what it means to inscribe remembrance and history. To write of time during the modernist era was to write of a quickly shifting world, to write the mutable and the vanishing; it was simultaneously to create a new time and to celebrate, mourn, and eulogize the passing of the old.

The choice to pair Eliot and Woolf is unusual. Eliot's conservatism and (late) religiosity have seemed to make his corpus incompatible with the work of a feminist, atheist, and avowedly leftist writer like Virginia Woolf. Indeed, Woolf and Eliot have never before been placed side by side, in dyadic conjunction, in a book-length study. Their work and their lives, though, reveal some striking proximities. Woolf and Eliot were almost exact contemporaries (born in 1882 and 1888, respectively), professional supporters of each other's work (Woolf's Hogarth Press, for example, published Eliot's second volume of poetry, *Poems*, in 1919, when he was still a relatively unknown poet, and Woolf herself set type for the Hogarth Press's 1923 edition of *The Waste Land*), and close friends for over twenty years. In 1936, in an astonishing letter to Woolf's sister, the painter Vanessa Bell, Woolf even expresses that she felt an erotic attraction to T. S. Eliot. Turning to the *memory* of a visit with Eliot through which to convey her desires, Woolf writes: "I had a visit, long long ago from Tom Eliot, whom I love, or could have loved, had we both been in the prime and not in the sere; how necessary do you think copulation is to friendship? At what point does 'love' become sexual?"[5] We have little other evidence of the eros of Woolf and Eliot's relation, but evidently their connection held some form of sexual charge, and I offer this as a delightful biographical fragment that supplements the contiguities in their thinking about the past. They each separately fashion a poetics of memory where translating one's experience of remembrance and historicity to textuality – what I will be calling *writing time* – occurs by concurrently exploring the erotic and the sensual. Further, just as Sigmund Freud proposes in *Civilization and Its Discontents* (1929) that we think of the psyche's mnemonic layering as analogous to palimpsestic, architectural remains and ruins, both writers stress that time and experience leave *material* and *retrievable* traces – not just in the mind and body but also in the physicality and designs of topography that we are then called upon to interpret. Both are far more present to each other's thinking and writing than we have yet imagined, and their texts offer deeply compelling instantiations of a modernist condensation of the bind between memory and desire. This study, then, considers especially what kinds of work memory does in Woolf and Eliot's literary experiments; how memory is constructed vis-à-vis sexual and textual forms of desire; what kinds of ethics Eliot and Woolf were developing around sites of memory and desire; and, where and why memory fails.

In Djuna Barnes's 1937 novel, *Nightwood*, Baron Felix announces that "To pay homage to our past is the only gesture that also includes the future."[6] Such a statement testifies to the profound complexity and convolution of a modernist predilection to express a time consciousness that looks backward *and* forward with equal, if ambivalent, intensity, all the while commemorating *and* rehabilitating the past as a necessary ingredient required to "make it new," as Ezra Pound notoriously commanded. Pushing toward imagined futures through reconfiguring memory and history was central to so many modernist projects, ranging from James Joyce's *Ulysses* (1922), to T. S. Eliot's *The Waste Land* (1922),

Gertrude Stein's *The Making of Americans* (1925), Virginia Woolf's *To the Lighthouse* (1927), Ezra Pound's *Cantos* (1930–69), William Faulkner's Yoknapatawpha novels, and Marcel Proust's *A la recherche du temps perdu* (1913–27), to name only a few era-defining texts whose authors found themselves compelled to turn to the past as their material, inspiration, and source. This was not simply because they were writing historical novels, or setting their poems in distant times. While their efforts evoke past ages, and make wide use of intertextual pastiche, for the most part modernist writers set their texts within a temporal frame that corresponds roughly with what they themselves had experienced. They shattered formal constraints, destabilized generic conventions, and relentlessly commented – both implicitly and explicitly – on the social, cultural, and political structures of their epoch.

There has, in fact, been an ongoing (albeit quiet) battle regarding modernism's relation to the past. Indeed, part of modernism's critical inheritance has involved a decades-long disavowal of its historical dimensions, along with repeated insistences that modernist aims and ideologies signify apolitical and overly aestheticized disavowals of previous work and culture – a turning away from the past in order to "make it new." Leo Bersani, Gregory Jay, Charles Altieri, Hayden White, and Paul de Man, for example, have each insisted on the modernist tendency to *revoke* history. Hayden White famously argues in 1978 that modernists possessed a "hostility towards history," rejected "historical consciousness," and held the "belief that the past was *only* a burden";[7] in his 1990 study, while discussing distinctly *modernist* writers (Walter Benjamin, Charles Baudelaire, and Friedrich Nietzsche, and specifically Eliot and Joyce in this instance), Leo Bersani claims that "the modern" of a "modernistic modernity" "retains an incomparable aura: that of being spiritually stranded, uniquely special in its radical break with traditional values and modes of consciousness";[8] in 1992, when Gregory Jay tries to distill what critics mean when they speak of "Modernism as a coherent event," one of the six features he outlines as its "distinguishing characteristics" is "a sense of rupture from the past,"[9] and in 1995 Charles Altieri stresses modernism's "antihistoricism."[10] Nicholas Andrew Miller has more recently noted that "Within certain strains of literary and cultural criticism, 'modernism' has come to be synonymous with a willful, even adolescent, ignorance of historical continuity in the pursuit of formal and stylistic innovation for its own sake" (2002).[11]

By contrast, a number of other critics – including Susan Stanford Friedman, Ronald Bush, Peter Fritzsche, Elena Gualtieri, Lawrence

Rainey, John Whittier-Ferguson, and James Longenbach, to name only a few – have directly contested arguments for modernist antagonisms to the past. Two decades ago James Longenbach pronounced that "It has long been apparent that the work of Eliot and Pound grows from an active interest in history."[12] Eliot, after all, makes some of his most influential critical pronouncements in "Tradition and the Individual Talent" (1919). Longenbach goes on, though, to point out that critics have focused preeminently on *literary* histories in Eliot and Pound's "poems including history," while "the question of the nature of their historicism itself has gone unanswered";[13] I would argue that this remains largely true today. Susan Stanford Friedman suggests in 1993 that "it is not the erasure of history but its insistent return as nightmare and desire which marks modernity's stance toward stories of the past,"[14] while Lawrence Rainey proposes in 2005 that "The modernists were obsessed with history. They mourned it and damned it, contested it as tenaciously as Jacob wrestling with the image of God."[15] Clearly this is contested territory, and we can still assert, more generally, that questions about a "modernist" relation to historicity and memory continue to be underexplored.

In this book I want to think of modernism's looking to the past as both a return *and* a departure, involving marked historiographical commitments to thinking the relations between memory, time, desire, and subjectivity, where present and past time are dialogically and endlessly engaged in a rearranging of the past's significations. Eliot and Woolf played with the vagaries of recollection, but still proposed that the past remains a fundamentally vital, retrievable, reinscribable, and often *pleasurable* residue. As Henri Bergson argues, "Our past . . . necessarily and automatically conserves itself. It survives completely whole . . . the past makes body with the present and creates with it without ceasing."[16] Evoking a bodily and material vitality of the past, where sensation and desire are at the core of memory's inscription and then return, the past always leaves its mark and it is up to the operations of chance and desire to determine which fragments will re-emerge as memory.

Both Eliot and Woolf render recollection not simply as a nostalgic, sentimental revisitation of lost time, but as the potent and ineluctable condition of possibility for writing the present. They disclose a passionate cathection to the past's abiding presence in part by affirming the past's profound temporal *and* spatial proximity – and even contiguity – with the present. The rupture between then and now, and the hiatal ground that such a break engenders, is acknowledged, but traversed and repaired – sometimes in a single gesture. In 1930 Eliot writes, "The new years walk, restoring / Through a bright cloud of tears, the years, restoring / With a new verse the ancient rhyme. Redeem / The time."[17] Both writers are compelled to repeat tropes of resuscitating, restoring, and even redeeming the past, while they reveal that such efforts never signify simple mimesis or reification. The fecund work of revisitation they trace means that if history (personal, literary, cultural, and political) is severed from the present, then the cut is only partial. The connectivity that remains leaves both the room and the desire to reconstitute and reclaim the past through its most intimate signs.

What I am describing is also not just the stance of the melancholic, where, if we follow Freud's 1917 proposals, melancholia develops through a failure to recognize and release an attachment to a beloved object-choice after a traumatic loss, involving "an extraordinary diminution in his self-regard, an impoverishment of his ego on a grand scale."[18] We certainly find elements of melancholia in some of Eliot and Woolf's dispositions to the past, but I want to insist that their engagement with the problem of anteriority is more nuanced than this, involving pleasures and pains, attachments and renunciations, and, above all, a recognition of the still-*becoming* life of the past within the present's only partial fullness. Their affective attachments to the past are distinct from both the sentimentality of a pure nostalgia unable to release its melancholic commitments, and from those of a transcendental idealization of past time. While recent trauma studies have focused preeminently on mourning and melancholia as modern and postmodern modes of memory, I want to propose that Eliot and Woolf's projects open up a different mnemonic record. The past in their work is a cherished, if occasionally dangerous, material that is urgently required to flesh out – sometimes in a flash – the fragile and fleeting (almost absent) fullness of the present. We find a palpable thematization of attempts to accept that, like a beloved Other, the past *cannot give itself to us* once and for all, no matter how much we might desire such a fantastic resolution. Much of their writing is driven by what it might mean to reapproach this kind of temporal alterity. For, memory, like an Other, manifests a separate and ongoing *coming-into-being* that demands a ceaseless reopening to the work of its translation and transfiguration.

For Eliot and Woolf the past also insists on a multiple rather than a singular hermeneutics. From Eliot's "The Love Song of J. Alfred Prufrock" to Woolf's *Orlando*, the past is always agitated with a slightly alienating current of the now, and simultaneously confronted with the (relatively) limited temporal domain of the present. Eliot and Woolf may refuse dis-attachment to the past, but they do so by recognizing a *good enough* accessibility to what remains. They each write out a past that can never be mastered, that is always ajar, and open to both reinscription and reexperience – open to the supplement of a perpetual (re)turn that would find in the past an always new object to confront. To remain connected to the past so that it does not become, as in Proust's closing vision of *Swann's Way*, a "fugitive" – a lost image in flight without a place in the present – is, I argue, one of the principle desires in Eliot and Woolf's oeuvre.

I divide the book into roughly two halves – the first I devote to T. S. Eliot, and the second to Virginia Woolf – to investigate, by juxtaposition, the startling correspondences in their renderings of mnemonic consciousness. In considering Eliot, I trace figures of sex, women, queerness, and desire in relation to historicity and remembrance in his canonical writings as well as in a series of bawdy poems that are still only partially published and have received very little critical notice. Nevertheless, it appears that Eliot composed this extensive body of pornotropic work over roughly fifty years. While these "Columbo and Bolo" verses may at first seem determinately at odds with Eliot's major poetry and essays, I propose instead that they illuminate – in a kind of hyperbolic relief – Eliot's persistent recourse to presenting the past thought lenses of eros and desire. They reveal some of the excesses of his poetic imagination and ask us to take on the burden of their provocation.

After a first chapter in which I investigate the complicated signs and motivations of these poems, I turn to instances from Eliot's pre-conversion (pre-1927) published poems and essays – from "The Love Song of J. Alfred Prufrock," to "Gerontion," "Portrait of a Lady," "Preludes," "Hysteria," *The Waste Land*, and "Tradition and the Individual Talent," among other pieces – where he conjoins memory with its sensual designations. As David Chinitz endeavors to do in *T. S. Eliot and the Cultural Divide*,[19] part of my task is to continue the work of exposing an "other" Eliot who reads very much against the grain of the asexual, straight, conservative, rigidly Anglo-Catholic, white, prudish "high" modernist "T. S. Eliot" we rather problematically still too often have come to "inherit" – to borrow a term Eliot disdains in "Tradition and the Individual Talent."[20] The Eliot I want to explore is sexy, dangerous, and crucially *uneven* in his investments and pronouncements.

I juxtapose these reflections on Eliot with a focus on Virginia Woolf by considering her similar explorations of the eros and desires implicit in thinking history and memory. While Woolf's poetics and metaphorics of corporeality and sexuality are still surprisingly underexplored in criticism, I suggest that some of Woolf's most erotic expositions occur in conjunction with her representations of recollection.[21] I emphasize her own preoccupations with rewriting and revisiting the eros of the past while she offers critiques of the political, cultural, and personal climates of her present. Indeed, I want to urge us to think of Woolf not only as a major modernist writer and feminist critic, but also as a complicated thinker of memory and history. To understand her better we would do well to place her ruminations on the past in dialogue with those of some of her immediate precursors and contemporaries like Sigmund Freud, Henri Bergson, Marcel Proust, Walter Benjamin, and Friedrich Nietzsche – some of whom she engaged with directly, and all of whom offer serendipitous illuminations. To this end I read Woolf unconventionally as a thinker of memory and history, and take up her contentions that we pay more attention to how the ostensibly three-dimensional spatiality of "the physical" is permeated and ridden with history. By considering *To the Lighthouse* (1927), *Orlando* (1928), *Between the Acts* (1941), "A Sketch of the Past" (1941), and her diaries, letters, and essays, and by placing personal memory in relation to more properly "historical" markers such as the Great War, colonialism, and the rise of Freudian psychoanalysis, I argue that Woolf discloses an intricate theory of writing the past that not only demands an ethics of remembering as necessary to modern subjectivity, but which evokes an ardent devotion to the past's materiality. Woolf repeatedly makes the (re)turn to memory emblematic of a kind of fertile desire, in part because memory stands as a replete ground of citation to which one is recalled to work through material from the past as a kind of palpable putty that is often sufficiently under the control of the conscious mind to be pleasurable.

Finally, I ask how Eliot, Woolf, and other modernists viewed and experienced historical, calendrical, personal, and epiphanic time. How did they articulate the time of memory? How does writing (the signification of the letter) help engender the abstract cohesiveness of a historical or remembered actuality? How is time bounded by language and language bounded by (and bonded to) time? How does time touch the modern(ist) subject? The coupling of memory and desire links what is past to the desires of the present, and always involves at least a double yoking, putting pressure on what Bergson sees as the distinction between the objective fact of time (*temps*) and its subjective experience (*durée*). Woolf and Eliot evince self-conscious historicizing gestures, eroticize reminiscence and its contents, and relentlessly approach the Otherness of "lost time," expressing a conviction that through memory firmly lodged in the body the most vital aspects of time remain undispersed. As in Julia Kristeva's reading of Proust, we find here "a new form of temporality" which "gives an X-ray image of memory, bringing to light its painful yet rapturous dependence on the senses . . . time is to be psychic time, and consequently the factor which determines our bodily life."[22] In this way, "mixing / Memory and desire" is done not by foregrounding a fear of their contamination, but with an almost lustful impulse to have reminiscence correspond with its sensual corollaries, all the while exposing the unrest between these figures. A palpable desire exists in Eliot and Woolf's work to *know* the heterogeneousness of the past. This represents not a repulsion from history, but a welcoming of its alterity as fundamentally (re)cognizable and desirable. What we find then is a copulative relation: to remember *is* to desire; to desire *is* to remember. This study considers the ways in which memory and history pressed themselves upon the minds of two exemplary figures who wrote under modernism's conditions – making time for writing, and in the process, writing time.

CHAPTER 1

An unexpected beginning: sex, race, and history in T. S. Eliot's Columbo and Bolo poems

I keep my countenance,
I remain self-possessed
Except when a street-piano, mechanical and tired
Reiterates some worn-out common song
With the smell of hyacinths across the garden
Recalling things that other people have desired.
Are these ideas right or wrong?

T. S. Eliot, "Portrait of a Lady"[1]

One day Columbo and the queen
They fell into a quarrel
Columbo showed his disrespect
By farting in a barrel.
The queen she called him horse's ass
And "dirty Spanish loafer"
They terminated the affair
By fucking on the sofa.

T. S. Eliot, *Inventions of the March Hare*[2]

One of the most striking instances of T. S. Eliot's mixing of memory and desire occurs in his rendering of the history, legacy, and cultural memory of early European colonial expansion. In the period from 1909 to 1922 when Eliot was writing and publishing poems such as "The Love Song of J. Alfred Prufrock," "Portrait of a Lady," "Preludes," and *The Waste Land* – poems that firmly established his reputation as one of the major poets of the century – he was simultaneously composing a long cycle of intensely sexual, bawdy, pornotropic, and satirical verse that has only recently come to light.[3] Centered on the seafaring adventures of an explorer named "Columbo" (Eliot uses an Italianate version of Christopher Columbus's name) and his encounters with two native inhabitants of Cuba, "King Bolo and his Big Black Bassturd Kween," these poems comically portray the history of early colonialism in the Americas as an orgy of uncontrollable desire and deviant sexuality. Columbo's voyages and his first contacts with the King and Queen of Cuba take place by, through, and for sex, as Eliot figures sodomy, masturbation, miscegenation, scatological rituals, and rape as the *modus operandi* of imperial conquest. The poems form part of an extensive cycle that Eliot continued to write throughout his life, and shared privately – in the teens and twenties especially – with a homosocially arranged coterie of male writers, including Conrad Aiken, Clive Bell, Bonamy Dobrée, James Joyce, Wyndham Lewis, and Ezra Pound. Taken as a corpus, the poems (untitled by Eliot) allegorize a number of concerns with Eliot's nascent reputation as a poet, his anxious desires for publicity, his exile from the United States, and his uneasy relation to race, sex, and colonialism. They explode still-prevalent myths about Eliot's asexuality, and they demand radical rereadings of the place of sex, race, history, and desire in his poetic and critical oeuvre.

Shockingly different in form, kind, and content from Eliot's canonical poems, the Columbo and Bolo stanzas – with sing-songy adolescent rhythms and rhyme schemes that seem more appropriate to schoolboy doggerel than to the poetry of a major literary figure – would hardly have done Eliot's literary reputation much good in the London literary scene of the nineteen-teens and early twenties. Nevertheless, Eliot actively tried to get them published. In what appear to be two of the early stanzas – at least chronologically speaking, in terms of the New World voyage of discovery that Eliot charts – Columbo is preparing to leave Spain, under the patronage of Queen Isabella and King Ferdinand, and the following scene takes place:

> One day the king & queen of Spain
> They gave a royal banquet
> Columbo having passed away
> Was brought in on a blanket
> The queen she took an oyster fork
> And pricked Columbo's navel
> Columbo hoisted up his ass
> And shat upon the table.
>
> Columbo and his merry men
> They set sail from Genoa
> Queen Isabella was aboard
> That famous Spanish whore.[4]

The penetrating "prick" of the queen's "oyster fork" is apparently enough to resurrect Columbo from a death-like pre-voyage unconsciousness: prodding him – marking him with the threat of rape – with her phallic utensil as she mixes sex and appetite to awaken him to his scatological act. Columbo returns the queen's "prick" with a contrary but commensurate response by marking his departure with a gesture of anal excrement. The whole contestation foreshadows Columbus's eventual fall from grace, and we are evidently meant to read her "prick" as phallic, since it intratextually cites a moment just seven lines earlier where Eliot writes anti-Semitically that when Columbo went to see a doctor in Spain, "Where doctors are not many / The only doctor in his town / Was a bastard jew named Benny," who "filled Columbo's prick / With Muriatic Acid."[5] Eliot thus begins his rendition of colonial history with a mocking critique of its origins: the signs of colonialism's beginnings are to be found in its performance of anal fantasies, involving a non-verbal exchange between patron and subject whose signification operates as erotic tribute *and* offensive rebuke.

Indeed, anal excrement will be the great, expendable form of currency and expression in these poems, with Eliot suggesting that "shit" is the fungible substance of colonialism par excellence: it is alternately deposited at formal occasions, thrown in play, the primary colonial cargo for import to Europe, while it is proposed as both the substance of a meal and as a sexual stimulant. Further, excremental homage turns out to be one of the dominant modes of a repeated mimicry that circulates between the colonists and the colonized. Within the indigenous social structure of Cuba that Columbo encounters, the natives partake of the same carnival of excremental expression with *their* royal head of state: "King Bolo's swarthy bodyguard / They numbered three and thirty," and while King Bolo is lying "down in the shade / His royal breast uncovering / They mounted in a banyan tree / And shat upon their sovereign."[6] Part insult, part sexual exhibitionism and even sexual flattery, the ubiquitous anal excrement of these poems asks us to rethink the relation between colonialism and waste, pillage and bodily excess. The colonial enterprise was girded with disrespect for the physical and sexual consent of others (sovereigns and colonized alike, Eliot insists), while the mockery Eliot makes of the project of discovery renders grabbing and shaming bodies as analogous to grabbing territories.

In the above stanza, Eliot is also already playing with the queer valences of "queen" – as he will do elsewhere in the poems – to suggest not only that colonialism's first conquests relied on hyperbolic registers of racist difference, but also that imperialism operated through deviant desire. Eliot is at once homophobic and homoerotically fascinated, and the poems' homoerotic content was crucial to the impetus for their creation and subsequent circulation among a group of all-male contemporary writers. Eliot depicts Queen Isabella, Christopher Columbus's Spanish-Catholic patroness, who favored his voyage while others looked more skeptically on his prospects, as both an ambiguously female and potentially queer "queen," and as a misogynistically portrayed "whore" who acted as Columbus's envoy. Historically, her support of Columbus – who hailed originally from Italy, and who was therefore already in some senses post-national in securing Spanish patronage – allowed him to become a principal Atlantic explorer for the Spanish royalty, and the "discoverer" of the "New World." Isabella also stands as something of a foil to her great English contemporary, the "virgin" Queen Elizabeth – another prominent female ruler whose cultural iconography has insisted on naming the degree of her erotic availability. In effect, Eliot is finding himself called upon to approach what Ella Shohat and Robert Stam have called the "primal scene of colonial intercourse,"[7] figuring history and sex, and memory and desire as inseparable, as though to write a history of New World discovery is also to write a sexuality.

To date, these Columbo and Bolo poems have received almost no critical attention. There has evidently been some temptation to leave them aside, and they have languished mostly unexamined since their respective dates of (still partial) publication in 1988, 1990, and 1996. As it now stands, with the exception of a few published reviews of Christopher Ricks's 1996 *Inventions of the March Hare*, in which the bulk of the stanzas first appeared,[8] and the occasional indication in biographies and critical guides that Eliot wrote some "bawdy" verses about Christopher Columbus, very few articles exist on the poems. It is, we might say, difficult to know where to begin with these bawdy verses, since they are as offensive as they are fascinating, and as dangerous as they are subversive. They play recklessly on prohibitions while offering a satirical poetics of desire and memory whose comic edge is always in danger of collapsing into the outright racism, homophobia, and misogyny that they ventriloquize, repeat, and critique.

Given Eliot's desire to publish these poems, the protracted period of their composition, and the range of issues they invoke, we cannot, though, dismiss them as "mere" juvenilia.[9] The Columbo and Bolo stanzas are hardly an occasional literary preoccupation, and their composition appears to have extended throughout Eliot's adult life. Eliot wrote a major part of the poems from about 1909 to 1929, a twenty-year span that coincides with one of his most productive periods, as well as with his permanent move to England, his marriage, and his conversion to Anglo-Catholicism in 1927. And the body of work these poems represent is incredibly vast, totaling at least seventy-five stanzas in all. So far, twenty-nine of these have been published – including nearly ten in Valerie Eliot's 1988 *The Letters of T. S. Eliot: Volume One, 1898–1922*, seventeen in Christopher Ricks's 1996 *Inventions of the March Hare*, two in *The Faber Book of Blue Verse* – and many more sit unpublished in archives.[10]

PUBLIC DESIRES AND PRIVATE CIRCULATIONS: ELIOT'S COTERIE

> One day Columbo went below
> To see the ship's physician:
> "It's this way, doc" he said said he
> I just cant stop a-pissin" . . .

or

> King Bolo's big black kukquheen
> Was fresh as ocean breezes.
> She burst aboard Columbo's ship
> With a cry of gentle Jesus.[11]

Who, we might ask, were Eliot's intended readers for these remarkable poems? Eliot had been writing the Columbo and Bolo verses at least since he was an undergraduate at Harvard (1906–9), and it is likely that he shared them aloud with several of his male friends from that time onward.[12] The earliest record we have of their circulation is from July 1914, immediately before the beginning of the Great War, when Eliot began to include them in his letters to Conrad Aiken, with whom he had worked on *The Harvard Advocate.* At the time, Eliot was studying German at a summer-language program in Marburg that would soon be cut short by Germany's declaration of war against Russia on 1 August 1914. The timing of the poems' composition and circulation is thus extraordinary: Eliot began sharing his parody of early European colonialism with others at precisely the moment when Europe was entering the Great War, a war that would, in part, mark the necessity of colonialism's demise. As such, the Columbo and Bolo verses gesture backward to relatively distant historical "origins" at the very moment when a new era of European national and international politics was unfolding.

That is, they look backward while reflecting the preoccupations of the new, using a historical rendition to critique the continued operations of early twentieth-century colonialism.

Eliot gradually expanded the circle of friends with whom he shared the poems to include not just Aiken, but other major writers, ranging from Clive Bell to Bonamy Dobrée, James Joyce, Wyndham Lewis, and Ezra Pound. Although at present it is difficult to assess all of Eliot's correspondence after 1922 (which is the end point of Valerie Eliot's excellent 1988 *The Letters of T. S. Eliot: Volume One*; a second volume has not yet appeared), from smatterings of letters in archives and from correspondence sent to Eliot by these interlocutors, we know that Eliot wrote about Bolo throughout his life. In the John Davy Hayward Bequest at Cambridge University, for instance, Bolo emerges in a letter to Clive Bell in 1941, nearly fifteen years after an intense correspondence on the subject with Bonamy Dobrée reaches its peak in 1927 – astonishingly, the year of Eliot's conversion – and roughly thirty years after Bolo's first incarnation. Furthermore, Conrad Aiken indicates in December 1964, less than a month before Eliot died on 4 January 1965, that Bolo was still a topic of interest. Writing to Eliot at the time, Aiken expresses regret that this year they would not have their usual exchange of Columbo and Bolo poems: "But o dear we shall miss our annual meeting in New York and the exchange of Bolos and lime rickeys at the River Club or Vanderbilt."[13] Aiken's phrasing suggests that Aiken, too, might have composed Bolo verses. I have, however, been unable to find any evidence of this in Aiken's writings. Perhaps Aiken offered the lime rickeys and Eliot offered the poems. What perhaps is most astonishing about this body of work, then, is that Eliot continued to write and circulate the Columbo and Bolo verses through his whole life. Though their "temperature and ambience is callow," as Hortense Spiller suggests,[14] they are the verses to which he most consistently returned, and they constitute his most sustained poetic output.

The poems' circulation in these letters seems to have been initially prompted by conditions of both literary and personal history – in part by the arrival of Wyndham Lewis's first issue of *Blast* on the London literary scene in June of 1914, and in part by Eliot's growing skepticism and disillusionment with the academic establishment of which, in 1914, while still a PhD student in philosophy at Harvard, he believed he was destined to be a part. Their dissemination thus stems from overlapping public and private desires: on the one hand they evidence his wish to participate in the public moment of *Blast*, while on the other hand they symptomatically indicate a wish to parody and distance himself from what he perceived to be a pedantic academic milieu that he was soon to leave.

The circulation of the Columbo and Bolo poems begins, importantly, with mimicry – a mode they will continue to reflect as they alternate between parody, satire, and outright repetition of racist codes and *topoi*. Deliberately echoing the "Blast Humour" from Lewis's new journal, in which Lewis alternately mocks and praises public personalities and cultural institutions, offering an iconoclastic and impetuous genre of humor that would either "Blast" or "Bless" depending on a satirical moral judgment of the figure in question, Eliot begins his July 1914 letter to Aiken with the following heading:

BLESS

COLUMBO
BOLO BLUBUNG CUDJO
THE CHAPLAIN BRUTUS SQUIRTY PANSY

BLAST

THE BOSUN COUSIN HUGH THE COOK
PROF. DR. KRAPP[15]

A jocular letter ensues that pokes fun at academics and includes some of Eliot's accomplished comic-like pen drawings (see Figure 1.1). In Eliot's visual depiction of Bolo he is a large, bald man of ambiguous race, smoking a cigar, decked out with a monocle and a polka-dotted bowtie. Beneath him the subscript reads – in an imperative pastiche form that blends aspects of Latin, Italian, and Spanish – "VIVA BOLO!!"[16] Bolo seems rather pleased with himself, and gives the impression that he is ogling something or someone outside the frame of the drawing. Behind him is a mountain, as Eliot mixes locales as well as historical moments to place Bolo in what is probably the German landscape Eliot inhabited at the time – a mountainous landscape he again depicts a week later in a letter to his American cousin, Eleanor Hinkley.[17] Bolo is thus curiously *distant*, geographically and temporally speaking, and *present*: he is simultaneously the imaginary native King of Cuba from Columbus's day, and a timeless caricature of sovereignty with infinitely changeable historical locations.

Figure 1.1. "VIVA BOLO!!" *The Letters of T. S. Eliot*, vol. 1, 43.

He alternately inhabits the present moment, and several centuries ago in the past – a gesture that asks, in another way, that we read Eliot's fascination with Bolo as reflective of Eliot's engagement with the relation between contemporaneity and history.

Most of those whom Eliot chooses to "Bless" or "Blast" are historical or stock figures that he fictionalizes and parodies in the cycle. David Chinitz points out that Eliot adapted the pieces from a folk ballad entitled "Christopher Columbo" – versions of which he may have heard sung during his adolescence in St. Louis.[18] While Christopher Columbus is the most explicitly historical figure, in his interpretive notes to Eliot's poems, B. C. Southam suggests that King Bolo may also be modeled on a historical figure named King Shamba Bolongongo who died in 1628, "ruler of the Kuba tribes, legendary for the number of widows and children he left."[19] Christopher Ricks contends it is also likely that Eliot was aware of some early comedic ballads by W. S. Gilbert (later of Gilbert and Sullivan), whose poem, "King Borria Bungalee Boo," describes a "man-eating African swell" with a small quarry of all-male "subjects." Gilbert's ballads are disturbingly racist without showing the least evidence that they are aware of being so, detailing the story of King Burria's tribe going to war with a tribe of Amazon women ruled by "Queen Loo" in order to satiate their cannibalistic urges. The Amazonian women decide they will try to seduce the all-male tribe peacefully with their coquettish ways, but their flirtatious advances do not persuade King Burria, who eats Queen Loo, while his tribesmen eat her subjects. As in Eliot's Columbo and Bolo poems, appetite and sex are in basic parity, as Gilbert offers an interpretation of the racial Other that imagines the two ends of the spectrum of war and peace as a choice between two forms of incorporation: cannibalism or sex, both involved with death and desire.

The other figures Eliot chooses to "Bless" or "Blast" are again either historical or representatives of a type. According to Southam, Cardinal Bessarian (1395–1472) "was Papal Legate to Venice, remembered as founder of the Library of St. Mark's. Eliot would have met the name in his Italian Renaissance course at Harvard."[20] "Cardinal Bessarian" may also commemorate a North African desert hermit, St. Bessarian, who was credited with many miracles, including bringing rain during a drought. Perhaps Eliot "blesses" this namesake partly because Bessarian was master over the elements whose failures would lead to the yearning for rain in *The Waste Land.* "Squirty Pansy" invokes the playfulness of slang to praise a sexually ejaculative homosexual male. The *Oxford English Dictionary* cites 1929 as the first time "pansy" takes on a queer valence in English, where pansy is defined as "effeminate; homosexual; affected." This means that Eliot's use of the term precedes the *Oxford English Dictionary*'s first example by fourteen years. That Eliot "Bless[es]" "Squirty Pansy" should alert us again to the homoerotic content of the Bolo poems, and to a recurring investment Eliot had at this time with the queer. The Germanic "Prof. Dr. Krapp," whom Eliot "blast[s]," is apparently named for the "Krapp" he produces, and is one of several fictional professors whom Eliot mocks at some length in the same letter, and then in his 1920s extensive correspondence with Bonamy Dobrée. We might also note the preponderance of the alliterative "B's" and "C's" in Eliot's "Bless" and "Blast" tribute to Lewis: with the exception of "Squirty Pansy" all of his designations begin with either a "B" or a hard "C" sound. Taking alliteration to ridiculous limits, then, Eliot joins Lewis's version of cultural critique to adopt *Blast*'s idiom in order to express his own humor of the time, which was satirically disdainful of imperialism, scatological, anti-academic, and only ambivalently respectful of the Church.

Although Eliot "Bless[es]" the chaplain, his attitude to religion in these stanzas is as vexed as his attitudes to colonialism. Sundays in particular seem to be good days for masturbation and rape in the cycle, and they represent the only day of the week that is ever named. The chaplain himself is hardly sexually pure, and he eagerly participates in the "spirit" of sex aboard the ship by whistling at King Bolo's Kween and buggering himself at sea: "K. B.b.b.b.k. [King Bolo's big black basturd kween] / Was awf'ly sweet and pure / She said 'I don't know what you mean!' / When the chaplain whistled to her;"[21] "He skipped so quickly round the mast / He buggered himself (in the asshole)."[22] Eliot's register of buffoonery about the religious should strike us as rather surprising given his conversion to Anglo-Catholicism in 1927, and his subsequent canonization as always-already enveloped in the fold of the Church. These poems reveal an Eliot who is more complicated and less resolved in his literary and religious convictions than we might now think.

Immediately after the imitative tribute to Lewis, Eliot appends a Columbo and Bolo stanza in his letter to Aiken:

> Now while Columbo and his men
> Were drinking ice cream soda
> In burst King Bolo's big black queen
> That famous old breech l(oader).
> Just then they rang the bell for lunch
> And served up – Fried Hyenas;
> And Columbo said "Will you take tail?
> Or just a bit of p(enis)?"[23]

Eliot gives no introduction or preamble to this stanza other than his mimicry of *Blast*, which strongly suggests that Aiken was already familiar with Eliot's Columbo and Bolo experiments. This happens to be a feature of the Bolo poems that runs through Eliot's correspondence with Aiken, Bell, Dobrée, Joyce, Lewis, and Pound: they are shrouded in learned allusions that inevitably include and exclude, carefully constructing a readership of insiders and outsiders that even persists today, with Eliot scholars referring to the Bolo poems as a kind of scurrilously funny open secret among those "who know."

The first stanza Eliot sends to Aiken is both disgusting and humorous, adolescent while it ventriloquizes racist and sexist stereotypes. Columbo and his all-male crew are evidently enjoying a dessert-like treat when suddenly "King Bolo's big black queen" "burst" upon the scene. This is apparently the queen's preferred mode of entry, and in another stanza she arrives on board in the same fashion: "King Bolo's big black kukquheen / Was fresh as ocean breezes. / She burst aboard Columbo's ship / With a cry of gentle Jesus."[24] An interruptive element, the queen is immediately sexualized and propositioned by Columbo as he wonders if she might "take" the strange (foreign?) food he offers – which in its own way emphasizes the hysteria underlying the encounter between Europeans and natives since it is nothing less than the "tail" of a hyena, an animal known for its uncontrollable laughter – or "just a bit of p(enis)?" Eliot here participates in a racist imaginary that figures blacks, and especially black women, as inviting and invoking sex and its discursive accoutrements, while we might say that fantasies predicated on cultural mythologies of racial alterity fuel these poems, as Eliot repeatedly binds the big "Others" of gender and race onto Bolo's queen.

Imagining the black body in this way, Eliot both uses and mocks phantasmatic perceptions that had been well in place from the time of early colonialism. Not only has the white imagination surcharged black and brown bodies with an excess of uncontrollable sexuality, but, such an imagination has also rendered this projected Otherness as bordering on homosexuality. bell hooks quotes Sander Gilman to propose that "'by the eighteenth century, the sexuality of the black, male and female, becomes an icon for deviant sexuality.'"[25] This date seems rather late, and Jonathan Goldberg pushes it back much further, pointing out that part of the rhetoric of the first European colonists involved classifying the native people of color as dangerously sexual, and often sodomitical. "'They are all sodomites;' so reads the dispatch sent from Vera Cruz, July 10, 1519, in the first so-called letter of Corté's . . . once made, few reports failed to repeat the charge."[26] Eliot was apparently well aware of these kinds of homophobic anxieties about New-World discovery, and his Columbo and Bolo verses historically recall these associations only to redeploy them as modernist humor, blending memory and desire in pornotropic renditions of colonial hysteria.

This is not too surprising, since, with so many other modernists on both sides of the Atlantic during this period – including James Joyce, Ezra Pound, William Faulkner, and Ernest Hemingway – Eliot was fascinated with ventriloquizing racism. With these poems he evidently takes pleasure in compulsively reiterating the moral abjection of prejudicial discourse, while repeating this racism with a palpable self-conscious mockery that exposes it at its most attenuated and outlandish limits, making fun of the extremities of nomenclature and prohibition in a parodic register replete with what Hayden White has called a "metadiscursive reflexiveness."[27] "King Bolo's Big Black Bassturd Kween" – the most potent moment of naming in the cycle – disturbs because of the element of racial hatred it speaks, while it also already troubles that racism by pointing to its own absurdity, turning the critical glance back upon itself to disclose more about the speaker than about the queen. Ventriloquizing as such is a kind of mimicry that takes pleasure in its model but revolts against it through simultaneously engaging mockery and parody, correcting bigotry and bias while exploiting them.

This, of course, does not get Eliot "off the hook" of racism. Yet by enacting the culturally popular racism of the teens and twenties while critiquing it, his stance toward racial difference – and toward what Frantz Fanon would later describe as the "phobogenic object" of colonial territory[28] – suddenly appears more complicated. While Eliot evokes stock racist stereotypes by representing the colonies as filled with "savages" and "cannibals," he also inverts and mocks these stereotypes. In the extensive anthropological commentary on Bolo and Bolovian customs he concocts for Bonamy Dobrée, Bolo is hardly a "savage" but is an eminent and quasi-originary specimen with excellent "blood" – the very emblem of "civilization": "many of our most eminent men have Bolovian blood."[29] Furthermore, in the first stanza he sends to Aiken that I cite above, "Bolo's big black queen" offers the disruptive element to the dessert party, but the obscene sexual advance comes from Columbo's *words* – as the representative of European politics and language – rather than from the queen's body. Columbo needs no prompting for his lewdness: he is sexually out of control, and his mission centers on sex on board and sex in the newly discovered colonies. The white colonial party carries and (quite literally) disseminates the mark of hyperbolic (bi)sexuality, and this functions as their most potent motivation for mixing with the native inhabitants. Yet the miscegenation of Columbo and the big black queen operates less as that worried marker of the meeting and mixing of races in the last century, charging sex with race, and race with sex, and stuttering on the ground of their mutual unreadability, than it does as a simple, albeit titillating, historical circumstance. The stanzas thus offer at least as much judgment on Columbo as they do on the native queen. That is to say, if there is a moral stance to be taken (which in Eliot's writings there usually is, somewhere), the obscenity lies with Columbo's perception of the queen, and not with the queen herself. Eliot therefore implicitly proposes that white colonial biases about native populations are perversely preoccupied with their own sexual projections and desires.

Anne McClintock suggests that "Controlling women's sexuality, exalting maternity and breeding a virile race of empire-builders were widely perceived as the paramount means for controlling the health and wealth of the male imperial body politic, so that, by the turn of the century, sexual purity emerged as a controlling metaphor for racial, economic and political power."[30] Eliot was well aware of the cultural valences around sexual purity, and he has been accused countless times himself of a stodgy puritanism. In writing his Bolo poems, though, he was calling a bluff, evacuating pretenses of sexual purity from the colonial project by parodying the lie of a noble imperialism conjured by Rudyard Kipling's infamous formulation of empire-building as the "white man's burden." Eliot's male and female colonists are hedonistic, miscegenating, cross-dressing, sodomizing, and bestialist: they are the inverse of the myth of sexual purity that McClintock and others claim was intrinsic to imperial power. Instead, racial and political power, the power of roaming the seas as Spain's (and, by extension, Europe's) ambassadors, depends on an uncontrollable sexual licentiousness whose outrageousness can meet no limit or prohibition, precisely because colonial expansion is coextensive with orgiastic desire. Eliot, then, seems to be saying that any phantasy of propriety in stories of European expansion can remain only that: a phantastic disguise that promotes its own misreading.

As Eliot expanded the group of friends to whom he sent the Columbo and Bolo material, his correspondents responded by affirming the poems' masturbatory qualities. In a rather slippery reference early in 1915, Wyndham Lewis wrote a letter to Pound that seems to allude to Eliot's pornotropic verse, but which does so only after careening anxiously through a detour about meeting the writer John Rodker. I will cite the paragraph in full:

> Thank you for Eliot poem. It is very respectable intelligent verse, as you say, and I found Rodker a most poisonous little bugger on Saturday, repellently hoarse (this may be a form of jealousy) and with abominable teeth, not to mention his manner. I am sure you cant [*sic*] say anything too bad about him. He told me he had written a lot of filthy sexual verse, which, if he sends it, I shall hang in the W.C. He described it as Verlainesque, damn his shifty little eyes. Well, well.[31]

The Wyndham Lewis correspondence from this time is difficult to date with absolute accuracy, but this letter appears during the same period in which Eliot had sent some Bolo poems to Lewis. Lewis, though, had deemed the Bolo verses unprintable. Through its awkward and abrupt textual juxtapositions, Lewis elides the distinction between his commentary on one of Eliot's poems and his meeting with another "bugger," John Rodker. Strikingly, Lewis remarks on a possible "jealousy" and on Rodker's "manner," performing a collision (separated only by commas) between personal competition, social presentation, and Eliot's verse. From there Lewis moves quickly to commenting that if Rodker (or Eliot?) sent him "filthy sexual verse" he would "hang it in the W. C." Whether these specific verses are Eliot's or Rodker's, Lewis's position is the same: pornotropic verse is masturbatory, and deserves to be read in poster-fashion on the bathroom wall. Pound thought of Eliot's poems this way too: in 1922, after Eliot had been sharing them with Pound for some years, he told Pound he was going to send some of his Columbo and Bolo poems to Joyce. With not-so-subtle masturbatory punning Pound retorted, "You can forward the Bolo to Joyce if you think it wont unhinge his somewhat sabbatarian mind. On the whole he might be saved the shock, shaved the sock [*sic*]."[32]

Eliot's willingness to circulate these poems only to male writers, while simultaneously parodying the queerness of colonial history, participates in the epistemological pairings of "secrecy/disclosure" and "public/private" that Eve Kosofsky Sedgwick has argued are constitutive of societal structures of gay closeting.[33] Eliot was both very much in the closet about his queer preoccupations, and halfway out of the closet because of his willingness to engage in homoerotic titillation among the members of his coterie. Columbo and his men are preoccupied with anal eroticism, and regularly sodomize both each other and King Bolo's campily named "Kween." In a scene that moves quickly from a masturbatory, narcissistic self-appraisal to an aggressive, public sodomization, Columbo "took his cock in both his hands / And swore it was a beauty" before pouncing on the cabin boy: "The cabin boy appeared on deck / And scampered up the mast-o / Columbo grasped him by the balls / And buggered him in the ass-o."[34] In another stanza, "Columbo slid along the deck / And raped the smoke-room steward."[35]

Eliot actually arranged his little coterie very much as they had been arranged in literary circles for centuries. As Wendy Wall writes in her discussion of Renaissance literature, "the coterie used the circulation of texts to consolidate the bonds formed among an elite and primarily male group."[36] Wall turns to J. W. Saunders in her article, who delineates the Renaissance coterie as

> a finishing school where members polished each other's art, which, like the taste for clothes, or the ear for a compliment, or the aptitude for dancing or fencing or riding, was very much a matter of doing the right things in the right way, in a game where every man tried to dazzle and out vie his competitors. More seriously a group restricted, ideally at least, to those who were equals or near-equals in social status . . . [they] cooperated in the formulation of critical principles, a sense of values.[37]

Although Eliot did not explicitly seek criticism from the members of his coterie for his Columbo and Bolo poems, he certainly sought to "dazzle and out vie his competitors" with the indecency of his verses. Their circulation participates in and offers a pornotropic extension of the collaborative effort Eliot made with Pound while crafting *The Waste Land* – a collaboration that Wayne Koestenbaum and others have read as emphatically homoerotic.[38] Their "dazzle" involved what I want to call *epistological* titillation: the poems evoked the pornographism of the comic strip in the space of his correspondence to his male contemporaries to try to shock and impress his peers with the language of obscenity. Eliot's efforts, though, to excite these contemporaries via the pornotropic letter seems to have been primarily one-way: apart from Pound and Dobrée the others do not appear to have reciprocated *epistologically* in the game of titillation. Pound, though, made up for any lack on the part of the others by marking Eliot's words about the crew with "the rest were jews and niggers," replying to Eliot, "Sweet Christ in hell, spew out some Rabelais / To belch and fahrt and to define the day / In fitting manner and her monument / Heap up for her in fadeless excrement."[39]

The sharing of pornotropic letters was not the only private, experimental exchange that took place in Eliot's correspondence. Michael North notes that Eliot and Pound made frequent experiments with American (and especially African-American) dialect in their letters, pointing out that "This dialect became in their correspondence an intimate code, a language of in-jokes and secrets . . . In the late 1930s Pound dubbed this private dialect 'epistolary.'"[40] Herbert Read, in "T. S. E. – A Memoir" (1967), famously cites a letter Eliot had sent him about how odd it felt to be

> an American who wasn't an American, because he was born in the South and went to school in New England as a small boy with a nigger drawl, but who wasn't a southerner in the South because his people were northerners in a border state and looked down on all southerners and Virginians, and who so was never anything anywhere and who therefore felt himself to be more an Englishman than a Frenchman and yet felt that the USA up to a hundred years ago was a family extension.[41]

Eliot's "family extension" included a deeply rooted ambivalence to the "strong brown god" of the Mississippi river he writes about in the opening lines of "The Dry Salvages" (1941) – the river which stands as a physical and symbolic rendering of the economics and fluid passages of the slave trade, conjoining the free and enslaved of North and South during the antebellum years (only a generation removed from Eliot himself), coursing through his birth town of St. Louis. Eliot even went so far as to sign himself "Tarbaby" when corresponding with Pound in 1925, when he was about to visit him in Rapallo, Italy.[42]

As I have suggested, Columbo's principal crewmembers are just as sexually obsessed as Columbo himself, including the cabin boy, the "bosun," and the chaplain (in a letter from 1916 to Aiken, the chaplain doubles as a version of Charlie Chaplin: "Charles, the Chaplain").[43] Eliot's rendition of colonial exploration thus imagines a pronounced sexual affiliation among sailors that extends the tradition of homoerotic "comradeship" found in sailor fiction – whose modernist culmination might be said to occur in Joseph Conrad's *Heart of Darkness* or *The Nigger of the Narcissus.* For the most part the Cuban natives also share the propensity to anal and excessive eroticism that the colonists do, and, as I have suggested, Columbo's crew find uncannily queer mirrors of themselves in the colonies. Offering an inversion of Homi Bhabha's model of mimicry, where the colonized subject responds "through the repetition of *partial presence*" to "the narcissistic demand of colonial authority," King Bolo and his Queen seem to belong, a priori, to the same confraternity of anal and scatological eroticism as the explorers.[44] The stanzas in effect partially level cultural difference by writing the colonial encounter as one in which the radical *sameness* of desire's surplus characteristics overrides dissimilarities of race, language, custom, history, and religion.

Yet the poems never once offer explicit judgment on their homosexual or bisexual practices (King Bolo and the queen are both alternately "bitches" and "bastards" through the cycle), and Eliot constructs queerness as simply intrinsic to the situational encounter.[45] The poems, I want to suggest, offer a version of Eliot's sexual discovery, charting the evolution of his queer poetics through an allegory of New World exploration. In only one instance does the speaker self-reflexively comment on the obscenity of Columbo's men, and this happens when the narrator accuses the "cabin boy," "Orlandino," of obscene *language*:

> A child of upright character
> But his language was obscene-o.
> "Fuck Spiders" was his chief remark
> In accents mild and dulcet.
> They asked him what there was for lunch
> And he simply answered "Bullshit."[46]

The censorious comment does not occur with reference to the violently sexual or scatological *acts*, but rather it notes the obscene *words* of one of the younger characters of the stanzas. Eliot is deconstructing his own game here by establishing a dichotomous and discontinuous set of values between himself as the writer of these verses and those who inhabit them. The speaker complains that Orlandino's language is "obscene-o," even though the stanzas themselves are much more hyperbolically smutty. This creates a *mise en abîme* structure of cascading standards that testifies to an almost endless play of possible allegories and critiques. Who is speaking for whom, and when, we have to ask. Meanwhile, Orlandino's *character* is considered "upright" despite the fact that he is one of the more repeatedly sodomized figures in the poems – in a stanza Eliot sent to Aiken in September 1914, the "cabin boy" is buggered after being "saved" from death: he "was sav'd alive / and bugger'd, in the sphincter."[47] This valence continues, especially if we take into account the unpublished stanzas at Yale, which are even more expressly homoerotic.

In his first Columbo and Bolo letter to Aiken, Eliot also mocks the projects of anthropology, history, and the academic establishment in general. In other words, he parodies his own location and interests, not least of which is his enchantment with Jessie L. Weston's *From Ritual to Romance* and Sir James George Frazer's *The Golden Bough* – two nineteenth-century anthropologically motivated treatises that would be enormously influential in the composition of *The Waste Land.* He glosses this particular Columbo and Bolo poem to write:

> The bracketed portions we owe to the restorations of the editor, Prof. Dr. Hasenpfeffer (Halle), with the assistance of his two inseparable friends, Dr. Hans Frigger (the celebrated poet) and Herr Schnitzel (aus Wien). How much we owe to the hardwon intuition of this truly great scholar! The editor also justly observes: "There seems to be a *double entendre* about the last two lines, but the fine flavour of the jest has not survived the centuries". – Yet we hope that such genius as his may penetrate even this enigma. Was it really the custom to drink ice-cream soda just before lunch? Prof. Dr. Hasenpfeffer insists that it was. Prof. Dr. Krapp (Jena) believes that the phrase is euphemistic.[48]

The "*double-entendre*" certainly refers to the homoerotic proposition of the lines in question, ("'Will you take tail? / Or just a bit of p(enis)?'"). At the same time, Eliot mocks the phony earnestness that can attend academic labor. Eliot's disillusion with the scholarly life began in full force while he was in Germany, and his stock Germanic professorial figures function as yet another caricature in this series. Academia, he suggests, is a dirty pursuit of the parenthetical, the excised, and the obscured. He writes a remarkable body of pornotropic poetry, and then laughs at us for considering it.

DESIRING PUBLICITY: ELIOT AS THE KWEEN OF "GOLDER'S [*SIC*] GREEN"

In addition to the pornotropic character of these Bolo poems what is startling is that Eliot actively tried to get them published. As it turns out, they are, *prima facie*, the first *face* that Eliot wanted to show the world.[49] After having participated *epistologically* in a teasing mimicry of Wyndham Lewis's important, though short-lived journal, *Blast*, and desiring inclusion within its moment, Eliot sent several Columbo and Bolo stanzas to Lewis early in 1915 for the second (and, what would be the last) issue of *Blast*. Lewis, however, rejected them, along with some of Eliot's other racy poems, "The Triumph of Bullshit," and "Ballade pour la grosse Lulu," which, like the Bolo verses, did not end up seeing publication until Ricks's *Inventions of the March Hare* in 1996. Lewis wrote to Pound to justify his decision: "Eliot has sent me Bullshit and the Ballad for Big Louise. They are excellent bits of scholarly ribaldry. I am trying to print them in *Blast*, but stick to my naif determination to have no 'words ending in -Uck, -Unt, and – Ugger.'"[50] Pound responded to Lewis by writing, "I dare say Eliot will consent to leaving blanks for the offending words."[51]

Eliot, in turn, reacted right away by writing a letter of complaint to Pound in February 1915:

> I have corresponded with Lewis, but his puritanical principles seem to bar my way to Publicity. I fear that King Bolo and his Big Black Kween will never burst into print. I understand that Priapism, Narcissism etc. are not approved of, and even so innocent a rhyme as
>
> . . . pulled her stockings off
> With a frightful cry of "Hauptbahnhof!!"
>
> is considered decadent.[52]

Eliot transforms Lewis's queasiness about overtly offensive language into a teasing charge that Lewis's "puritanical principles" will effectively keep him from finding the "Publicity" he desires. "Priapism" denotes the custom of placing a phallic god at the center of a decorative garden, as well as a more general licentiousness, and Eliot's naming of his activities in this guise reveals a self-mocking awareness of the exhibitionism he sought to deploy at this early stage of his career. Lewis's suggestion that Eliot's poetry was evidence of moral or sexual decadence, and his more subtle implication that Eliot was writing in a line of "decadent" poets might have been a veiled compliment. Lewis did, after all, publish some of Eliot's other verse in the forthcoming issue of *Blast*, accepting "Preludes" and "Rhapsody of a Windy Night [*sic*]."[53] Did Eliot consider "Preludes" and "Rhapsody" insufficient for the "Publicity" he hoped to achieve? Or, did Eliot find out after his grumbling letter to Pound that Lewis would include these two poems? Was he hoping that obscenity would do the work for him of "Publicity," as he offered a queer pornotropic poetics of colonialism to modernist readers several years before the bawdy sections of *Ulysses* appeared?

The young Eliot was hoping for a bit of capital "P" "Publicity" from the Columbo and Bolo poems, and he imagined them as his first "burst" onto the London literary scene. His desire for publication at this time was "keen," and he was willing to risk being dangerously flamboyant to find the publicity he wanted. In the grievance he sent to Pound, Eliot exactly echoes the language he uses in the Columbo and Bolo verses to describe the queen's mode of presenting herself: his poems could not "burst" upon the literary scene with the same ease that Bolo's "big black queen" "burst" onboard, and "burst" upon the party of colonists "drinking ice cream soda." That is, as elsewhere in his letters, especially to Pound, Eliot proposes that if writing is a sexual act, then publishing is its ejaculative fulfillment. Indeed, Eliot seemed to enjoy the valences of "burst[ing]" into print a great deal, and the term recurs in 1922 when he is about to publish *The Waste Land* in the first issue of his new journal, *The Criterion*. In this instance the tables are turned, and he gives Lewis a back seat, writing to Pound, "I think that if the *Waste Land* [*sic*] bursts out in the first number and you contribute to the second, that Lewis must remain behind the scenes until the third."[54]

Eliot's version of Lewis's charge against him as a still-unpublished poet was an excess of decadence, and a lack of puritanism – charges that are nearly impossible to imagine in the context of most later readings of Eliot. It is equally ironic and surprising that it was Lewis – something of a bad-boy iconoclast of English modernism – who policed these representations of race, sex, and ribaldry out of the nascent canon of literary modernism. If Eliot had been allowed to publish the Bolo poems, they would have arrived on the London scene as an interruptive element several years before the racy sections of *Ulysses* "burst" upon English literature and helped to make Joyce famous. This was not the only time that Eliot met the censor prior to publication among friends. When he was revising *The Waste Land* in 1921 he followed Pound's advice and excised the intensely sexual, scatological, and violently misogynistic sections which had initially begun "The Fire Sermon": "The white-armed Fresca blinks, and yawns, and gapes, / Aroused from dreams of love and pleasant rapes . . . Leaving the bubbling beverage to cool, Fresca slips softly to the needful stool, / Where the pathetic tale of Richardson / Eases her labour till the deed is done" (lines 3–4 and 11–14).[55]

After Lewis rejected his Bolo verses, Eliot persisted in trying to publish them for a number of years. Even as late as May 1921 Eliot was still hoping that the Bolo poems would someday find wider circulation. Although he did not know Joyce terribly well, and had only met him in 1920, Eliot offers him a sampling of the Columbo and Bolo poems in one of his letters of May 1921. He writes enviously to Joyce after having had a "taste" of the *Ulysses* manuscript for which he claims "nothing but admiration," particularly for the explicitly sexual sections, confessing to an anxiety of influence (as did others, including Virginia Woolf): "I wish, for my own sake, that I had not read it," complimenting Joyce on the news that "even a limited and very expensive edition is to appear," asking "Has it been properly circularised in England?"[56] He then admits that he has been having difficulty himself finding the publication and publicity he desires for his own "limited edition," exclaiming, "I wish that Miss Beach would bring out a limited edition of my epic ballad on the life of Christopher Columbus and his friend King Bolo, but 'Bolo's big black bastard queen / Was *so* obscene / She shocked the folk of Golder's Green.'"[57] Eliot had declared a serious admiration for the scandalous sections of *Ulysses* as soon as he read them in 1919, writing to his friend John Quinn, the New York lawyer and patron of the arts, "I should like to do everything I can about it over here. The part of *Ulysses* in question struck me as almost the finest I have read: I have lived on it ever since I read it."[58] The ribaldry of the scandalous, masturbatory, homoerotic, and copulative sections of *Ulysses* is not unlike that of Eliot's doggerel, and part of his frustrated admiration for Joyce could be due to the fact that Eliot met the censor before publication and "publicity," while Joyce met the censor after publication and the immense publicity of scandal.

As he does elsewhere, in Eliot's letter to Joyce he blurs the distinction between his "epic ballad" and "Bolo's big black bastard queen": both it (his poem) and she (the queen) are "so obscene" that they "shocked the folk of Golder's Green."[59] As such, Eliot makes Bolo's big black queen perform the allegorical work of obscenity; that is, she functions as a poetic-fictional "objective correlative" for his own desires for publicity. What Eliot is doing in this particular letter to Joyce is borrowing the shock-value of race and sex as markers of disruption in the precious atmosphere of suburban London in the teens, and applying these to the shock-value of his unpublishable poetry. In effect he constructs a tautological narrative about his inability to publish: the disruptive elements of color and sex are too obscene for the "folk of Golder's Green"; because the disruptive elements of color and sex are in my poems, no one will publish them; therefore my poems and I are as obscene as the "big black queen."

In another letter to Conrad Aiken in 1916, Eliot includes two more Columbo and Bolo stanzas as a gloss on his current situation after he reports that he is in a terrible state. Here, as elsewhere, Eliot explicitly uses the Columbo and Bolo poems to allegorize details of his own biography:

The news is that I am to be at Highgate School, near town, next term, that I am starting to rewrite my thesis, that my wife has been very ill, that I have been taken up with the worries of finance and Vivien's health, that my friend Jean Verdenal [to whom he dedicated the *Prufrock* volume in 1917] has been killed, that nothing has been seen of Armstrong, who is now a captain in Kitchener's army, that compulsion is coming in, that my putative publisher will probably be conscripted, that we are very blue about the war, that living is going up, and that

King Bolo's big black bassturd kween
That airy fairy hairy un
She led the dance on Golder's Green
With Cardinal Bessarian.[60]

King Bolo's queen has by this time moved from Cuba to London itself, to the fashionable Jewish neighborhood of Golders Green, no less, and she is physically on display as a dancer, paired with a powerful Catholic religious representative. The question is, what work is this queen doing for Eliot? Her status as a foreigner of color with no proper parentage would mark her as a "bassturd" in the strictures of British society of the time, while Eliot again implies that she might actually be a *male* (or transgendered) "queen" or "fairy" in drag. Both terms had come to mean "homosexual" by the late nineteenth century, and Eliot was well aware of their queer valences. The hair on the "airy fairy hairy un" recalls the "Arms that are braceleted and white and bare / (But in the lamplight, downed with light brown hair!)" (lines 62-3) from "The Love Song of J. Alfred Prufrock,"[61] although Bolo's queen is yet more hirsute.

The semiosis of her corporeality lacks the subtlety of being "downed with light brown hair," but still urges the dialogue between erotic attraction and physical repulsion that we find throughout the *Prufrock* volume.

In the same letter to Aiken, Eliot continues by claiming, "I am *keen* about rhymes ending in –een," and he appends the following stanza:

> King Bolo's big black bassturd kween
> Her taste was kalm and klassic
> And as for anything obscene
> She said it made her ass sick.[62]

Eliot here takes another linguistic step to incorporate himself into his poems, playing with sound and meaning by alluding to his feeling of being "keen" for the "een" sound, and thereby performatively enfolding himself into their rhyme scheme, and into the poems themselves. It is as if he himself is an extension of the "-een" rhymes in his cycle, or perhaps that he is just as *queer* as his verses – as if he just might be the "kween of Golder's Green." Invoking sodomitical metaphors to insist on the queen's distaste for obscenity – "anything obscene" "made her ass sick" – he again proposes that it is not the queen who is obscene, but it is the cultural dispensation that deems the fact of her large, queer, blackness which is obscene: the genteel "folk of Golder's Green" are thus the markers and makers of obscenity. The black queen functions as the sign of difference in the middle-class culture of Golders Green at a moment when foreignness was akin to obscenity, and the Jewish suburb did not necessarily give shelter to other displaced groups.

Hard as it is for us to imagine, Eliot perceived himself as an unwelcome foreigner in London in the teens – he was classless in British society, and he felt very much without family, having strained relations terribly with his father when he left America and then decided in the following year not to complete his doctorate at Harvard. In his letters Eliot was frequently preoccupied with a sense of alienation from Anglo-Saxon European culture generally, and already in the summer of 1914 he had written to Aiken, "I think that this will be a very pleasant exile on the whole, – though I cannot look upon a summer in Germany as anything but an exile."[63] This attitude changes little during the first years he lives in England, and he writes to his cousin Eleanor Hinkley in the fall of 1914, "I don't think that I should ever feel at home in England, as I do for instance in France . . . I should always, I think, be aware of a certain sense of confinement in England, and repression."[64] Eliot's very English wife, née Vivien Haigh-Wood, considered Eliot deeply "American," and in 1918 made excuses for missing a dance party hosted by their friend Mary Hutchinson by explaining, "Tom is impossible at present – very American and obstinate."[65] Then in 1919, in his own letter to Mary Hutchinson, Eliot writes, "But remember that I am a *metic* – a foreigner, and that I *want* to understand you, and all the background and tradition of you."[66] Less than three weeks earlier he had written to Ottoline Morrell – hostess extraordinaire of Bloomsbury in the country: "I feel completely exhausted and especially depressed by my awareness of having lost contact with Americans and their ways, and by the hopelessness of ever making them understand so many things."[67] Eliot never really felt he belonged anywhere, and this permanent state of cultural hybridity and even isolation is part of what he stages and negotiates through the transatlantic sexual *mélange* that emerges in the Columbo and Bolo cycle.

Instead of finding the publicity he desired for his bawdy poems Eliot shared them very privately over the years, often as a satiric way to negotiate his dealings with the public world of publishing and notoriety, and the private world of his identity as an *émigré*. Instead of the Bolo verses, Eliot's first publications, all in 1915, were "The Love Song of J. Alfred Prufrock," "The Boston Evening Transcript," "Aunt Helen," and "Cousin Nancy" in *Poetry*, "Preludes" and "Rhapsody of [*sic*] a Windy Night" in *Blast*, and "Portrait of a Lady" in *Others*. At the beginning of 1915 he was a young struggling poet, lucky to be befriended by the more established Ezra Pound. At the end of the year he was on his way to becoming the T. S. Eliot who would be canonized by such events as the *Dial* prize in 1922, the intense critical attention his writing received in little magazines and reviews in the teens and early twenties, and then by the nascent school of New Criticism in the 1920s and 1930s. These became the early basis of Eliot's reputation, and began to shape the character of English and American modernism. But now that we have Eliot's pornotropic verses in print, rereadings of his canonical poems are almost mandatory. We will inevitably come to understand a remarkably different Eliot – a pornographic Eliot, a smutty Eliot, and an Eliot committed to investigating the tensions between satire, sex, and race, as well as between memory and desire.

Although he was initially willing to come out of the closet with these poems, and to circulate them not simply to his coterie but to seek their publication, this attitude changed with his growing fame. By late 1922 Eliot's desire to publish the Columbo and Bolo poems seems to have entirely subsided. After the immense critical success of *The Waste Land,* Eliot could have published almost anything he wanted. Instead of finally then "coming out" with the Columbo and Bolo poems, Eliot decided to become his own censor. Not only did he choose not to publish his bawdy poems at this time, but when John Quinn asked if he could purchase Eliot's early notebooks, Eliot excised the leaves that contained the explicitly sexual and scatological material. Eliot had wanted to give Quinn the manuscript of *The Waste Land* as a gesture of thanks for Quinn's efforts – since 1917 – to support Eliot's work. His desire to publish in the United States was linked to a strong wish for familial approval, and he wrote to Quinn in January 1919, within two weeks of Eliot's father's death: "I explained to you when I wrote last how important it was to me for family reasons to get something in the way of a book published in America. Since then my father has died, but this does not weaken the need for a book at all – it really reinforces it – my mother is still alive."[68] Quinn was instrumental in Knopf's publication of *Poems* in 1919, and he appreciated Eliot's generous offer of *The Waste Land* manuscript, but Quinn wished to give Eliot financial as well as critical support, insisting that he *buy The Waste Land* leaves. Yet even though Eliot was financially strained during this period he refused to accept any funds for the manuscript, wanting to maintain the gesture of gift giving. Eliot did eventually agree, however, to Quinn's purchase of an early notebook that contained the Prufrock manuscripts and other juvenilia.[69] This notebook contained many of the Columbo and Bolo verses, along with some of Eliot's other pornotropic verse. Something startling happened at this juncture, though: before Eliot gave the notebook to Quinn he tore out what he feared might be offending pages. Apparently by 1922 Eliot had developed a heightened sense of shame at his explosively sexual experiments. He was by this time much less "keen" to have the Bolo verses "burst into print," and he suppressed them by not circulating them to his patron. That he did so while leaving the traces of these leaves (holding the notebook one sees obvious remnants of torn-out pages), and without destroying the poems suggests that while he wanted to withhold the explicit material, he also left room for these excisions to be discovered.

THE HERMENEUTICS OF HUMOR: ELIOT'S BAD BAWDY VERSE

Although Virginia Woolf may not have known about Eliot's Columbo and Bolo poems, she did manage to diagnose rather presciently his penchant for poetic critique coupled with humor. After a meeting with him in 1920 she records in her diary: "His turn is for caricature. In trying to define his meaning ('I dont [*sic*] mean satire') we foundered."[70] Earlier that year, Eliot made a similar comment about his role as a "satirist" in a letter to his brother, Henry. After Eliot had finally found publication in the United States with Knopf's collection of his work, simply entitled *Poems*, Eliot wrote to his brother about his worry that "Sweeney Erect" might "shock" their mother. Eliot also confessed he was ashamed to have her read some of his other poems, admitting that he had considered ripping out "Ode" from his English "Limited Edition" of *Ara Vos Prec* so she would not see it. This phantasy of keeping aspects of his verse hidden from the gaze of the maternal repeats Eliot's self-censorship with his patron/pater John Quinn. In his own defense to his brother, Eliot alluded to his perceived role in England as a satirist: "Some of the new poems, the Sweeney ones, especially 'Among the Nightingales' and 'Burbank' are intensely serious, and I think these two are among the best that I have ever done. But even here I am considered by the ordinary Newspaper critic as a Wit or a satirist, and in America I suppose I shall be thought merely disgusting."[71] Eliot evidently wants, all at once, to report his reception as a satirist, and to assert that his poems are *not* composed as mere satire. Satire, of course, can be "intensely serious," though its nuances are difficult to decipher, and its proliferating double meanings defer accountability. Indeed, only a few reviews have alluded to the Columbo and Bolo poems within *Inventions of the March Hare*, but among them, James Graham and Jan Gorak both emphasize Eliot's satirical stance. Graham claims that "The poems collected here are, in short, his treasure chest, the raw material he would work for years to come . . . He is determined to get satire, the critical stance, back into English verse."[72] Gorak, in turn, writes of "the fusion of dream and satire that drives these early poems."[73] In an essay contributed to Allen Tate's *T. S. Eliot: The Man and His Work* (1966) Bonamy Dobrée, who had gradually, over decades, become uneasy in his epistolary exchange with Eliot, downplays the extent of his familiarity with the poems. In the same piece, though, Dobrée notes their satiric character: Eliot "did not tell me much about those characters . . . but I was given portions of a Bolovian Epic (not always very decorous) and something about their religion. This latter was in part an amiable satire on the way people, anthropologists especially, talk about the religion of others."[74]

To read these verses without addressing their comic-book-like humor would be to oversimplify them radically. In *The Dialect of Modernism* Michael North affirms that much of the "new" language of modernism "was to be found in movies, comic strips, and smutty stories," and, in a discussion centered on Pound and T. S. Eliot, he cites a remark from

Conrad Aiken to indicate the modernist fascination with colloquial expression: "'The very language of the street had genius in it.'"[75] To take these poems too seriously would be to refuse the playful interruption they offer to the still-dominant but very narrow reading of T. S. Eliot as the most conservative emblem of high literary modernism and its critical correlative, the New Criticism. Eliot's doggerel not only mocks historical and quasi-historical figures, but it also parodies poetic form and expression: it reads itself reading history and desire by exposing both form and cultural conquest as riddled with intersecting excesses and absurdities. He experiments with stock bawdy humor and word play, managing to make us laugh in part because his verses show themselves up as utterly inane, disclosing the limits of the obscene as he pushes at the limits of the humorous. The poems are as ridiculous as they are offensive, and they stretch the boundaries of obscenity to make us question its very hermeneutics and construction.

As in his other poems, Eliot pushes traditional generic boundaries beyond their accepted limits, in this case by mixing aspects of several forms of light bawdy verse, including the limerick and the clerihew, to offer a peculiarly modernist, self-conscious form of pornotropic experiment. He called his Columbo and Bolo poems "ballads," and imagined setting them to music one day. Jonathan Gill points out that the verses exhibit an "affiliation with songs found in any number of popular anthologies of Negro song," and claims that they borrow conventions from minstrelsy song by featuring "phonetic spelling, improper syntax, and highly charged and malleable rhythms," as well as a "double tone."[76] As Francis Teague writes of the clerihew, we might also say that these lines provide "a cockneyed look at the great." The clerihew "differs from other light verse forms by its roughness: while other light verse is polished, the clerihew is deliberately clumsy, and might be said to burlesque a form such as the limerick."[77] The form in effect mirrors the poems' content, burlesquing traditional literary genres at the same time that the verses parody received narrative histories about the legend of Columbus.

In a 1998 review of *Inventions of the March Hare*, Alex Zwerdling makes the important point that "The cultural dispensation from which Eliot emerged demanded virtual silence on the subject of erotic life. Though he would free himself from it in part, the unpublished poems show that his imagination constantly brooded on the forbidden subject in ways that would have shocked his original readers."[78] Zwerdling also notes that in the sexually explicit sections of the draft for "The Love Song of J. Alfred Prufrock" – "Prufrock's Pervigilium," which appears in

Inventions of the March Hare for the first time – one "finds not only 'lonely men in shirtsleeves, leaning out of windows,' but 'women, spilling out of corsets,' standing in the entries of 'evil houses leaning all together' and 'pointing a ribald finger at me in the darkness.'"[79] Zwerdling's observations might equally apply to the more shocking Columbo and Bolo verses. In these, Eliot goes much further than invoking sex with female body parts "spilling out of corsets" and male torsos "leaning out of windows" – each pushing beyond confinement toward a sexual encounter. Instead of remaining within the strictures of synecdoche Eliot revels in lampoon, with his indestructible cartoon-like figures capable of superhuman feats: "A bullet came along the road / And up Columbo's asshole"; when Columbo is "sick-o" he "filled the pump with argyrol / And rammed it up his prick-o"; Columbo "spun his balls around his head / And cried 'Hooray for whores;'" and following the dictates of navigation, the crew "turned [Columbo's] asshole S. S.W."[80] As we discover when reading the Columbo and Bolo verses, Eliot was hardly a passive victim of sexually suggestive finger pointing: he shakes quite a "ribald" finger at his contemporary and later readers in these verses with a fusion of pornography, satire, and titillation that insistently intertwines the cultural memory of colonialism with a theory of its underlying modes of desire.

ELIOT'S *PARERGON*

How can we negotiate the existence of these poems alongside the body of Eliot's published material? We can no longer argue, as does Colleen Lamos, that "the gender anxieties and homosexual desires that pervade" Eliot's works were always "displaced or disavowed," nor that Eliot during this early period "sought to contain" his "errant impulses."[81] Instead, we might think of the Columbo and Bolo poems as a pornotropic *parergon* for Eliot's work. I borrow the term directly from Conrad Aiken's designation of the Bolo poems as "parerga" in a short essay called "King Bolo and Others" that he wrote to celebrate the occasion of Eliot's sixtieth birthday in 1948. Aiken's piece actually gives scant attention to the Bolo poems, but he refers to them as a knowing insider, participating in the quaint closeting of Eliot's verses that had by now been going on for decades. It is unlikely that many other contributors to the collection, with the exception of Clive Bell, knew the content of these verses. Aiken's title then operates as a titillating (and perhaps irritating) piece of knowledge about Eliot for which epistemological access was denied to most of the collection's readers and contributors.

Although he does not amplify his remarks with a sample from the Columbo and Bolo compositions, Aiken does give a rather interesting brief interpretation of the import of the poems to Eliot's oeuvre. He is especially reminiscent of their days together at Harvard:

> What did we talk about? or what didn't we? It was the first "great" era of the comic strip, of Krazy Kat,[82] and Mutt and Jeff, and Rube Goldberg's elaborate lunacies: it was also perhaps the most creative period of American slang, and in both these departments of invention he took enormous pleasure. How delighted we were with the word "dinge" for negro! This rich native creativeness was to be reflected, of course, in his poetry, notably in Prufrock.[83]

Eliding the boundaries between the humor of the comic strip and racist "slang," Aiken brings racism and humor together under the single banner of undergraduate delight. But where did Aiken get this slang from? Why were he and Eliot so excited to borrow racist humor and terminology? As Hortense Spillers proposes, they would not have *known* many blacks at all, but "what they did know was that 'dinge' named a limit, a neologism and, therefore, an unnamable, beyond representability."[84] These poems also offer the mnemonic trace of Eliot's own American-ness and his always ruffled sense of a generalized unbelonging – of being, somehow, originally traversed with "America," its dialects, and its painful legacy of originary and continuing racial violences, while always being at a loss for (re)possessing his American lineage. Turning to an allegory of New World discovery precisely at the moment when he was choosing the Old World over the New himself, these poems forcefully worry the limits of Eliot's self-representation as a racial Other and expose the hauntedness of his genealogical history as an American.

Aiken continues his tribute by recalling that Eliot's relish for slang and comic-book-like characters "gave rise to the series of hilariously naughty *parerga* which was devoted spasmodically to that singular and sterling character known as King Bolo, not to mention King Bolo's Queen, 'that airy fairy hairy- 'un, who led the dance on Golder's Green with Cardinal Bessarion.'"[85] Quoting from Eliot's 1916 letter, sent to him over thirty years earlier, Aiken again effaces race and obscenity from the equation to portray the "queen" simply as "Bolo's Queen" rather than his "big black queen," or his "big black bassturd Kween." He thus teases us and any fellow contributors who were not "in the know" about these verses by exposing only a glimmer of a sophomoric-sounding rhyme without context, offering Eliot a birthday gift coded in the registers of secrecy and intimacy, disavowing full accountability, but delighting in insider allusions.

Aiken's notion that the poems operate as *parerga* is a fitting description: the poems are "an extra ornament in art" (*Oxford English Dictionary*) that surprise us by revealing more about what we deem to be central to the text (whether literary or otherwise) than the center itself. Jacques Derrida articulates it in this way:

> A parergon comes against, beside, and in addition to the *ergon*, the work done [*fait*], the fact [*le fait*], the work, but it does not fall to one side, it touches and cooperates within the operation, from a certain outside. Neither simply outside nor simply inside. Like an accessory that one is obliged to welcome on the border, on board [*au bord*, *à bord*]. It is first of all the on (the) bo(a)rd(er) [*Il est d'abord l'à-bord*].[86]

Eliot's Columbo and Bolo poems situate themselves for us on the "border" or the boundary of his other canonical poems, touching them by illuminating new limits of interpretation; neither entirely "outside nor simply inside," they "inscribe[] something which comes as an extra, *exterior* to the proper field . . . but whose transcendent exteriority comes to play, abut onto, brush against, rub, press against the limit itself and intervene in the inside only to the extent that the inside is lacking."[87] The pornotropic poems shock us, highlighting and foregrounding Eliot's obsessions with sexuality, race, and the corporeal, so that we now know to read for traces of an intricate sexual imagination in his other poetry.

In his birthday tribute Aiken gives scarcely any further attention to the Columbo and Bolo poems. He does, though, insist on their value as social and academic critique: "These admirable stanzas, notable at times for their penetrating social criticisms were to continue for years as a sort of cynical counterpoint to the study of Sanskrit and the treatise on epistemology. Their influence on the development of a Style will no doubt come in due course to the attention of Herr Dr. Krapp of Wien."[88] Again, many of Aiken's audience of fellow contributors – not to mention his readers – would have had no idea what he was talking about: who might "Herr Dr. Krapp" be exactly? As it turns out, we are he: academic scholars who are only now uncovering these poems to give them critical attention. Eliot writes a bawdy *parergon* to his poems, and then laughs at us for considering it, embracing us into the fold of humor and titillation as its newest objects of satire. The Columbo and Bolo poems highlight his ongoing obsessions with sex, race, and history – concerns that recur in more moderate incarnations through his canonical writings – and they will necessarily change the ways we read T. S. Eliot.

CHAPTER 2

Mixing memory and desire: rereading Eliot and the body of history

> The world seems a complete nightmare at times; nothing that could happen would be surprising. I wonder if there will ever come a time when we shall look back and find that the period we are living through seems quite unreal in retrospect.
>
> T. S. Eliot, letter to his brother, Henry Eliot, 23 March 1917[1]

> In this alone we suffer:
> cut off from hope, we live on in desire.
>
> Dante, *The Inferno*[2]

THE WASTE LAND: A POESIS OF MEMORY

Where, one might ask, do we find anything commensurate in T. S. Eliot's canonical writing to the game of sexual display enacted on the scene of global history and cultural memory that he offers us in the sustained experiment of his Columbo and Bolo poems? We might not find the same erotic or histrionic excesses, but the Columbo and Bolo verses are still far closer in their bearings to his well-known poems than we might think, tempting as it is to concentrate on the astonishing gulf between what was "public" about Eliot's poetic output, and what has remained "private" even until now. A major line of continuity between these two bodies of work is to be found in their mutual and persistent blending of memory and desire, history and sexuality, the past and eros. That is, as with the Bolo poems, in Eliot's canonical texts we find a prevailing tropological substructure in his readings of the past which insists that approaching the enigma of anteriority means simultaneously reading desire. We find, then, a historical and mnemonic poetics of desire, and an eroticized, sensual poetics of history and memory, where memory and desire function analogically as inseparable aspects of Eliot's modernist historiography.

Let us turn for a moment to the opening of *The Waste Land*, in which the phrase, "mixing / Memory and desire," occurs. Eliot's poem begins with "The Burial of the Dead":

> April is the cruellest month, breeding
> Lilacs out of the dead land, mixing
> Memory and desire, stirring
> Dull roots with spring rain.[3]

In these lines, Eliot's speaker insists that April is cruel because it breeds flowers from death, it mixes the pastness of memory with the futurity implicit in desire, and it stirs what is dull and buried with a rain that promises rebirth. April is cruel because in its temporal pull it performs a zeugmatic function: it yokes together what is painfully opposite and seemingly unrelated through a dramatic revolution of the earth's cycles. I am borrowing the term "zeugma" from critical terminology which in turn takes zeugma from the Greek, where it signifies "means of binding" or "yoke." A zeugma may refer to a simple agrammatical yoking where a singular and plural are bound together in colloquial use: the common phrase "one or two *years* ago" should read "one year or two years ago," and thus yokes the singular with its double. Zeugma may also sylleptically bind the figurative and the literal, stimulating us to read metaphor as *equally* straddling two planes at once. It is principally used today as a poetic term to describe the yoking together of parts of speech in such a way that more than one semantic sense is evoked in a single phrase; this binding then produces a double meaning, or a momentary sleight of hand – a kind of linguistic double consciousness. The device was especially popular in the eighteenth century, and a frequently cited example comes from Pope's *The Rape of the Lock*: "[Anna] Dost sometimes Counsel take – and sometimes *Tea*."[4] The verb "take" is grammatically correct in both parts of the sentence, and without repeating itself links actions that are not usually thought of on equal footing: even though one certainly does "take" both "tea" and "council," the verb anticipates an object to do with advice that is not found. In its effect, a zeugma performs a semantic trick that makes us double back to reread language from an estranged place; a zeugma deceives our expectations for how language works, and through doing so commands that we rethink how words mean.

Here I want to push the term zeugma beyond its traditional rhetorical and poetic boundaries toward zeugma as epistemology. In this sense a zeugma names the place in which otherwise incongruous ideas are suddenly and forcefully yoked or "taken together" (as syllepsis) in such a way that produces a confusion, hesitation, and an almost violent opening to unmanageable meaning. Part of what Eliot is saying as he elaborates the agony of springtime – perhaps a rendition of modernism itself, as the late, never-really-expected blossoming out of a post-Victorian world – is that when newness and change happen, memory and desire mix. Woolf communicates a similar sentiment – perhaps deliberately echoing Eliot – when she writes in *The Years* (1937): "Spring was sad always . . . it brought back memories."[5] Recollection, both writers suggest, acutely touches the subject in instances of rebirth, while a poesis of forward-moving desire is intrinsic to any act of looking backward.

In this way, part of what Eliot is describing in the opening of *The Waste Land* is the necessity of reading history alongside its erotic and sensuous counterparts. That is, to understand the very difficult connotations of "mixing / Memory and desire" – which has become something of an unexamined, dead metaphor – we might do well to think of it as zeugmatically binding not two parts of speech, but two markedly different categories of human experience. Eliot's phrase, "mixing / Memory and desire," links what appear to be tragically incompatible: memory is inherently backward glancing (it considers anteriority, it provides a legible – if unpredictable – archive of what has been), while desire propels us to act, compels thought, and produces futurity; desire is the mysterious sap that stirs "Dull roots with spring rain," even while the land appears to be dead. Part of the pain of April, then, stems from the "breeding," "mixing," and "stirring" of the *copulating* land, whose love pangs generate nothing less than a potent mixing of eros and thanatos: a gerund-inflected resurrection from a landscape of death. This "zeugma" thus stresses the alienation of memory from desire while crucially announcing their closeness.

Part of what I hold myself responsible for in querying the "mixing" of "memory and desire" involves asking why and how Eliot's epoch-defining poem happens to begin with this gesture. Certainly one can think of the past and feel desire, but if one tries to untangle what it means to feel such a desire in relation to what is ostensibly finished and irretrievable, then the prospect becomes more troubling. What I want to propose is that Eliot's work here is striking past a poetics of nostalgia that would seek, and then mourn, a lost phantasy of a retrievable past. Eliot's poems show us again and again that nostalgia's leanings toward a surplus, or perceived plenitude, of the past can never be satiated: the remains of the past will again emerge, psychically and even materially, but they will return as a charged detritus that demands renegotiating if we are to discover its "breeding" and flowering. Eliot thus points to a poetics of desire and memory that would claim a porous, interdependent affiliation between the two figures: coordinating memory and desire's syllepsis means to observe and accept their interdependence and fundamental coupling.

Because April stands as the month when this forward–backward temporal dialectic is writ large in the "natural" world of the west, the time of year of this first section of *The Waste Land* conjures a traditional, even Romantic, conception of desire that would be in sync with natural and calendrical cycles. In Eliot's writing, however, "nature" is always included with hesitation. Following Baudelaire, whom Eliot acknowledged as a major poetic influence, nature often emits "confusing speech," and can never be read simply "naturally": "*La Nature est un temple où de vivants piliers / Laissent parfois sortir de confuses paroles.*"[6] Later in "The Burial of the Dead" the speaker observes the undead who, as if in opposition to the natural laws of gravity, "Flowed up the hill" (line 66). He then addresses "Stetson" – a ghostly representative of the mythic past of the first Punic War (*c.* 264–241 BCE) between Rome and Carthage – to inquire about rebirth from the remnants of the dead: "'That corpse you planted last year in your garden, / 'Has it begun to sprout? Will it bloom this year? / 'Or has the sudden frost disturbed its bed?'" (lines 71-3). Eliot's perspective on springtime proposes not the clear structuring of nature as analogous to personal experience by which Romanticism at least in part defined itself, but a subtle disruption of nature vis-à-vis the social and the psychic at the very moment when nature appears unproblematically to mimic these spheres. As such, Eliot's rendition of April also points to a prevailing modernist alienation from late nineteenth- and early twentieth-century epistemological and symbolic codes.

April is cruel because by prompting memory it reminds one of the inevitability and necessity of change. Its function is both anamnestic (helping rather than hindering memory) and recuperative – through its annual repetition it recalls to consciousness what might have been forgotten. After the seeming immutability that winter grants by freezing time – along with landscape and memory ("Winter kept us warm, covering / Earth in forgetful snow, feeding / A little life with dried tubers," lines 5-7) – spring forces us not only to remember, but to participate in change. Winter keeps us "warm" because it allows us to survive in the illusory forgetfulness of what feels like a stilled temporality. We become so forgetful in fact that we do not mind being fed by "dried tubers," failing to recall that spring's rebirth and summer's growth can bring forth more desirable fruit. These first lines thus function as a foundational and unifying trope for *The Waste Land* as a whole, indicating from the outset that the poem will be concerned with suffering, regeneration, and cyclic time, as well as with (re)negotiating a future from the past. These lines also work as a distilled referent for Eliot's underlying interests in the intersections of time, memory, and desire that run through his poetic works, and they begin to illuminate the project of modernism reading itself in relation to historicity.

ENGENDERING "GERONTION"

While critics have considered the texture of the cityscape in Eliot's poetry fairly extensively, and resonances of specific locales sound deeply in many of his poems (we might think of both London and Boston in "The Love Song of J. Alfred Prufrock," London in *The Waste Land*, and both rural England and New England in the *Four Quartets*), in some instances the physiognomy of place is superseded by the physicality of the human body – especially the female body – as a correlative that helps to underscore the spatiality of memory. In "The Metaphysical Poets," written in 1921, the year in which he began to draft *The Waste Land*, Eliot intimates a special interest in this tropological pattern by drawing attention to a moment in Donne's "A Valediction: Of Weeping" where Donne renders spatiality and contemporary geography in terms of the human body. Tracing the movement of the poem, Eliot notes that Donne shifts adroitly "from the geographer's globe to the tear, and the tear to the deluge."[7] That is, Eliot's modernist sensibilities were sensitive to the ways in which Donne identifies the cartography of globalism and the evolving science of maps in terms of a quick shift to a legible bodily and emotional product (tears), with the poem then cycling back to a natural phenomenon ("the deluge," which is Eliot's word) that physical and human geography might have been seeking to manage.

In "Gerontion" (1920) Eliot indicates a similar predisposition for metaphors of mapping history as it meets the body. The poem opens with a desire for rain that almost begs for an allegorical reading, prefiguring the need for personal and cultural salvation and regeneration that *The Waste Land* will make one of its principal *topoi*: "Here I am, an old man in a dry month, / Being read to by a boy, waiting for rain" (lines 1-2). The juxtaposition of "age and youth," the passive "waiting" of the elder figure who refers to himself narratologically with the demonstrative phrase, "Here I am" – as though considering himself from outside a strict interiority that nevertheless feels called to mark being in the first-person for the (exterior) reader of the poem – and the boy's contrasting *activity* of reading aloud, all ask us to link the desire for rain and wetness with desires for mythical and psychosexual communication, cleansing, and sexual refertilization. Unlike the "spring rain" that stirs "dull roots" in "The Burial of the Dead," however, and in contrast to the exquisite tension Eliot builds in "What the Thunder Said" around a sustained desire for rain that finally comes "In a flash of lightning" (line 393), no rain ever falls in "Gerontion." Instead, the poem negotiates sexual dryness and the death of passion through anatomizing and finally eviscerating the troubled body of history.

At the structural heart of "Gerontion" – indeed, at exactly the halfway point – we find an imperative command to "think" history and memory. The central verse paragraph begins:

> After such knowledge, what forgiveness? Think now
> History has many cunning passages, contrived corridors
> And issues, deceives with whispering ambitions,
> Guides us by vanities. Think now
> She gives when our attention is distracted . . .
>
> (lines 32-6)

This passage refers rather explicitly to female genitalia as a metaphor for the permutations and unpredictable curvatures of history. As with his Columbo and Bolo poems, Eliot's phrasing and tone invoke both an erotic playfulness and a disturbing misogyny. Punning in multiple registers on history's "cunning passages, contrived corridors / And issues," we find history evoked both as the secret(ions) and fluids of female sexual desire and as the birth event itself. Deriding female sexuality as he does through much of his poetry, this passage embodies a crucial ambivalence about writing the past in Eliot's work, as we feel a palpable disgust and protest against the entrapment, slipperiness, and spiraling excesses that history threatens with her (multiple) "cunning passages" and "contrived corridors."

If, as Paul Veyne suggests, "every event is worthy of history,"[8] perhaps part of Eliot's discomfort here stems from history's potential for endless and excessive proliferation and reproduction. History is uncontainable and (sexually) messy; we are never quite in control of its meaning because so much of it has existed by way of a metaphoricity that remains always just slightly ajar. Michel de Certeau reminds us that "every true historian is a poet of meticulous detail who plays, as does the esthetician, on the thousand harmonic levels that a rare piece awakens within a broad network of knowledge."[9] De Certeau insists, too, on the endless "deviations" of *narratives* about history from what we might deem historical *facts*, and he stresses the epistemological impossibility of arriving at any final "truth" about the past. Eliot knows full well that casting (or recasting) a version of history depends on the vicissitudes of memory and the limits of narration, and this section of "Gerontion" attests to a worry that the complications of historiography might be analogous to the unreadable signifiers of elusive, hidden, female sexual organs.

The poem's logic further proposes that history as a woman is not to be trusted – she dissembles and "Guides us by vanities" (line 35). Like the women in the *Prufrock* volume, whom Eliot's speaker finds discomforting because they are never quite what they appear to be – "Arms that are braceleted and white and bare / (But in the lamplight, downed with light brown hair!)" (lines 63-4) – history in "Gerontion"

> gives when our attention is distracted
> And what she gives, gives with such supple confusions
> That the giving famishes the craving. Gives too late
> What's not believed in, or if still believed,
> In memory only, reconsidered passion. Gives too soon
> Into weak hands, what's thought can be dispensed with
> Till the refusal propagates a fear. (lines 36-42)

History gives when we are not ready for the gift, and she gives in such an indecipherable manner that her gift is insufficient to desire, which hopes for a radical readability of its object. History in this schema is repellent because of her cleverness, contrivances, and disorderliness. History lies, expects too much, maps an excess, and proceeds by way of the "vanities" of narcissistic self-interest. The mixing of memory and desire, then, is not always an easy exchange, and history as a woman does not satisfy.[10]

Unlike Eliot's question in "Prufrock," "Is it perfume from a dress / That makes me so digress?" (lines 65-6), the speaker in "Gerontion" is vulnerable to history-as-femininity only when he is *already* "distracted." In this state of half-attention he experiences her advances as confusing, her gift prolonging and extending desire, stirring but not satiating it. Such a titillation condemns the subject to the hellish punishment conjured in Dante's lines from *The Inferno* that I cite at the beginning of this chapter, with which Eliot strongly identified: "In this alone we suffer: / cut off from hope, we live on in desire." Eliot's feminized embodiment of history gives her subject not living "passion," but a stale substitute that starves under the guise of an offering (communion?) that is either no longer "believed in," or, if it is (he is uncertain), only through the subjective archive of memory. Desire has lost the vitality that nevertheless still throbs in history's sexual contours with her game of giving. Eliot thus writes history and desire as chiasmatically engaged in an endless loop:[11] history is vitally sexual, but that vitality is not necessarily vitally desired. Memory, in this section of "Gerontion," marks the repository of old, abandoned beliefs and passions that can be recalled but not relived, and the wish to explore history – so palpable elsewhere in Eliot's oeuvre – collapses when directly confronted with the logic of history as *heterosexual* sex. This should not surprise us too much, since in Eliot's work what is specifically *undesirable* about desire are most often its heteronormative and authorized forms, and he persistently works through this unease by expressing "inverted" queer desire in a much more positive light – a point to which I will return.

In "Gerontion" the speaker negotiates sex, memory, and history by remembering a failed sublime of love and a failed erotic cathection to remembrance. By its second half the poem begins to sound very much like an elegy for the lost possibility of romantic encounter:

> I that was near your heart was removed therefrom
> To lose beauty in terror, terror in inquisition.
> I have lost my passion: why should I need to keep it
> Since what is kept must be adulterated?
> I have lost my sight, smell, hearing, taste, and touch:
> How should I use them for your closer contact?
> (lines 54-9)

As though recovering from heartbreak, Eliot's speaker catalogues the "lost objects" of a failed relationality, moving deftly from the aesthetic category of lost "beauty" to lost "terror" and "passion," and then to the intensely personal vehicles of the five senses that are responsible for subjective appreciation, with each sense enumerated, sight coming first. Just as in the erotically charged moment of *The Waste Land* when Eliot paraphrases a passage from Sappho's fragment thirty-one – "I could not / Speak, and my eyes failed, I was neither / Living nor dead" (lines 38-40) – desire makes the senses run aground, and memory, as the legacy of history's "cunning passages," seals the failure. In *To the Lighthouse* Woolf's narrator asks, "how could one express in words these emotions of the body?",[12] and Eliot's speaker pronounces a similar failure of language when confronted with passionate excess. Akin to Edmund Burke's eighteenth-century ideas of the sublime, where the rift between the sublime and the beautiful is absolute – "A mode of terror, or of pain, is always the cause of the sublime," while "the beautiful is founded on mere positive pleasure, and excites in the soul that feeling, which is called love"[13] – beauty is lost in terror to approach a sublime that is the inverse of Romantic desire. Quite significantly, Eliot's speaker does not ask why should I keep it? (passion), but "why should I *need* to keep it?" (my emphasis), as though he seeks answers from an external necessity of the order of a god, or at least a law – a law that also ordains "what is kept *must* be adulterated" (my emphasis).

Personal recollection in this way indicates a loss and adulteration of desire, as Eliot constructs the past in terms of what Christine Froula has identified in *The Waste Land* as "the translation of remembered passion and desire into repugnant, implicitly repudiated forms."[14] That is, while Eliot explicitly links history and desire, desire for him is so regulated and controlled that it often becomes, de facto, the emotive object to be forever modified and displaced. Desire, after all, entails an excess that we wish (but inevitably fail) to know, and our very longing to control it points to desire's unrepresentable and unruly psychic value. In Jacques Lacan's terms, desire involves an endlessly unsatisfied "desire of the Other,"[15] with the wish of and for the Other existing at the very etiology of subjectivity: "the first object of desire is to be recognized by the other."[16] Desire, too, is always mediated by language and the chain of signification that metonymically represents the endless distance between the ostensible *thusness* of the signified and the emptiness of the relational signifier. But what are we without this *full and empty* opacity of the signifier, whose mystery simultaneously enchants and alienates us? It is through the very structure of our relation to words, that is, that we find language all at once estranging, desirable, and fundamentally poetic. For Lacan, as for Eliot, desire is always bound up in compulsion, and in wanting what lies beyond the sphere of transparent choice: it involves our need for recognition and reciprocity from that Other who nevertheless will always remain an absolute alterity. Desire needs the cooperation and even co-opting of an Other in order to be met, and it therefore sits at one of the limits of human freedom. Patrick Fuery puts it this way: "Whereas 'need' and 'demand' can be tied to specific objects and relations, 'desire' always exceeds those objects and the subject's relationships to them."[17]

Perhaps it is precisely because desire's fulfillment is endlessly regulated for us by an Other that Eliot turns to a Christian-Buddhist renunciation of desire in later poems like "Ash Wednesday" (1930) and the *Four Quartets* (1935–42). His opening lines of "Ash Wednesday" – "Because I do not hope to turn again / Because I do not hope / Because I do not hope to turn / Desiring this man's gift and that man's scope" (lines 1-4) – attempt to relinquish hope and desire at the text's outset, as though by forsaking this apparatus he may start somewhere closer to the purified intention of prayer. This gesture, though, collapses again by the poem's end into desire for the Other of the divine, as though Eliot manages only to transpose desire from the human to the sacred in these crucial years around his conversion: "Suffer me not to be separated // And let my cry come unto Thee" (lines 218-19). Then, a decade later in "East Coker" (1940) Eliot writes intratextually about striving to live without desire or expectation: "I said to my soul, be still, and wait without hope / For hope would be hope for the wrong thing" (lines 124-5). Within desire's structure, Eliot seems to be saying, is both the hope for its realization alongside a maturing awareness in the subject (chained to temporality and remembrance) that such a realization must, paradoxically, not be anticipated. As Eliot proposes in "Little Gidding," (1942) "This is the use of memory: / For liberation – not less of love but expanding / Of love beyond desire" (lines 157-9). Such a renunciation and displacement of desire, then, equals a freedom from time and memory: a "liberation / From the future as well as the past" ("Little Gidding," lines 159-60).

MEMORY AND/AS HISTORY

He who has once begun to open the fan of memory never comes to the end of its segments.

Walter Benjamin, "A Berlin Chronicle," 1932[18]

If history deceives, then what work does memory do, and how do these two figures differ in Eliot's writing? I want to argue that modernist writers tended to conflate history and memory, intertwining the acts and facts of the past with the conscious and unconscious narrations and renditions of such events. For their part, Eliot and Woolf both blurred the distinction between recollection and the historical, and the boundaries between memory and history are frequently slight in their work.[19] Memory and history bleed into each other's parameters, and even global events are often conveyed through lenses and allegories of personal experience. "History" in the modernist sense stands as either an absolute, unlimited temporal designation for all the facts of past thought and occurrence – the impossible sum total of all that has ever happened, and the reality of the vastness of the past – or, more realistically, history is any one of many possible narrative renditions of "the truth" of past time.[20] History in this second sense relies on framing, chance, and discursivity to convey ideas about the past in legible terms. As Fredric Jameson contends, "history is *not* a text, not a narrative, master or otherwise, but . . . it is inaccessible to us except in textual form."[21] Roland Barthes, for his part, suggests that "Historical discourse does not follow the real; rather, it only signifies it, endlessly reiterating that *it happened.*"[22] Contrary to notions that a modernist historical sense generally involves peremptory and totalizing narratives (as critics are especially fond of noting through the case of Eliot's "Tradition and the Individual Talent"), Eliot and Woolf both generate a self-reflexive and metaphorically intricate hermeneutics and poetics of the past. Each plays the game of being attracted to the possibility of resuscitation from the dead, and thereby accessing a still-numinous vitality of the past; however, each recognizes that what we claim to know or recall about the past depends on the aleatory motivations and desires particular to given subjective (dis)positions. "History" both *describes* the time of the past – signaling a discursive representation of ostensible knowledge about past events, thought(s), tendencies, and socio-cultural predispositions – while it also *constitutes* the past. As Michel De Certeau affirms, "What we initially call history is nothing more than a narrative," but, from there, "another history begins. It tends to establish heteronomy ('That's what happened') within the homogeneity of language ('That's what they say,' or 'That's what we read'). It produces the historical dimension within the element of a text. More strictly speaking, it is tantamount to *making history.*"[23] History involves a convoluted layering of event and discourse, even while it often holds onto claims to "objectivity" and "factuality."

Memory, in contrast, will sooner confess its dependence on subjectivity and the unreliable ways in which conscious and unconscious domains register experience. Memory denotes a relation with anteriority that is negotiated more explicitly through a lens that is deemed at least partially "private" and singular, while it assumes some experiential connection with a contemporaneity that extends into an idea of the past. Concomitantly, what one conventionally knows as a kind of capital "H" "History" claims to bear testimony to a (theoretically) shared and agreed upon knowledge about facts of the past: others have recognized the significance of certain episodes or cultural features that take root in the collective mind as marks of previous time. Still, once one moves beyond the sphere of strictly personal recollection, distinctions collapse, particularly when we take into consideration cultural memory. Jan Assman offers a wonderfully lucid formulation of cultural memory, which he sees as involving

> that body of reusable texts, images, and rituals specific to each society in each epoch, whose "cultivation" serves to stabilize and convey that society's self-image. Upon such collective knowledge, for the most part (but not exclusively) of the past, each group bases its awareness of unity and particularity . . . Through its

cultural heritage a society becomes visible to itself and to others. Which past becomes evident in that heritage and which values emerge in its identificatory appropriation tells us much about the constitution and tendencies of a society.[24]

We are also well aware since Freud that memory may be real or imagined – an archive of actual experience, ridden with what Assman calls the archive's "potentiality"[25] – or almost entirely overwritten by phantasy. Freud, for example, proposes that memories may be "altered and falsified, and . . . put into the service of later [psychic] trends,"[26] while elsewhere he wants to "assure" us that this falsification does not necessarily mean an innate predisposition to dissembling: "people often construct such things unconsciously – almost like works of fiction."[27] Memory from this perspective becomes a partially fictional encryption, ridden with Assman's "potentiality of the archive" (punning, perhaps, on its *potency* and *power*) that is always already overdetermined by what the psyche is capable of instantiating.

Of course, as Paul Veyne insists, "History with a capital H," properly speaking, "does not exist. There only exist 'histories of' . . . The idea of History is an inaccessible limit or, rather, a transcendental idea. That History cannot be written."[28] Veyne also suggests, "All that consciousness knows of history is a narrow fringe of the past whose memory is still living in the collective memory of the present generation; it also knows – Heidegger seems to set great store by this – that its existence is existence with others, collective destiny."[29] Memory, on the other hand, is more subjective and fragile; as collective as cultural memory may be, it tends to shift, rewrite, and forget in ways that an idealized notion of an objective history does to a lesser degree. Once an idea or an event makes it into the realm of the so-called "historical," it is very hard to unwrite such an utterance; memory, though, is notoriously more prone to vicissitudes. In "Leonardo da Vinci and a Memory of His Childhood," Freud draws the analogy between memory and history by asserting,

A man's conscious memory of the events of his maturity is in every way comparable to the first kind of historical writing [which was a chronicle of current events]; while the memories that he has of his childhood correspond, as far as their origins and reliability are concerned, to the history of a nation's earliest days, which was compiled later and for tendentious reasons.[30]

The two categories are always open to undoing, and both Woolf and Eliot persistently transgress and break down distinctions between memory and history. Michel Foucault, for one, has taught us that history exists equally in the interstitial gaps of life and experience as it does in the cultural, technological, military, aesthetic, and economic shifts that continue to be most noted by historians: a "history, guided by genealogy . . . seeks to make visible all of those discontinuities that cross us."[31]

What we find Eliot and Woolf already expressing in the early part of the twentieth century is that to *know* history means to bring it into the folds of psychic time and to relate it to the (erotic and sensuous) implications of memory. As Michael Steinberg proposes in a discussion of Walter Benjamin, "In its existential import, history converges with memory."[32] Eliot and Woolf each shows that *both* history and memory rely on narration, and are thus vulnerable to fissures, "cunning passages," and displacements; history, they repeatedly insist, is as subjective as memory. When Woolf writes of her childhood, she frequently remembers feelings, images, and sensations rather than major events. In "A Sketch of the Past" she describes the formation of memory in this way: "we are sealed vessels afloat upon what it is convenient to call reality; at some moments, without a reason, without an effort, the sealing matter cracks; in floods reality; that is a scene."[33] When a "scene" is registered it then becomes the indelible *matter of memory* – a point to which I will return – that will remain to be unearthed. Further, Woolf and Eliot both juxtapose the briefest moments of time with global politics and shifting historical conditions. Homi Bhabha's words here have prescience: "We need another time of writing that will be able to inscribe the ambivalent and chiasmatic intersections of time and place that constitute the problematic 'modern' experience of the western nation."[34] Such a writing would be both "historical" and mnemonic, but it would write history without invoking a monolithic notion of a singular and tellable past. For Woolf and Eliot what *matters* for both personal and cultural memory is any instance that generates a sufficient cathection between the person and the "scene" (or fragment) imposed on the archive of the psyche. Neither writer was after any kind of "total history" that claimed to describe every nuance of the past; both were aware that the histories and memories they wrote depended upon the changing operations of phantasy, citation, chance, and forgetting.

What place does desire have in Eliot and Woolf's modernist engagements with history and remembrance? In their texts, desire and eros endlessly invite themselves into the dynamic of approaching the past and its inscription – as though to affirm that the past *cannot* be told without their sensational supplement. Several years before writing "Gerontion" or *The Waste Land*, Eliot draws "memory and desire" together in "Rhapsody on a Windy Night" (1915). In this instance, memory (like desire elsewhere in his texts) meets a limit of manageability and decipherability. As if to categorize and encase memory within *chronos*,

"Rhapsody on a Windy Night" situates recollection within the arbitrary but strictly regulated divisions of clock time over the space of a single night, and the demarcation of the hours operate formally to separate the stanzas. The march of clock time provides one of the few stable anchors in a poem concerned to express the chaos of desire vis-à-vis memory within an alienating modern cityscape:

> Twelve o'clock.
> Along the reaches of the street
> Held in a lunar synthesis,
> Whispering lunar incantations
> Dissolve the floors of memory
> And all its clear relations,
> Its divisions and precisions.
> Every street lamp that I pass
> Beats like a fatalistic drum,
> And through the spaces of the dark
> Midnight shakes the memory
> As a madman shakes a dead geranium.
> (lines 1-12)

Memory, like a grammar or a calculus, is, like chronological time, arranged by "clear relations" and "divisions and precisions" that are nevertheless delicate and prone to dissolution. The specific time of "midnight" (repeated twice; in the second instance by *naming* it rather than by citing its number on the clock dial) "shakes the memory," as if recollection is destabilized by meeting a conjunction of the dead of night with the carefully notated framework of clock time. While every memory is made *in time*, Eliot figures memory's disruption by the temporal with a simile that pronounces the likeness between this disruption and madness. In this way, the vanished vitality of the "dead geranium" offers an objective correlative for the waste of memory's fecundity.

What version of memory is Eliot presenting us with here? One approach critics have taken in reading Eliot's "use of memory" (to borrow Eliot's phrase from "Little Gidding" which Grover Smith makes the title of a 1996 study)[35] is to think of his work in juxtaposition with that of the French philosopher, Henri Bergson. Eliot attended Bergson's weekly lectures at the Collège de France through the Sorbonne in 1911, when Eliot was just twenty-three. Bergson's lecture notes seem not to have survived,[36] but his thinking about memory was fairly consistent through this period, when he was building on the theories put forth in his highly influential *Matter and Memory*, first published in 1896, but already in its fifth edition by 1908, two years before Eliot arrived in Paris. Bergson's approach to memory is pseudo-scientific and intensely materialistic: he repeatedly stresses, in a very literal sense, that the past leaves material traces in the psyche, whose deposits then become the "matter" of memory. An endless "exchange" of "substance"[37] also occurs between present "perception" and one's "recollection" of the past: "if there be memory, that is, the survival of past images, these images must constantly mingle with our perception of the present and may even take its place."[38] For Bergson, "Memory, inseparable in practice from perception, imports the past into the present, contracts into a single intuition many moments of duration, and thus by a twofold operation compels us, de facto, to perceive matter in ourselves, whereas we, de jure, perceive matter within matter."[39]

In the case of "Rhapsody on a Windy Night," Donald Childs finds Eliot's use of memory decisively un-Bergsonian, agreeing with Gertrude Patterson that Eliot wants to repudiate Bergson's understanding of memory as biologically based and lacking a coherent philosophic system.[40] Patterson, Childs points out, "suggests that the poem finds the Bergsonian ideal – pure memory – useless: clearly, 'memory' in this poem only serves to make the present more sordid, more meaningless; this is the only 'illumination' which it can offer: it can urge the observer to no meaningful activity since its contents are useless to him."[41] I would, though, urge us to reconsider this claim. Surely Eliot often presents memory as a figure of barrenness and failed potential, but within the lament for a plenitude that the past did not bring forth, we find that memory and desire mix because what one remembers – and then labors to record through writing about that experience in time – are none other than sites of intense desire. And, part of Eliot's turn to memory involves what Frank Kermode has brilliantly explored as Eliot's profound *surrender* to poetry – a giving himself over to "the bewildering minute"[42] of the enigma of experience, a facing of the past's contents that is made especially possible through the mediation of poetry. It is through the act of remembering that we reanimate earlier desires through a longing to recuperate something of the never-achieved promises the past seemed to hold. That is, through recollection we mimetically re-enact and re-stage desire.

Eliot's speaker in the last section of *The Waste Land* surrenders and confesses this remembrance to the reader:

> *Datta*: what have we given?
> My friend, blood shaking my heart
> The awful daring of a moment's surrender

> Which an age of prudence can never retract
> By this, and this only, we have existed
> Which is not to be found in our obituaries
> Or in memories draped by the beneficent spider
> Or under seals broken by the lean solicitor
> In our empty rooms (lines 402-10)

The process of recollection, then, means foundering, and undergoing repeated, compulsive longings for the desires of the past, for a blood that shakes the heart, for the surrender that is the ground of our existence. This chronic, faltering turn to remembrance coincides with an anxiety about facing (again) time's most existentially charged moments: "The awful daring of a moment's surrender" is the key and the means, the only means, for how – "we have existed."

This link between memory and desire – where each is dialectically and dialogically involved in the disequilibrium and unevenness of memory as failed desire, and where memory and desire continually anticipate each other's limits – remains true in Eliot's later poetry. In "Burnt Norton" (1935), we discover something akin to a testament of love about Emily Hale, the woman with whom Eliot had an "understanding" before he left Harvard for France in 1910, with whom Eliot engaged in an extended correspondence, and who still hoped Eliot would marry her after his first marriage with Vivien Haigh-Wood collapsed in the early 1930s. In "Burnt Norton" the speaker mourns the failed possibility of their relationship, lamenting the "passage which we did not take / Towards the door we never opened / Into the rose-garden" (lines 12-14).[43] The roses of this garden, loaded with traditional associations with love, courtship, and desire, stand as a beyond that was "never" approached and perhaps as a "surrender" that never occurred, reminding us of the shriveled potential of the "dead geranium" in "Rhapsody on a Windy Night."[44]

HYSTERY AND DESIRE

Eliot's little-known prose poem, "Hysteria," found in the *Prufrock* volume, boldly enunciates the repeated fear of contamination from the feminine that Eliot evinces in a great deal of his poetry, and uses this repulsion as a way to approach the feminized dangers of history. The poem is one of Eliot's funniest pieces, and it deals with the confrontation that emerges when (male) decorum meets the contagion of (female) hysterical laughter. In the poem a man and a woman are seated for tea in the very public space of a restaurant when the woman undergoes a fit of uncontrollable laughter. Despite his efforts at resistance, the male speaker experiences an excessive identification with the laughing woman even as he struggles against the threat of incorporation "in the dark caverns of her throat" (line 4). The narrative subsequently follows and parodies the spectacle of their hysterical assimilation, concluding with the speaker's attempts to resist emasculation and hysteria by controlling the "shaking" (line 9) of the female body in order to resume normative codes of behavior. The poem is short, and I will reprint it in full here.

Hysteria

As she laughed I was aware of becoming involved in her laughter and being part of it, until her teeth were only accidental stars with a talent for squad-drill. I was drawn in by short gasps, inhaled at each momentary recovery, lost finally in the dark caverns of her throat, bruised by the ripple of unseen muscles. An elderly waiter with trembling hands was hurriedly spreading a pink and white checked cloth over the rusty green iron table, saying: "If the lady and gentleman wish to take their tea in the garden, if the lady and gentleman wish to take their tea in the garden . . . " I decided that if the shaking of her breasts could be stopped, some of the fragments of the afternoon might be collected, and I concentrated my attention with careful subtlety to this end.

In his intense identification with the woman's impulsive laughter, the male speaker does nothing less than confess to his own propensity to the dangers and contagions of hysteria. Echoing a scene of fellatio, he is taken inside her throat, "lost finally in the dark caverns," and "bruised" in a violent, sado-masochistic phantasy of incorporation and devourment.

As a partial answer to the fascination with "female smells in shuttered rooms" from "Rhapsody on a Windy Night" (line 66), where the speaker experiences "smell" as a double entrapment within confining interior spaces, the male speaker in "Hysteria" renders an oscillating repulsion and attraction to the female body by allowing himself to imagine his own engulfment. Given Eliot's preoccupations elsewhere with history as cavernous, slippery, and explicitly linked to female genitalia, we have to wonder whether history itself operates as a species of "hysteria" for Eliot. Freud and Breuer had proposed in 1893 that hysteria emerges as a persistent physical symptom which marks an inability to release a prior traumatic effect: "*Hysterics suffer mainly from reminiscences.*"[45] Freud and Breuer theorize that "the psychotherapeutic procedure" is "curative" because it "*brings to an end the operative force of the idea which was not abreacted in the first instance, by allowing its strangulated affect to find a way out through speech.*"[46] Both history and hysteria threaten engulfment because they entreat us to face the unending and potentially undiscoverable limits of desire and forgotten history. Eliot, in effect, asks us to wonder how far back we may trace the flesh of memory, or the bodies that constitute the corpus and the opus of the past, without being engulfed in the small death that comes from the closeness of eros and thanatos – the "two chief subjects – in fact, the only subjects of the Professor's [Freud's] eternal preoccupation," as H. D. insists in her account of her analysis with Freud.[47]

The intrusion of the elderly male waiter in "Hysteria" (whose description takes up nearly one third of the poem) offers the speaker a forgiving and recognizable cultural and social stability in contrast to the panic of incorporation. After the waiter's banal stuttered words ("'If the lady and gentleman wish to take their tea in the garden, if the lady and gentleman wish to take their tea in the garden'") – a repetitive speech that attests to his own horror of the social gaffe – the speaker seizes the chance to collect himself, seeking respite from the psycho-sexual encounter through a transposition to a more stable social realm. But the speaker is only capable of focusing on "the shaking of her breasts," wishing they would "stop," and evidently taking ambivalent delight in reporting their continuing disturbance. The poem thus expresses both the fear and phantasy of being swallowed by an overpowering femininity associated with the uncontrollability of the hysteric, the womb-woman.

In the poem we have no access to the woman's speech, only to the extra-verbal language of her shaking, laughing body. The two men, meanwhile, are allied in their contra-identificatory protest. The narrative voice gives us access to the silent speaker's inner monologue – a retrospective, poetic self-talk that alternates between resistance and submission. What we do not learn is the history/hystery of just why he has developed this terror of entrapment and identification with the female body and its eruptions; this anxiety is nevertheless legible as the symptom of his own corporeal archive. Rather strikingly, the speaker does not suggest that he *knew* what it was like to laugh hysterically, he reports a self-conscious awareness of "*becoming* involved in her laughter," and, further, of "*being* part of it" (my emphasis). The poem thus registers and reports an ontological experience of a self-alienating synecdoche – "becoming" and "being" "*part*" of the affect of an Other – as it marks an early stage in Eliot's ongoing fascinations with femininity and the hazardous ground of sexual taboo.[48]

In *The Waste Land* a similar concern with the instability of sexual identifications is staged once again when Eliot establishes ambivalently gendered speakers as the narrative voice(s) of his major poem. The poem does not allow us to discern, once and for all, when the speakers are men or women (or both/neither) since he/she constantly changes genders as well as locales. Even though by the end of the first verse-paragraph of "The Burial of the Dead" he/she is named "Marie," the speaker then identifies himself as a comrade to "Stetson:" "You who were with me in the ships at Mylae!" (line 70). In 1952 John Peter, in a now-famous article that was way ahead of its time, identified the dominant speaker's voice as that of a young man, possibly in love with Phlebas: "At some previous time the speaker has fallen completely – perhaps the right word is 'irretrievably' – in love. The object of this love was a young man who soon afterwards met his death, it would seem by drowning."[49] Eliot's deliberately unreliable footnotes to the poem also advise us on the transgendered nature of the poem's perspective on identity and sexuality:

> Tiresias, although a mere spectator and not indeed a "character," is yet the most important personage of the poem, uniting all the rest. Just as the one-eyed merchant, seller of currants, melts into the Phoenician Sailor, and the latter is not wholly distinct from Ferdinand Prince of Naples, so all the women are one woman, and the two sexes meet in Tiresias. What Tiresias *sees*, in fact, is the substance of the poem. (footnote to line 218)

It is the blind and aged *seer* from the ancient past of Greek mythography, whose body is literally traversed with memory and desire (and its witnessing), who performs the poem's unifying function. Encrypted with the signs of both male and female gender and sexuality, along with time's mnemonic and destructive effects – "Old man with wrinkled female breasts," and "old man with wrinkled dugs" (lines 219 and 228) – Tiresias is a parergic "spectator" called upon from long ago to tell the fortunes and futures of the poem's present. *The Waste Land* thematizes such gender slippages as part of the general unpredictability and even volatility of desire, which, it proclaims, never fully knows either its object or its subject. "Hysteria" likewise represents the pervasive transgenderism of desire as part of the mutability, contagion, and collapsibility of gender difference.

Sandra Gilbert and Susan Gubar's critique of "Hysteria" focuses on the contractibility of hysterical disease, arguing, "this man suffers from a hysteria he has caught from his female companion, a hysteria about her *hyster*, her womb and its mysterious 'hystery.'"[50] One of the keys to the mystery of the historical in Eliot's writing might just reside in the inscrutability of Eliot's readings of the feminine. Wayne Koestenbaum goes so far as to contend that Eliot himself was a hysteric, arguing that Eliot allegorized his own suffering by portraying hysterical women who possessed all kinds of ailments, including – like Anna O. – a loss of speech.[51] Discussing the conclusion of *The Waste Land*, Koestenbaum sees not a spiritual resolution of the disparate voices and desires in the poem, but an "extreme retreat from desire into hysteria,"[52] with yet more confusing tongues than the earlier sections. Even a critic as reserved as Harold Bloom discerns hysteria in Eliot, contending that "the lines beginning 'Lady of Silences' in *Ash Wednesday* convey a sense of controlled hysteria."[53] It is also possible to think of this "hystery" that Gilbert and Gubar diagnose as nothing less than history itself.

MISREADING MEMORY, MISTAKING HISTORY

In Eliot's case the paradox of modernism's simultaneous forward and backward temporal fixations is complicated by the critical tendencies that have informed his canonization. Despite the reflections on memory and/or history we find in almost every one of his poems, an interpretive mode persisted for decades that read Eliot and other modernists as manifesting a strident indifference to the claims of history.[54] Critics proclaimed Eliot's absorption in a tight, narcissistic formalism that had little interest in cultures or views outside of its form for form's sake. That is, not only has Eliot come to stand – until very recently, and within a relatively small group of scholars – homogeneously and statically as *the* paradigmatic representative of the privileged, white, male, Anglo-Catholic, modernist poet, he has predominantly stood as the emblem, par excellence, of an ahistorical modernism preoccupied with form above all else. This tendency has primarily taken two different forms: either critics have refused to see the historical in Eliot at all, or, if they do, they have attended primarily to literary histories. But as his Columbo and Bolo poems preeminently show, and as we ought to glean from his persistent turn to the past in his poems and his cultural-historical criticism in his essays, Eliot was endlessly preoccupied with the interplay between national and cultural histories, personal memory, literary intertextualities, and libidinal (and other) desires. It is thus part of my task here to help dismantle – or at least to unsettle further – the auratic imago of "T. S. Eliot" that many of us still inherit, and to proffer a turn in critical reading.

The blindnesses critics have manifested (and perhaps cherished) in relation to the crises and obsessions around writing the historical that abound in Eliot's work date to some of his earliest readers. In one of the first reviews of Eliot's second book, *Poems* (1919), published by Woolf's Hogarth Press, John Middleton Murry gave a lukewarm response in the *Times Literary Supplement*, writing, "We may guess that he is fastidiously on his guard against echoes. There shall not be a cadence in his few verses that will remind anyone of anything. His composition is an incessant process of refusing all that offers itself, for fear that it should not be his own."[55] While that very same year Murry had announced and celebrated the benefits of an amnesiac consciousness to modernism, here he finds fault with what he perceives to be a refusal of the past. Enmeshed in the aesthetics of *newness* in Eliot's style, and riveted by Eliot's radical departures from earlier poetic modes, Murry simply could not see the presence of cultural memory and the past's "echoes" in Eliot's early verse. He did not see that *Poems* is as backward-looking as it is pushing at the confines of the present poetic. Stylistically and formally Eliot shattered old patterns of writing, and gave the world of poetry a shock it hadn't experienced since Mallarmé declared that the Symbolists had done violence to verse. Apparently, Murry had not yet read (or else simply disbelieved) Eliot's "Tradition and the Individual Talent."

Nearly two decades later, on the basis of Eliot's startling abandonment of conventional poetic form, W. B. Yeats also aligned Eliot with disavowals of anteriority. In a lecture he gave in 1936, "Modern Poetry," Yeats asserts, "In the third year of the War came the most revolutionary man in poetry during my lifetime, though his revolution was stylistic alone – T. S. Eliot published his first book. No romantic word or sound, nothing reminiscent . . . could be permitted henceforth."[56] Yeats's statement is part homage and part critique; it distances Eliot's generation from Yeats's by emphasizing Eliot's efforts to prohibit gestures toward a lost past. Yeats sees Eliot as authoritatively drawing a line between the poetry of his time and that of even a few years before: nothing "romantic" or "reminiscent" "could be *permitted* henceforth" (my emphasis). Yeats's interpretation also separates Eliot from a "Traditional" capital "R" "Romantic" ethos with which Yeats identified long into the modernist era: in 1931 he writes in "Coole and Ballylee," "We were the last Romantics – chose for theme / Traditional sanctity and loveliness."[57] Yeats mourned lost time more fastidiously and less ambivalently than did later modernist writers; imagining a vanished heroic age, grieving for love's failures, and resuscitating the local of Irish and Celtic mythologies that Graeco-Roman dominance had displaced, Yeats's view of the past might be called preeminently nostalgic. As it turns out, Eliot had more flattering comments to offer about Yeats, and these centered on Yeats's *historical* significance to the modernist period. In a phrase that he might have equally applied to himself, Eliot argues in 1957 that Yeats "was one of those few whose history is the history of their own time, who are a part of the consciousness of an age which cannot be understood without them."[58]

PROJECTING THE FUTURE

In Eliot's correspondence we find a decided tendency to writing contemporary time as a fragile interstitial point between dangerous, slippery, yet almost magnetically *desirable* histories that he contrasts with elusive, frightening futures. Including regretful, ruminative expositions about what has been, he concomitantly projects the future as a dystopic illness, already in need of remedy. As early as 1917 Eliot was anticipating how the present of an England in the midst of the Great War would be remembered, gazing to an uncertain future to help him name and diagnose the conditions of war, the maladies plaguing him and his wife, and the effects of their ongoing financial difficulties. In his efforts to discover a stable vantage point for thinking of present time, Eliot expressly coveted a return to prewar conditions, hoping that one day the nightmarish wartime period would appear as anomaly – as insubstantial as an "unreal city." In 1918 Eliot writes to his mother, "The strain of life is very great and I fear it will be for the rest of the lives of anyone now on earth. I am very pessimistic about the world we are going to have to live in after the war."[59] Two years later he writes to her on the same theme, lamenting that "[t]he future is always precarious," and disclosing to his brother a few months later that "One feels now, at I imagine a much younger age than people ever had to before, a responsibility toward the next, unfortunate generation."[60] This is Eliot reading his generation in the face of history, placing himself in a model of historical continuity that can no longer abide fantasies of progress that fueled the Victorian imagination.

Despite Eliot's solicitude for the future, and his ambivalent sexing of the past as a fraught, but ultimately more desirable temporal ground, the past remained for Eliot an always-only partially unearthed object. Lyndall Gordon notes in her most recent biography of Eliot that he had affirmed "the past is 'a pit for us still to explore.'"[61] Like the "dark caverns" of the hysteric's throat in "Hysteria" which threaten to consume the poem's speaker, the past's obscurity nevertheless offers an irresistible temptation for Eliot to "explore" poetically. The endeavor was laden with the difficulties of rendering a historicity that Eliot persistently figured as erotogenic.

Walter Benjamin once pronounced that "He who seeks to approach his own buried past must conduct himself like a man digging," insisting that "He must not be afraid to return again and again to the same matter."[62] Eliot's oeuvre testifies to precisely such a conscientious labor of "digging" – not only at the past, but at what it would mean to find a passage to a fearless embrace of the past's alterity. The whispering, "paralysed," "shade[s]" of "The Hollow Men" (1925), for example, entreat a form of forgiving remembrance from the dead:

> Those who have crossed
> With direct eyes, to death's other Kingdom
> Remember us – if at all – not as lost
> Violent souls, but only
> As the hollow men
> The stuffed men.
>
> ("The Hollow Men," lines 13-18)

This "other Kingdom" that Eliot imagines is, though, a place where one would still be vulnerable to longing: "Trembling with tenderness / Lips that would kiss / Form prayers to broken stone" (lines 49-51). The transition from the intimate desires of the dead, through a synecdochic physicality, to the language and surrender of prayer, designates desire's structure as still fundamentally prone to interruption. Deflecting the conditionality of the kiss onto a colder physicality than the human returns these inhabitants of the afterlife to a riven materiality. In this light, Benjamin's formulation might help us to think through Eliot's relation to the past in his poetry – a relation that we might, in fact, call *archaeological*.

The first section of *The Waste Land*, "The Burial of the Dead," ends with a chance encounter with the shade of Stetson that marks the possibility of just this kind of archaeological and physical labor vis-à-vis the past. The meeting collapses more than two thousand years of human history as Eliot's speaker, having just crossed London Bridge, sees Stetson, and calls out to him by identifying his place in memory:

> "Stetson!
> "You who were with me in the ships at Mylae!
> "That corpse you planted last year in your garden,
> "Has it begun to sprout? Will it bloom this year?
> "Or has the sudden frost disturbed its bed?
> "O keep the Dog far hence, that's friend to men,

"Or with his nails he'll dig it up again!
"You! hypocrite lecteur! – mon semblable, – mon frère!"
(lines 69-76)

Next to the evocation of the still-potent buried corpse we can feel the physicality of the human-sounding dog's "nails" (rather than claws) that threaten to dig up the "planted" body that promises regeneration, repair, and rebirth from death. The dog presumably desires the corpse as he would desire the return of a lost master, believing firmly in the prospect of raising (and perhaps eating) the dead. The speaker gives a stern warning to keep the dog "far hence" lest the dog, by animal accident and curiosity, perform the archaeological work of disinterment.

This admonition then accrues further nuance through Eliot's concurrent intertextual "digging" up the past of English letters, as he deftly "steals" (to use Eliot's preferred term) and inverts two lines from John Webster's *The White Devil.* In Cornelia's dirge we find a wolf in place of the dog, and an enemy rather than a friend when she sings, "*But keep the wolfe far thence, that's foe to men / For with his nailes hee'l dig them up agen.*"[63] While the speaker of this point in *The Waste Land* warns against a strictly animalistic archaeological procedure, Eliot himself is lusting after literary history with a kind of insatiable desire for its incorporation – its bodily inclusion – in his own work's design. The dog "that's friend to men" may, in fact, be just what is needed to make sense of what the past has covered.[64] On the other hand, by digging up the corpse the dog might be preventing the possibility of rebirth – the "sprout" and "bloom" from the "dried tubers" of human entombment. The dog's "nails" also intratextually anticipate the breakdown of consciousness that will be dramatized toward the end of the third section of *The Waste Land,* "The Fire Sermon," when the speaker claims, "'On Margate Sands. / I can connect / Nothing with nothing. / The broken fingernails of dirty hands" (lines 300-3).[65] Indeed, in *The Waste Land,* images of pastness and recollection are nestled so firmly amid place, anchored so ineluctably to locale, that we begin to wonder whether place stands as another instance of the sensuous registering of memory.

But, whose corpse is this anyway? Perhaps it is Stetson's own lost body, divided from the "shade" who is being directed to discover a reflowering into the spirit world. Christine Froula suggests that the regulating voice of the poem (the "Police" of Eliot's original title, taken from Dickens's phrase from *Our Mutual Friend,* "He Do the Police in Different Voices") demands "the murder and burial – of the Lover," who stands as an erotic counterpoint to the authoritative "Police" who dominate the dialectic of danger and obedience in the poem.[66]

The "corpse" that Stetson "planted last year" could also be the corpse of a failed love affair, signifying the painful psychical damage that remains after the demise of a romantic relation. The whole image, in any case, astutely attests through metaphor to the return of the repressed. Eliot is well aware that what is buried has the potential to return again, either through the seasons of regeneration, or through the mind's repetitive processes and patterns – a kind of Freudian compulsion to repeat. This is part of the meaning of Eliot's phrase in "Little Gidding," "What we call the beginning is often the end / And to make an end is to make a beginning. / The end is where we start from" (lines 215-17). In the unburying that the poem portends, Eliot suggests that memory can be "stirr[ed]" from the "dead land" just as "dull roots" are stirred with "spring rain." In both cases, the past both threatens and promises regeneration: the infertility of the waste land demands the influence of desire to (re)discover and recover/uncover its potency.

To go at such a past "digging" would be to disinter traumatic memory, and to take on the labor of "remembering, repeating, and working through," that Freud posits in 1914 is the work of the talking cure.[67] This method of healing rekindles and re-approaches emotions of the past in order to expose hitherto "forgotten" states to the possibility of speech and, thereby, release. Freud employs recurring metaphors of lucidity to describe the cure: the "abreaction" – a term he coined with Breuer in "Studies on Hysteria" in 1895 – effected by the emotive discharge brings hidden, obscure, unconscious material to "light." Much later, in one of her major studies on trauma, Cathy Caruth probes Freud's methodology by asking the crucial question, "what can it mean that history occurs as a symptom?"[68] Eliot approaches nearly an identical problematic when he closes "The Burial of the Dead" with the past emerging as both the psychic and material symptom of a failed burial. The corpse's anticipated blossoming repeats the past as a still vital physical effect *and* affect. Elsewhere Caruth frames trauma as "an overwhelming experience of sudden or catastrophic events in which the response to the event occurs in the often delayed, uncontrolled repetitive experience of hallucinations and other intrusive phenomena."[69] Central to her analytic is the repressive response that trauma produces: there is "a period of forgetting that occurs after the accident" that leaves a "legacy of incomprehensibility at the heart of catastrophic experience."[70] The "shock" of trauma causes "a break in the mind's experience of time";[71] it produces a repeated desire to return to and re-experience the scene of abjection to try to grasp cognitively what only the body and the unconscious have come to know.

In *Blindness and Insight* Paul de Man points to a place in Nietzsche's "Of the Use and Misuse of History for Life" (1874) where Nietzsche proposes that a capacity to forget is essential to "the good in human affairs."[72] De Man notes that in Nietzsche "the ability to experience life in a nonhistorical way [is] the most important and original of experiences, as the foundation on which right, health, greatness, and anything truly human can be erected."[73] Nietzsche is more ambivalent than de Man stresses here, and he does concede that "at times this very life that requires forgetfulness demands the temporary suspension of this forgetfulness."[74] Still, forgetfulness – and "illusion" – for Nietzsche are major conditions necessary to consciousness if one is to achieve happiness: unlike the blissfully forgetful animal, the human being "wonder[s] about himself and how he was unable to learn to forget and always clung to what was past; no matter how far or how fast he runs, that chain runs with him."[75] Plotinus, as Richard Macksey shows us in his study of time in Proust, "dismisses memory": "The more the Soul strives after the intelligible, the more it [will] forget[] . . . In this sense, therefore, we may say that the good soul is forgetful."[76] In light of current trauma studies, we could phrase Nietzsche and Plotinus's advice in another way: the ability to disallow trauma its potentially limitless and haunting effects is *the* precondition for future being, becoming, and authentic existence. Such a state of experience, lightened of the "burden of the past" (to borrow Walter Jackson Bate's phrase), is almost impossible to attain.[77] Nietzsche expounds an unachievable Letheian phantasy of *being-without-anteriority*, where human beings could approximate an animalistic consciousness whose happiness depends on an *incapacity* for remembrance. In his model we find one of the most important proto-modernist revocations of the abuses of history and memory on the psyche of a given singularity. In stark contrast, *The Waste Land* presents a series of subject positions that reveal a stuttering inability and a desire-laden refusal to flee from the histories that pervade them. The poem stands as a major modernist example of the tropological and affective presence of the past within a consciousness, a form, and an aesthetics that push toward a different futurity by insisting on the "newness" of the present traversed with the dead.

LANDSCAPES AND BODYSCAPES

When Eliot renders the labyrinthine city in "Prufrock" as erotically charged – "Streets that follow like a tedious argument / Of insidious intent" (lines 8-9) – he proposes that the constructed passageways of the city are desire incarnate. In a letter to Conrad Aiken in 1914, just a few months after he had arrived in England, Eliot writes, "One walks about the street with one's desires, and one's refinement rises up like a wall whenever opportunity approaches. I should be better off, I sometimes think, if I had disposed of my virginity and shyness several years ago: and indeed I still think sometimes that it would be well to do so before marriage."[78] When Alan Marshall cites the first part of this passage in his chapter in *The Cambridge Companion to T. S. Eliot*, he remarks, "It is an image of highly sexed metropolitan isolation. The city is mapped and traced by desire – defined by the current of need that flows through it or is blocked by it."[79] Marshall disregards Eliot's confession of being, in fact, uncomfortably *undersexed* (rather than "highly sexed"), and significantly sur-charged with "desire," but he does touch on the important point that Eliot charts and "map[s]" the convolutions of desire's architecture onto the city's contours.

In an excised section of "The Fire Sermon" in *The Waste Land*, Eliot writes of London as a murderous and wildly proliferating sexual force: "London, the swarming life you kill and breed, / Huddled between the concrete and the sky, / Responsive to the momentary need, / Vibrates unconscious to its formal destiny."[80] As French poets like Charles Baudelaire and Jules Laforgue had already done before him, Eliot concerns himself with writing the time of his particular modernity, locating his figures in contemporary cityscapes and allegorical waste lands, describing anxious subjectivities and frustrated lovers while always offering a critique of culture. In 1915, immediately after Eliot had simultaneously made four of the most momentous decisions of his life – to remain in England, to pursue a career as a poet, to marry Vivien Haigh-Wood, and to give up academia – Pound suggests in a letter to Eliot's father that Eliot "has gone farther" than either Browning or Pound himself in terms of changing modern sensibilities because he had "begun with the much more difficult job of setting his 'personae' in modern life, within discouragingly 'unpoetic' modern surroundings."[81]

In the "Death By Water" section of *The Waste Land* Eliot moves to a different kind of physicality of memory. In this case he traces the body's disintegrating skeleton – like the "corpse" "planted last year" in "The Burial of the Dead," a remainder that is not-yet-cipher – and discovers this remnant as a call to recollection. As in the imperative mode of "Gerontion" we are commanded to remember "Phlebas the Phoenician, a fortnight dead" (line 312), even while Phlebas is entering a "whirlpool" of anti-memory and released into an oblivion where he "Forgot the cry of gulls, and the deep sea swell / And the profit and loss" (lines 313-14). The sea's current "Picked his bones in whispers" (line 316), offering the ghostly presence of language only as murmurous undertones semiotically resistant to interpretation. The picked bones – whose delicacy reminds one of John Donne's delightfully alliterative lines from "The Relic" that Eliot cites in "The Metaphysical Poets," "A bracelet of bright hair about the bone"[82] – lead the speaker from amnesia back to recollection through dissolution: "He passed the stages of his age and youth" (line 317). Phlebas forgets sound, nature, movement, and capital ("the cry of gulls," "the deep sea swell," "the profit and the loss"), but remembers "stages of his age and youth," as though life were best recalled in segments – a conception Woolf would fight against a few years later in "Modern Fiction" (1925) when she insists "Life is not a series of gig lamps symmetrically arranged."[83] We, the *hypocrite lecteur*, either "Gentile or Jew" (line 319), are called to forget racial and religious differences, and to participate in a shared memorial for the many dead who populate *The Waste Land*, with Phlebas acting as a kind of synecdochic signifier for the crowd, the masses, and the more generalized dead: "Consider Phlebas, who was once handsome and tall as you" (line 321). This prompting further petitions us to recall the fragile nature of our own relation to time and mortality. History and desire are as inseparable for Eliot here as eros and thanatos are for Freud. The life drive at the core of psycho-sexual existence finds, inevitably, a counterweight in the death drive, while the transmutation of (past) life into history and memory means that something vibrant has ceased to be outside of the parameters of pure experience: history, that is, marks both the death and the dying of the passionate body. The speaker's request yokes death and youth, and recalls another modernist figuration of this same binding in Yeats's homage to "The young / In one another's arms" in "Sailing to Byzantium," where the young are both always ourselves and always Other, precisely because youth is eternally impermanent: "Those dying generations."[84] Eliot entreats us to "Consider Phlebas" not by what he did, thought, or accomplished, but by his physicality. What is left of Phlebas's beauty are swirling bones in an eddying, unlocatable whirlpool – the unconscious and the ocean as a vast tabula rasa, where beginnings and endings are undiscoverable, and where culture is displaced by the signs of longing.

Jean-Jacques Rousseau argues that "the Greek alphabet derives from the Phoenician, and is indebted to it,"[85] and Eliot may well have been aware of this claim when he was writing his version of a drowned, male,

Ophelia-like beloved, whose identity is linked with the origins of the earliest Western inscriptions. In Michel Foucault's thinking about the human corporeal, the body stands as "the inscribed surface of events (traced by language and dissolved by ideas)," while he proposes that the "task" of genealogy is "to expose a body totally imprinted by history and the process of history's destruction of the body."[86] *The Waste Land* does exactly this, exposing not simply the history of literature in its intertextual fragments, but writing out a poetics of memory that relies on a constant return to both the body (and its remains after death) as well as to the correlatives of a corporeally imagined landscape. In addition to an archaeological poesis of disinterring memory, then, *The Waste Land* anticipates a Foucauldian model of genealogy.

While death or the threat of death haunts the poem, *The Waste Land* also signals a turn to remember not only ghosts and skeletons, but also instances of desire. In a surprisingly Romantic section of *The Waste Land*, taken directly from both Sappho's fragment 31 and Richard Wagner's *Tristan und Isolde*, Eliot's speaker reveals a profound vulnerability to the (heterosexual) desire he repudiates in other texts:

> *Frisch weht der Wind*
> *Der Heimat zu*
> *Mein Irisch Kind*
> *Wo weilest du?*
> "You gave me hyacinths first a year ago;
> "They called me the hyacinth girl."
> – Yet when we came back, late, from the hyacinth garden,
> Your arms full, and your hair wet, I could not
> Speak, and my eyes failed, I was neither
> Living nor dead, and I knew nothing,
> Looking into the heart of light, the silence.
> *Oed' und leer das Meer.* (lines 31-42)

Addressing his Irish "kin" or "child" with the personal "du" immediately introduces a familiarity and even intimacy to these lines, and the sight of the lover, with full arms and wet hair, returning "late" from the garden, is moving enough to cause a collapse of both language and vision. As elsewhere in Eliot's poems, wetness suggests both sexuality and regeneration; the "waste land," after all, is desolate, in part, because of its literal dryness – there is "no sound of water" (line 24). Charged with sensual desire, this scene is one of the most sexual in all of Eliot's canonical poetry. Overwhelmed by his feelings, the lover experiences a sexual-spiritual emptiness (signifying heaven, Buddhistic nirvana, or orgasm?), "Looking into the heart of light, the silence."[87] As in the *Prufrock* volume, though, which I will explore, desire recognizes its own failure even in the moment it is felt; the moment of desire is already strange and estranged from the subject. In his response to desire the lover turns *not* toward the ostensible object, but inward, away from the "hyacinth girl," to a desolation borrowed from Wagner's *Tristan und Isolde: "Oed' und leer das Meer"* – desolate and empty the sea.

MAPPING MEMORY

The movement of memory in "The Burial of the Dead" follows an interesting order. First, we are told, with indicative sentences, of the cruelty of "mixing / Memory and desire," and of the paradoxical warmth of winter's "forgetful snow" – an inattentive, barely sustaining pleasure that differs from the awakened call to being we find in Nietzsche's arguments for a balance of forgetfulness and historical consciousness. Then we progress through a childhood memory of sledding down unnamed European mountains (probably the Alps) – "Marie, / Marie, hold on tight. And down we went" (lines 15-16) – to the cultural and mythic content of Old-Testament wisdom whose present tense again collapses millennia to bring Judeo-Christian mysteries into the current moment: "Son of man, / You cannot say, or guess, for you know only / A heap of broken images, where the sun beats, / And the dead tree gives no shelter, the cricket no relief" (lines 20-3).[88] A more personal memory of desire and its failure then takes place in the "hyacinth girl" section. These recollective shifts are immediately followed by an interlude that looks to the *future* via remembrance: the speaker, who is obsessed with memory, goes to "Madame Sosostris, famous clairvoyante" (line 43), to have his fortune told. Madame Sosostris, though, is unable to prognosticate without taking recourse to the language of Shakespeare and Dante, so that, like Tiresias, her very way of diagnosing the future is through reading the past. At this point in the poem, intertextual literary memory begins to dominate, reaching its peak in the last verse paragraph of "The Burial of the Dead," where Eliot compiles Dante, Blake (according to Pound), Webster, and Baudelaire to produce a palimpsestic literary layering whose fractured coalescence comments both on Eliot's personal past and the past of the poem's characters.

Memory in *The Waste Land*, though, devolves quickly into nightmare, particularly in the memories it records of violent or "undesired" (line 218) sex. There is one rape in the poem – that of the mythical Philomel, whom

Tereus rapes and then silences by cutting out her tongue – while the encounter with "the typist" (line 222) and "the young man carbuncular" (line 231) uncannily echoes that trauma, rendering heterosexual physical intimacy as a male "assault" on a passive woman: "Flushed and decided, he assaults at once; / Exploring hands encounter no defence; / His vanity requires no response, / And makes a welcome of indifference" (lines 239-42). Michael Levenson suggests that "The barbarous king who rudely forced Philomela is the terrible figure for the politics of intimacy; power between bodies, whose effects are written throughout the poem,"[89] while Harriet Davidson points out that "The poem returns again and again to 'improper' sexual desire, temptation, and surrender and their often tragic consequences."[90] The dramatically staged failure of memory in the second section, "A Game of Chess," when we are privy to a neurotic exchange between two lovers (who may be husband and wife), offers not consolation, but a constellated moment in the collapse of intimacy and communication, two products of desire. In their respective notes to Eliot's drafts, Pound named this portion of the poem "photography" and Vivien Eliot labeled it "WONDERFUL," each testifying to its resemblances to Eliot's domestic life.

This intensely personal segment erupts immediately after a contemplation of Ovid's myth of Philomel – a story that moves from quasi-incestuous and illicit sexual violence to sisterly revenge, matricide, and cannibalism before the gods intervene to send Philomel, her sister Procne, and Tireus all into flight by transforming them into birds. After returning to the excitation and inflammation of a language of the body – "her hair / Spread out in fiery points / Glowed into words, then would be savagely still" (lines 108-10), we shift to a bleak modern scene where speech, but not understanding, is possible:

> "My nerves are bad to-night. Yes, bad. Stay with me.
> Speak to me. Why do you never speak. Speak.
> What are you thinking of? What thinking? What?
> I never know what you are thinking. Think."
>
> I think we are in rats' alley
> Where the dead men lost their bones.
>
> (lines 111-16)

The ways in which their failure of communication negotiates both memory and desire is made clearer if we look at the drafts of the poem. Here, in two versions of "A Game of Chess" (which had been titled, "IN THE CAGE"), when implored to "Think," the interlocutor does not reply with the present tense – "I think we are in rats' alley" – but he responds to describe the hellscape of their initial meeting: "I think we met first in rats' alley / Where the dead men lost their bones."[91] This moment also anticipates the "rats' feet over broken glass" (lines 9-10) from "The Hollow Men," published a few years later. The final version of the poem stresses the present agony of the relationship by transforming the past into the present through an editorial amendment; perhaps Eliot was uncertain whether current or previous dysfunctionality is worse. Part of the horror also stems from the "dead men" having "lost their bones," which would present the insoluble difficulty of having lost the archive before it can "breed" or "sprout" to a future that might redeem. In Eliot – as in Woolf – repression is bound to fail, and the archive can always bloom again. Woolf writes of her present in 1925, for instance, "(over all this the bloom of the past descends as I write – it becomes sad, beautiful, memorable)."[92]

In a draft version of a slightly later part of "A Game of Chess," the wind is "Carrying / Away the little light dead people."[93] This again heralds the removal of the body, and hence the dispersal of the evidence and *matter* of memory that Eliot's poetry, like Bergson's philosophy, suggests it is crucial to avow. In his poetic, mnemonic inscriptions, corporeal remains almost always leave their trace, and when they do not, we find his speakers distressed at this unnatural dissolution of the body's testament. As Nicholas Andrew Miller points out in a discussion of Giambattista Vico's *The New Science* (1744), "knowing . . . is a poetic process of re-membering bodies; implicitly, therefore, all rational knowing has an erotic aspect, a production rather than a mimicking of experiential organizations and configurations. The body is never for Vico the prerequisite to erotic experience, but its result, an arrangement of organs invested by desire."[94]

The dialogue between the estranged lovers continues with an abrupt slip from the personal back to the cultural and literary, when the interlocutor falters under the strain of remembering:

> "Do
> You know nothing? Do you see nothing? Do you remember
> Nothing?"
>
> I remember
> Those are pearls that were his eyes.
> "Are you alive, or not? Is there nothing in your head?"
> (lines 121-6)

Instead of "nothing," the interlocutor remembers Ariel inciting Ferdinand in *The Tempest* with his trickster song to grieve the father he fears is dead. This recollection of an archetypal moment from Shakespeare that is itself a false provocation to mourn what is *not* in fact gone, what is not subject to the "current under sea" that "Picked his bones in whispers" (lines 315-16), has affinities with the intra-individual agony the speakers suffer in their inability to communicate. Eliot thus discloses a modernist study in heteroglossic voices and consciousnesses that each cry out that the past in all its guises is impossible to flee.

In "The Fire Sermon" the unusually clean river Thames bears no "testimony of summer nights" (line 179), as though we have reached a clean slate of memory, mirrored by the topographic correlative of the river. But this part of the poem is again filled with bones. Half-citing Andrew Marvell's "To His Coy Mistress," and preserving Marvell's end-rhymes as well as his focus on the auditory, instead of hearing "Time's wingèd chariot hurrying near," the speaker hears "The rattle of the bones:" "at my back in a cold blast I hear / The rattle of the bones, and chuckle spread from ear to ear" (lines 185-6). Then, after the speaker muses "upon the king my brother's wreck / And on the king my father's death before him" (lines 191-2), and thus on what may be his own position to inherit the throne, the poem continues, "White bodies naked on the low damp ground / And bones cast in a little low dry garret, / Rattled by the rat's foot only, year to year" (lines 193-5). In this case, despite the disturbance the bones suffer from the synecdochic feet of passing animals, the bones do not threaten resurrection; further, because the garret is "dry," we are assured of their preservation rather than decay. While much of the poem longs for a redemptive rain, dryness, too, can be a condition of serenity. As Eliot writes in the final section of the poem, "Dry bones can harm no one" (line 390), calling on his reader to think again of the Book of Ezekiel – "Oh ye dry bones, hear the word of the Lord" (37.4) – and, very likely, alluding to Emerson's gesture of anti-memory in his short booklet, *Nature*, "why should we grope among the dry bones of the past?"[95]

In his handwritten notes to *The Waste Land*, Eliot's close friend John Davy Hayward, with whom he lived from 1946 to 1957 and whom Richard Badenhausen considers "Eliot's consummate collaborator,"[96] proposes to Eliot that the key "theme" of the poem is "death in life."[97] With the proliferation of bones throughout the poem, and the dialectic between the body's waste and its regeneration, another major theme is certainly *life in death* – or, futurity and fruition from the past, memory charged with desire. After all, death quite literally hangs over the poem, with its epigraph reading, in a mixture of Latin and Greek, "I saw with my own eyes the Sibyl at Cumae hanging in a cage, and when the boys said to her: 'Sibyl, what do you want?' She answered, 'I want to die.'" This particular Sibyl, a prophetic old woman, guided Aeneas through Hades in *The Aeneid.* Given eternal life by Apollo, she tragically neglected to ask for perpetual youth, and so was condemned to aging forever in an undying body. Sibyl's desire for death finds itself transliterated into all the strained desires of the dead throughout the poem not to be lost to the social codes and physical forms of the living. The dead of *The Waste Land* insist on not being forgotten, and consequently reappear within the realm of the living. From the shade of Stetson, to Tiresias, to the anonymous "rattle of the bones," to Phlebas the Phoenician, "a fortnight dead" (line 312), and even to the evocation of a resurrected Christ "Gliding wrapt in a brown mantle" (line 363), we are asked to feel the presence of these former lives as shadows that overwrite the present with their urgent desires for redemption.

By the end of *The Waste Land*, the question of whether Eliot is offering a bleak portrait of death in life, or, more redemptively, of life *from* death, is again staged, though critics differ radically in their readings of the closing line, "Shantih shantih shantih" (line 433). In interpretations that see the poem's close as embracing the possibility of new life after the existence in the desert that *The Waste Land* describes, part of the redemption occurs by disavowing the uncontrollable aspects of desire and death, choosing instead order and acceptance. When the "thunder" finally speaks after the protracted dryness of the poem, its simple, monosyllabic "DA," repeated three times, moves the speaker or narrator (it is unclear which at this point) to utter the Sanskrit triumvirate, "*Datta,*" "*Dayadhvam,*" "*Damyata,*" translated by Eliot as "give," "sympathize," "control." "DA" simultaneously invokes the German "gone"/"there" (made much of by Freud in his "fort"/"da" episode in *Beyond the Pleasure Principle*), the Irish word for "father," and the Sanskrit root of these imperatives. "*Datta,*" "*Dayadhvam,*" "*Damyata*" together command an offering, and the important lines about "blood shaking my heart" (line 402) place passion and desire at the core of being. Eliot suggests in "The Metaphysical Poets" that we should understand "desire" in its broadest effects: "Racine or Donne looked into a good deal more than the heart. One must look into the cerebral cortex, the nervous system, and the digestive tracts."[98] Eliot wants us to think of desire and history through nothing less than the body. And, as I have shown, for Eliot it is *only* through a surrender potent enough to mark the body that we exist. This "awful daring," however, is illegible in a historical sense – it is written in the body, its memory instructs our desires, but its trace resides beyond a decipherable semiotic residue. Outside the written, beyond the well-intentioned weaver – "the beneficent spider" (line 407) – and inscrutable to law, desire is "not to be found in our obituaries" (line 406).

From this section guided by the Sanskrit imperative "give" (*Datta*), the leading principle becomes "sympathize" (*Dayadhvam*), and the speaker offers a pre-existentialist vision of autotelic cycles of psychic self-imprisonment: "We think of the key, each in his prison / Thinking of the key, each confirms a prison" (lines 413-14). Still, what follows are "aethereal rumours" (line 415) that "Revive for a moment a broken Coriolanus" (lines 415-16). The pronounced ambiguity leaves it uncertain whether the speaker is proffering a hope for redemption and sympathy – extended even to "a broken Coriolanus," who betrayed his beloved city of Rome when he led an army against it – or whether it is only the memory of Coriolanus that is revived, perhaps as a paradigmatic instance of the tragedy of fighting oneself. After a short section guided by "control" (*Damyata*), where finding reciprocity in the heart of a beloved is compared to the temporary control achieved over a boat on a calm sea, the penultimate lines of *The Waste Land* take place in this seascape: "I sat upon the shore / Fishing, with the arid plain behind me" (line 423-4). Intratextually reminiscent of the other waterways that thread their ways through the poem, from the alternately dirty and clean river Thames, to the scene of sexual encounter in the "narrow canoe" at Richmond, and to "Death by Water," the shore offers a "calm" hiatus or tableau that briefly supplants chaos. This temporary "order," however, finds hesitation intrinsic to its very condition of serenity, and such tranquility does not stand as the resolute closure to the poem. To end, then, the relaxed vulnerability of the fisher king, who exposes his back to the waste land, gives way to what is arguably the most chaotic section of the poem. In a mayhem of counterpoint, where the speaker multilingually and maniacally reports ruins, fragments, abandonment, and madness (beginning with the sing-songy nursery rhyme that scarcely knows what it prophesizes: "London Bridge is falling down falling down falling down" (line 426)), any attempt to discern a single speaking voice again becomes impossible. But then, in the poem's last lines, Eliot offers the Hindu prayer (like the nursery rhyme, lacking any punctuation) – "Shantih shantih shantih" (line 433), which he roughly translates in his notes as the Christian "Peace which passeth understanding." The phrase performatively declares a spiritual resolution, proposing that even amidst destruction and abjection, the language of peace exists. The gesture marks an end point – or at least a stalling – of the relentless repetition of desire unmet.

CHAPTER 3

Eliot, eros, and desire: "Oh, do not ask, 'What is it?'"

"Sibyl, what do you want?" "I want to die."

T. S. Eliot, epigraph to *The Waste Land*

Memory!
You have the key,
The little lamp spreads a ring on the stair.
Mount.
The bed is open . . .

T. S. Eliot, "Rhapsody on a Windy Night"[1]

In September of 1914, shortly after Eliot's arrival in England from Germany, where he had been studying until the outbreak of what would become the Great War, and in a letter that includes a sodomitical stanza that he (perhaps jokingly) claims he submitted for a hundred-dollar prize, Eliot writes to Conrad Aiken praising the kindness of Ezra Pound, his new friend, and noting Pound's support of Eliot's poetic endeavors. In the same letter Eliot expresses a deep anxiety about his poetic career and his level of productivity:

Pound has been *on n'est pas plus aimable*, and is going to print "Prufrock" in *Poetry* and pay me for it. He wants me to bring out a Vol. after the War. The devil of it is that I have done nothing good since J. A[lfred] P[rufrock] and writhe in impotence . . . I think now that all my good stuff was done before I had begun to worry – three years ago.[2]

Eliot's self-critical judgment about the quality of his work is allied with a discomfort which he describes in terms remarkably akin to the corporeal frustrations of sexual "impotence" – explicitly associating poetic productivity with a more youthful blithe spirit and virility. If Eliot failed to write more "good stuff," it would be because "petty worries"[3] had ruined his sexual fertility.

Eliot then proceeds to include a queer, bawdy poem toward the end of this letter. Borrowing a phrase from the Duke of Wellington that Joyce makes much of in *Finnegans Wake*, Eliot entitles the piece "UP BOYS AND AT 'EM!"[4] with instructions that it is to be "Adapted to the tune of C. Columbo lived in Spain." The verse paragraph offers additional comment on his writerly predicament:

Now while our heroes were at sea
  They pass'd a German warship.
The captain pac'd the quarterdeck
  Parading in his corset.
What ho! they cry'd, we'll sink your ship!
  And so they up and sink'd her.
But the cabin boy was sav'd alive
  And bugger'd, in the sphincter.

Eliot continues his letter to Aiken by writing,

> The poem was declined by several musical publishers on the ground that it paid too great a tribute to the charms of German youth to be acceptable to the English public. I acknowledg'd the force of the objection, but replied that it was only to be regarded as a punitive measure, and to show the readiness and devotion to duty of the British seaman.[5]

Inviting a parallel between his own anxieties about publication and the worry of rivaling "Prufrock" due to his "impotence," Eliot uses the material of war to thematize unstable masculinities of transnational affiliations, leaving it somewhat unclear whether the cross-dressing captain, proudly on display in "his corset," is part of the British, Spanish, or German fleet. Are "our heroes" the British, or the Spanish of Columbo's ships? Does the pacing captain belong to the "heroes," or to the "German warship"? For Eliot to "writhe"/write "in impotence" meant that he felt compelled to defer and counter his feared de-tumescence by producing more pornotropic work in the vein of his Columbo and Bolo bawdy verses – again, sharing it with a specifically male audience. The cabin boy is violated as a matter of "duty," while later in the same (astonishingly rich) letter, Eliot turns to still another mode of bodily violation, proclaiming the benefits of self-mutilation: "it's interesting to cut yourself to pieces once in a while, and wait to see if the fragments will sprout."[6] The metaphorical phrasing anticipates the fertility of corpses in *The Waste Land*, and again affirms that material wounding, scarring, and ruin can lead to new, even redemptive, growth in the future.

Equating poetic performance with sexual fecundity once more establishes the eros bound up with writing time. Poetic expression (about culture, about war, and about sensational desires) is a supplemental sexual act, and, as Wayne Koestenbaum argues, one that Eliot frequently understood to be most successful between men.[7] Indeed, as Koestenbaum first stressed, when Eliot was completing *The Waste Land*, he and Pound would engage in overtly sexual banter about their transgendered roles in the poem's production. In these exchanges both feminize each other, with Pound referring affectionately to Eliot as a "bitch," and to himself in the third person as the willing midwife or doctor who "performed the caesarean Operation" on the pregnant Eliot to allow for the birth of the poem.[8] Eliot reciprocates by agreeing with Pound's metaphor (while inverting the capitalization) to claim that he wishes "to use Caesarean operation in italics in front" – as an epigraph for the "front" (the genitals?) of *The Waste Land*.[9] A few days later Pound replies, "Do as you like about my obstetric effort."[10] This feminization of Eliot as the birthing mother who is unable to deliver his/her baby without Pound's incisions again circumvents the perilous "corridors" of female genitalia (and history) that Eliot elaborates in "Gerontion," preferring a cutting of the body and text to the physiological labor of birthing alone. To follow the analogy, Pound, in effect, reaches *into* Eliot's womb via textual emendation and excision – breaking past tissue and skin – to lay hold of a poem fundamentally concerned with the topographics of "waste." Indeed, allusions to the birth process continue when Eliot admits to a kind of post-partum depression after the operation and delivery. Responding in kind to Pound's Christmas Eve Italian–English phrase on the successful completion of the poem, "Complimenti, you bitch," Eliot writes, "Complimenti appreciated, as have been excessively depressed."[11]

The reciprocal feminization we find in this correspondence is highly unstable and subject to transgendered revisions. Within the same letter in which Pound refers to his "obstetric effort," Pound praises Eliot's verse by extolling Eliot's virility: "May your erection never grow less."[12] Six months after the exchange about Pound's obstetrics and Eliot's erection Eliot again reciprocates in their ribald register, signing off from a letter to Pound by hailing him: "O Student of the Kama Sutra."[13] Well-noted for its yogic-sexual techniques, offering advice on a dozens of topics from kissing to biting, harems, sexual positions, and courtship, the ancient Hindu manual would have been accessible to Eliot through his studies of Sanskrit and Eastern religions at Harvard. Then, during this same period, Eliot offers Pound another colloquial, belated, post-coital compliment in praise of their mutual passionate – and now also incestuous – act: "Good fucking, brother."[14] He ends the letter there, and, rather unusually, does not sign it. Perhaps such a comment cannot quite bear his signature.[15]

Eliot's sexualized anxieties about equaling "The Love Song of J. Alfred Prufrock" bothered him on more than one occasion. In 1916, two years after his letter to Aiken in which he complains of "writh[ing] in impotence," he writes to his brother, Henry.

> I had a very good review in the London *Nation* which I will send you. I feel a sort of posthumous pleasure in it. I often feel that 'J. A. [lfred] P. [rufrock]' is a swan song, but I never mention the fact because Vivien is so exceedingly anxious that I shall equal it, and would be bitterly disappointed if I do not. So do not suggest to anyone how I feel. The present year has been, in some respects, the most awful nightmare of anxiety that the mind of man could conceive, but at least it is not dull, and it has its compensations.[16]

In the mid-teens Eliot could still agonize that "Prufrock" might be all that he would produce of the stature of poetry to which he aspired. A "swan song," the *Oxford English Dictionary* tells us, is "a song like that fabled to be sung by a dying swan; the last work of a poet or musician, composed shortly before his death; hence, any final performance, action, or effort." In framing "Prufrock" this way Eliot confesses a fear to his brother that he is unable to convey to his wife: this might be his farewell appearance, a poetic death that conjoins the poignancy of birth, early triumph, and exhaustion. We should also remember that, as Jewel Spears Brooker points out, Eliot sent this letter just two days after one of the worst blitzes London suffered during the First World War – a bombardment he did not witness, but one that left traumatic aftereffects in the besieged city.[17] Ruminating on his poetic mortality in the context of war and death, Eliot imagines his debut on the London literary scene as his epitaph, proposing that "Prufrock" would do the work of elegy as well as the work of beginning.

PRUFROCK AND INTERROGATIVE DESIRE

The *Prufrock* volume is full of meditations on the ways in which the body, desires, and memory constantly infiltrate each other with their relations – with the ways that they mutually write each other, and change each other inter- and intratextually through that inscription. In "The Love Song of J. Alfred Prufrock" Eliot renders the impulses and limits of desire in a number of ways: in the desire for propriety, for a language of accurate expression, for lost time, and in the latent sexual desires of a young or middle-aged man. The poem also discursively enacts a dynamics of desire by repeatedly addressing questions to an unspecified Other to whom there can be no adequate responses. After attempting to dispense with an unspecified "overwhelming question" by displacing the query with an insistence on a shared social act instead – "Oh, do not ask, 'What is it?'/ Let us go and make our visit" (lines 11-12) – the poem contains no less than fifteen question marks in its 131 lines. Each question initiates another step in a dialectical dance between the epistemological, the ontological, and the social that the poem almost rhythmically enacts for its audience. Yet each of these fields will be marked by spectacular failure through the poem. In addition, the speaker *refers* to a "question" no less than three times in the poem: twice to indicate the "overwhelming question" (lines 10 and 93), and once to say there will be time "for all the works and days of hands / That lift and drop a question on your plate" (lines 29-30). Structurally, then, "Prufrock" is written as an unanswerable series of interrogatives. And what does a question imply but a desire for an answer? We also have to wonder to whom these questions are posed. Perhaps to a larger-than-life cultural superego with godlike answers? The speaker's identification with the beheaded John the Baptist in the desperate lines that begin with a double hesitation – "But though I have wept and fasted, wept and prayed, / Though I have seen my head (grown slightly bald) brought in upon a platter, / I am no prophet – and here's no great matter" (lines 81-3) – prefigures Eliot's own conversion to Anglo-Catholicism in 1927, and we might think of the secular uncertainty and incessant philosophical questioning that shadows "Prufrock" as forecasting Eliot's more fervent desire for answers that would culminate in his turn to the Church.

A little over a third of the way through the poem Prufrock asks the immense and unanswerable question "Do I dare / Disturb the universe?" (lines 45-6). What would it mean for Prufrock to disturb the universe? We wonder if in his dramatic rendition of a modern neurotic Eliot is proposing that asking too much disturbs the order of things. And, which universe does he refer to, that of his social "world," that of the larger cosmos, or both? This question, borrowed from one of Jules Laforgue's letters of 1881, is originally hinted at simply as a repetitive, stammering, "'Do I dare?' and, 'Do I dare?'" (line 38). It then evolves and recurs throughout the poem, shifting from this unspecified daring to the question about the "universe," and finally to the presumably much simpler question, "Do I dare to eat a peach?" near the poem's close (line 122).

Found outside the quotation marks that distinguish the dramatic voice of the poem's speaker(s), the second and third reformulations are framed as glimpses into the speaker's interiority. The simultaneous pathos and bathos in the question about the "peach" pose the quandary of disclosing one's desire for the object. Imbibing it, and exhibiting appetite by taking something messy but luscious – that might drip down his chin – into his body, might incite a distressing embarrassment. Indeed, so much of Eliot's poetry speaks precisely to the crisis that is staged when the erotic and phantasmatic desires of a modern, self-conscious subjectivity encounter conventional codes of conduct and must acknowledge a troubling call to respond to regimes of social and cultural control. Do I dare risk sexual, social, or sensual vulnerability? "Do I dare to eat a peach?" both parodies the grandioseness of the question about the universe, while it asserts that questions about the cosmos and sexuality are equally puzzling. Asking these questions puts the speaker in a stance of humility where desire is so regulated that both the immense question about the universe and the quibbling questions of propriety and behavior testify to an anxious subjectivity, apparently afraid of desire itself – looking ahead already to the "torment / Of love unsatisfied / The greater torment / Of love satisfied" that we find years later in the second part of "Ash Wednesday" (lines 76-9).

When Lacan suggests in "Of the Subject of Certainty" that "Desire, more than any other point in the range of human possibility, meets its limit somewhere," he is urgently offering a contrast between his vision of the function of desire with that developed in the "register of traditional psychology," where, he argues, psychologists have tended to emphasize the *limitless* character of desire.[18] Of course, it is precisely due to its limitlessness nature that desire restricts us most acutely. In "Prufrock" the confines posed by social necessity (verging on the *ananke* of the "universe['s]" claims on us) meet with an intimidating infinity of possible aberrations, protests, and even perversions. Certainly, as Lacan claims, desire is that which most definitively "finds its boundary, its strict relation, its limit,"[19] but desire discovers this limit because of the immeasurable nature of its drive. As Eliot contends in his essay on "Baudelaire" (1930), "in much romantic poetry the sadness is due to the exploitation of the fact that *no human relations are adequate to human desires*, but also to the disbelief in any further object for human desires than that which, being human, fails to satisfy."[20] He cites a similar comment from St. John of the Cross as his epigraph for an unfinished poem, "Sweeney Agonistes": "*Hence the soul cannot be possessed of the divine union, until it has divested itself of the love of created beings.*" This, in some ways, might be said to be the miraculous remedy Eliot's work is always seeking and resisting. For Eliot, the human is inadequate to desire because desire carries with it the illusion that its interminable thirst may be satisfied. He quite strikingly confirms Lacan's view that desire will always find its failure, since built into desire's structure for Eliot is the law that its response will be insufficient to the request. We could then consider Eliot's poetry as the expression of desire that has reached its limit and knows it. Or, that what Eliot explores through the *Prufrock* volume and *The Waste Land* are desires that claim to have lost the will to desire, and yet still ardently, fiercely protest such a disavowal; insatiable desires that are themselves undesired. To invoke Eliot's terms from "Burnt Norton": "Desire itself is movement / Not in itself desirable" (lines 164-5).

A great deal of Eliot's poetry allegorizes being in love *not* with another human being, but with the idea of overcoming desire itself. His poetry thematizes and eroticizes the very tension and excitation of his speakers' protests and *resistances* to desire. For Eliot, desire is faithfully pitted against itself. His speakers feel desire, and in the same instant meet the desire not to desire (sexually, or otherwise). In the solicitude to overcome this unrest, we find a strikingly modernist portrait of failure: the attempts to repudiate an erotic grammar of experience only end by deepening that articulation. Indeed, Eliot's speakers seem to crave a state in which neither desire nor its mnemonic archive would haunt the subject, but where desire's effects would become the purified "destroyer, reminder" ("The Dry Salvages," line 8) of a new, courageous opening to what would finally be an *un-awful* "daring of a moment's surrender" (*The Waste Land*, line 403). This then turns the equation of undesirable desire around, for we find, also, that longings to instantiate an ideal or realizable eros bubble up through the cracks of Eliot's all-too-fragile repressive gestures. Instead of a discourse of anti-sexuality, the efforts within his poetry to overcome the uncomfortable presumptions of eros only succeed in performing and exceeding their own resistances. Far from constituting an oeuvre of counter-erotics, then, Eliot's poems articulate the urgency of desires that exist in the brimming agons between inhibition and exhibition, sublimation and expression, censorship and pornotropism.

The intense anxiety about behavior and the ends of desire in "Prufrock" also attests to a general conviction in Eliot's writing that every moment is history, and that there is no undoing time. To surrender to desire would mean surrendering to the tousled anarchy of time, for time is as unruly as sex.

Near the beginning of "Prufrock" Eliot offers a sustained meditation on time:

> And indeed there will be time
> For the yellow smoke that slides along the street
> Rubbing its back upon the window-panes;
> There will be time, there will be time
> To prepare a face to meet the faces that you meet;
> There will be time to murder and create,
> And time for all the works and days of hands
> That lift and drop a question on your plate;
> Time for you and time for me,
> And time yet for a hundred indecisions,
> And for a hundred visions and revisions,
> Before the taking of a toast and tea. (lines 23-34)

Recalling the opening line of Marvell's "To His Coy Mistress" ("Had we but world enough, and time"), and thereby placing itself within a literary-historical tradition that laments the paucity of time, Eliot's speaker nevertheless insists that "there will be time" to realize all the desires that might occur. This repeated assertion – "there will be time" (eight times in different guises in this verse-paragraph alone) – both affirms the certainty that time *will be* (philosophically, mathematically, in the abstract), while it imagines the possibilities that will unfold for the speaker in time. The repeated insistence that "there will be time," though, discloses a profound worry that there might *not* be time. Why insist upon it if it is certain? The pronouncement, as a partial response to all the poem's questions, begins to sound suspiciously performative, as though Eliot hopes to make time by asserting not simply that there *is* time, at present, but that there *will be* time into a futurity that such a phrase promises. Again, as though involved in a pre-conversion confrontation with the difficulties of faith, Eliot's speaker tries to enact a faith in time by speaking it.

This anxiety about the lack of time, and the attendant desire for the promise of time, also stand as regretful, premature contemplations about Eliot's passing youth. The worry is that later years will devolve into repetition, stripped of newness. Like the teacher son of David, King of Jerusalem, who grieves in Ecclesiastes, "there is no new thing under the sun," Eliot's speaker has already lived long enough to discover life as repetition: "For I have known them all already, known them all – / Have known the evenings, mornings, afternoons, / I have measured out my life with coffee spoons" (lines 49-51). Even so, he regrets the loss of the time of youth: "I grow old . . . I grow old . . . / I shall wear the bottoms of my trousers rolled" (lines 120-1). Eliot was just twenty-six when the poem was finally published in 1915, and twenty-two when he finished it in July or August 1911 (the dating is unclear). As for the question of how to ascertain Prufrock's age, Eliot attested to the autobiographical content of the poem in 1962 when he said in an interview that Prufrock was in part an older man of about forty, and in part "himself" when he wrote it.[21]

QUEERYING PRUFROCK

In "Little Gidding" Eliot unites the gesture of poetry with memory and desire once again with the phrase, "Every poem an epitaph" (line 226). Every poem is, in a sense, an homage to someone or something we have lost – a means of bringing memory to the field of present experience. "The Love Song of J. Alfred Prufrock" also functions as a homoerotic elegy and "epitaph" for Eliot's slightly younger friend, Jean Verdenal, to whom the poem is dedicated: "For Jean Verdenal, 1889–1915 / mort aux Dardanelles." The phrase indicates Verdenal's tragically short life (he was a year younger than Eliot) and the site of his death at the battle of Gallipoli, invoking the romantic myth of Hero and Leander – a precursor to Shakespeare's *Romeo and Juliet* tale of "star-crossed" lovers – who loved each other so passionately that Leander swam across the Hellespont (the modern-day Dardanelles) nightly in order to see her, a priestess to Aphrodite. When Leander drowned on his way to visit Hero she committed suicide. Importantly, Eliot places an inscription from Dante's *Purgatorio* immediately beneath his dedication to Verdenal, although the quotation is rarely translated or discussed: "*Or puoi la quantitate / comprender dell'amor ch'a te mi scalda, / quando dismento nostra vanitate, / trattando l'ombre come cosa salda*" (I translate it as, "Now you can understand / The quantity of love that burns me for you / When we undeceive our vanity / Treating shadows as something solid"). The juxtaposition of the dedication to Verdenal – whom some have convincingly posited was a lover of Eliot's – and the yearning romantic regret found in Dante's lines asks that we consider the relation between the two epigraphs as a comment on the homoerotic unrest in the remainder of the poem. We might, then, read the "love song" of J. Alfred Prufrock as a veiled articulation of homosexual desire that could not yet be sung, either by Eliot or by many of his contemporaries. As Marja Palmer notes, "It is indeed amazing how the aspect of love in 'The Love Song' has been neglected by critics throughout the years. It should be evident that love is the main theme of the poem."[22]

The Great War was killing hundreds of thousands of Europe's youth as Eliot was publishing this poem, and Eliot was deeply sensitive to this tragedy. In the first Battle of the Somme alone, in July 1916, Paul Fussell tells us that 60,000 British soldiers were killed in a single day, "the record so far."[23] On 21 March 1918, during Germany's "Michael Offensive" that began the second Battle of the Somme, "The British lost 150,000 men almost immediately; 90,000 as prisoners; and total British casualties rose to 300,000 within the next six days."[24] Fussell later remarks that "even in the quietest times, some 7,000 British men and officers were killed and wounded daily, just as a matter of course. 'Wastage,' the Staff called it."[25] It is almost impossible for us to imagine this particular form of mass slaughter, and to understand from our vantage point the ravaging intensity the Great War wreaked on the generations who lived through it. Eliot was personally acquainted with many of the enlisted, he tried unsuccessfully to volunteer himself (he was turned down for service, as Lyndall Gordon explains, "on account of tachycardia and his old hernia"),[26] and he seems to have suffered a kind of ongoing melancholia about the shock of his various personal losses during the war.[27]

In a letter to his mother on 18 November 1915 he describes his fondness for his brother-in-law, Maurice Haigh-Wood, who was briefly back in England while on leave from the front:

> It seems very strange that a boy of nineteen should have such experiences – often twelve hours alone in his "dug-out" in the trenches, and at night, when he cannot sleep, occupying himself by shooting rats with a revolver. What he tells about rats and vermin is incredible – Northern France is swarming, and the rats are as big as cats. His dug-out, where he sleeps, is underground, and gets no sunlight.[28]

Eliot's most painful loss occurred in early 1916: on 10 January he wrote a letter to Conrad Aiken telling him "my friend Jean Verdenal has been killed, [and] that nothing has been seen of Armstrong, who is now a captain in Kitchener's army."[29] From the evidence of Eliot's letters, Jean Verdenal seems to have been one of Eliot's most significant attachments during his lifetime. His dedication of "The Love Song of J. Alfred Prufrock" to this friend affects the way we read the poem, mixing a very special, private tribute with the global historical fact of the still-ongoing war, asking whether there will be time beyond the time of crisis.

After this highly evocative beginning, the homoerotic subtext of the poem continues to build, with Eliot alluding almost exclusively to artistic predecessors who have been linked to homosexuality: Michelangelo, Shakespeare, and Whitman are the most obvious. Still, queer desire, and the questions the speaker dares not ask, are discursive confessions in and of themselves, even while Eliot's expressions of homoeroticism in his canonical verse remain muted, like a "love that dare not speak its name." Once we are attuned to the queer predilections of the poem, though, it becomes difficult to read it entirely straight. The statement just after the midway point of the poem, "Shall I say, I have gone at dusk through narrow streets / And watched the smoke that rises from the pipes / Of lonely men in shirt-sleeves, leaning out of windows?" (lines 70-2) begins to resemble a tentative proclamation of the forbidden delights of homosexual cruising. In case we miss the implications of this terrain of intimacy between "lonely" male bodies, we need only recall that from the outset of the poem Eliot figures the "narrow" urban streets as analogous to seduction, with "insidious intent" (line 9). The speaker's tentative confession also points to a highly regulated world of boundaries and confinement: the "narrow streets" seem barely to contain the peripatetic speaker, the "smoke" escapes from the bowls of "pipes," and the half-clothed "lonely men" seem to be precipitously on the brink of encounter, "leaning out of windows." Then, at the close of the poem, in seeing the mermaids – a homosocial *female* community – the speaker proclaims, "I do not think that they will sing to me" (line 125). Neither will the speaker sing a "love song" to them.

We begin to see that Eliot's repulsion from sex – and both memory and history's eroticism – was coded. He was sexier and more dramatically invested in representing sexuality than critics have acknowledged until only very recently. Yet we do not need his Columbo and Bolo *parergon* to tell us that T. S. Eliot wrote physical and somatic desire in the teens and twenties; the Columbo and Bolo poems only help us see that our scandalous suspicions are correct. It might, in fact, be time to look back to the prescience of one of Eliot's earliest critics, I. A. Richards, who urged people to read Eliot in terms of "sex," suggesting that to understand *The Waste Land* readers should turn to "Canto xxvi of the *Purgatorio* . . . It illuminates his persistent concern with sex, the problem of our generation, as religion was the problem of the last."[30]

LANGUAGE AND DESIRE

Central to the question of desire in T. S. Eliot is the desire of language to press beyond semantic and semiotic limits to touch upon some other bodily or existential truth. This desire to press beyond the limits of language is invariably present in poetry, and certainly latent in the structure of metaphor, and it is particularly acute in the attention Eliot gives to etymology and philology. As we see from Eliot's arguments in his critical essays, the past is radically coextensive and contiguous with the present, and this is perhaps most discernible in the tangible traces the past deposits within the fabric of language. In a little-known essay called "The Three Provincialities" that he wrote in the same year as *The Waste Land* but which remained unpublished until 1951, Eliot explains his poetic method in terms of a philological historical:

> Whatever words a writer employs, he benefits by knowing as much as possible of the history of these words, of the *uses to which they have already been applied.* Such knowledge facilitates his task of giving to the word a new life and to the language a new idiom. The essential of tradition is in this; and in getting as much as possible of the whole weight of the history of the language behind his word.[31]

The modernist "newness" Eliot was after still demanded a thorough knowledge of the history of language, literature, and culture – up to the very point of composition. That is, while he was iconoclastic formally, he wanted to include the rustle of the past in his poetic efforts through recognizing that previous terms, idioms, phrases, and language systems should always haunt their present uses.

Quite strikingly, Virginia Woolf presciently diagnosed Eliot's fascination with a kind of historiography of language after her very first meeting with him in 1918. After their encounter she records the following rather astute interpretive comment: "I think he believes in 'living phrases' & their difference from dead ones; in writing with extreme care, in observing all syntax & grammar; & so making this new poetry flower on the stem of the oldest."[32] Although Woolf writes this sentence several years before Eliot began drafting *The Waste Land*, she proves to be remarkably attuned to her new friend's preoccupations with finding life from death, and with "mixing / Memory and desire," even anticipating his "breeding / Lilacs out of the dead land" with her analogy to poetry's "flower[ing] on the stem of the oldest."

Woolf and Eliot happened to meet exactly as the Great War was ending, so that the historical consequences and circumstances of one of the century's major traumatic events shadowed their early acquaintance. The dates occurred like this: Woolf received a letter from Eliot on 28 October 1918, asking if they could get together; she agreed to a visit, and they scheduled one for 15 November; in the meantime the Armistice was signed on Monday 11 November. On the morning of Eliot's arrival on the fifteenth Woolf was in the midst of recording her thoughts on war and peace in her diary, trying to discern whether the atmosphere in England had changed substantially with the return of peace. She observes,

"Peace is rapidly dissolving into the light of common day . . . We are once more a nation of individuals."[33] When Eliot appears she is forced to stop her musings on the historical present, and she resumes her diary writing after his stay to cite his visit precisely as an *interruption*:

> I was interrupted somewhere on this page by the arrival of Mr Eliot. Mr Eliot is well expressed by his name – a polished, cultivated, elaborate young American, talking so slow, that each word seems to have a special finish allotted it. But beneath the surface, it is fairly evident that he is very intellectual, intolerant, with strong views of his own, & a poetic creed. I'm sorry to say that this sets up Ezra Pound & Wyndham Lewis as great poets, or in the current phrase "very interesting" writers. He admires Mr Joyce immensely. He produced 3 or 4 poems for us to look at – the fruit of two years, since he works all day in a Bank, & in his reasonable way thinks regular work good for people of nervous constitutions.[34]

This meeting with one of her most significant contemporaries ironically causes her to suspend her writing about nothing less than personal reminiscence about a major moment in global history. Within the week she also finished writing her second novel, *Night and Day* (1919).

Woolf aligns Eliot's reverence for the past with an attention to the formalities and formalisms of language. However, unlike the appraisals of John Middleton Murry or W. B. Yeats that I discuss in chapter 2, she discerns that Eliot's formalist allegiances specifically embraced a historical dimension: he was committed to granting attention to the letter of the past in terms of its differences and deferrals from the letter of the present. Although punctilious in "syntax and grammar," Eliot was acutely aware of the deadness of overused phrases, and he shared Joseph Conrad's aspiration in the Preface to *The Nigger of the Narcissus* to bring "the light of magic suggestiveness . . . to play for an evanescent instant over the commonplace surface of words: of the old, old words, worn thin, defaced by ages of careless usage."[35] Much of Eliot's writing of the past involved reading "tradition," allowing words to carry the historical and cultural moment they inevitably contain, and being ready to revise and re-order the waste of the past.

Language carried history for Eliot, but he was also deeply impressed by the ways in which language limits and confines our knowledge of the past. Again, as though anticipating a Lacanian awareness that subjects are formed by and through language, in "Prufrock" the speaker bemoans:

> And I have known the eyes already, known them all –
> The eyes that fix you in a formulated phrase,
> And when I am formulated, sprawling on a pin,
> When I am pinned and wriggling on the wall,

> Then how should I begin
> To spit out all the butt-ends of my days and ways?
> And how should I presume? (lines 55-61)

Eliot's poetry insists from the beginning on a desire to move beyond language as a carrier of convention, proposing instead that language may operate as a vehicle of play. To "pin" signification down is to rein in the infinite and fecund possibilities of language, and, as part of his effort to write through aporias of desire, Eliot deliberately refuses to bind the meaning of so many of his poems, leaving them open to reinterpretation and change. No reader can come to *The Waste Land* for the first time entirely prepared to read it, in full grasp of each allusion Eliot entreats us to know or discover, and there can be no "ideal" reading of the historical plenitude the poem contains. Our readings must endlessly participate in rereadings of the past literary traditions that he reifies and redeploys. Furthermore, Eliot's compilations of linguistic tissues that are loaded with traces of the past *and* with the residues of 1922 England must always be reread through the prism of our own contemporary cultural and historical locations. One of Eliot's desires then also anticipates Roland Barthes's heralding of the "birth of the reader," which must come at the cost of the "death of the Author."[36] This includes the desire to have the reader partake in (re)creating the poem: to both become and resist becoming the dissembling reader whom Eliot both appeals to and admonishes at the end of "The Burial of the Dead" as his likeness and kin: "'You! Hypocrite lecteur! – mon semblable, – mon frère!'" (line 76).

Part of the desire for the supple elusiveness (and allusiveness) of language that is so acutely tangible in Eliot is made clearer if we look to Julia Kristeva. She suggests, in her readings of Barthes, that literary writing offers the subject a unique relationship to the signifier: "The desire of a subject that ties him to the signifier obtains through this signifier an objective, extraindividual value, void-in-itself, other, without, for all that, ceasing (as it does in science) to be the desire of a subject. This happens only in literature."[37] The signifier is empty, but we still desire it, and in his poems Eliot thematizes the tie and the distance between a writer or a speaker's desire and the signs he or she succeeds in enunciating. Eliot is frequently frustrated by the limits of language, and he will "interrupt" his verse in dramatic fashion to tell us so. In the last third of "Prufrock," for example, we find a thrice-expressed, echoing pronouncement about the exasperation of transposing meaning to language. The first occurs after the speaker wonders about the "worth" of vocalizing the "overwhelming question." This happens as a female lover passively attests – in a domestic, nocturnal (or somnolent) space, via the subjunctive – to the perils and aporias of attempted communication: "If one, settling a pillow by her head, / Should say: 'That is not what I meant at all. / That is not it at all'" (lines 96-8). Six lines further on, while still ruminating about the "worth" of trying to express the ineffable, the speaker mimics the woman's phrasing with an echolalic turn, appending an exclamation mark: "It is impossible to say just what I mean!" (line 104). Then, still in the bedroom scene, the woman inverts her own phrasing to pronounce, "'That is not it at all, / That is not what I meant, at all'" (lines 109-10). We might juxtapose here Walter Benjamin's comment in "The Task of the Translator" that "In all language and linguistic creations there remains in addition to what can be conveyed something that cannot be communicated . . . And that which seeks to represent, to produce itself in the evolving of languages, is that very nucleus of pure language."[38] In the structure of Eliot's repetition, meaning appears to be unreceived (and perhaps even unreceivable), while language as the vehicle of enunciation betrays a semantic barrenness that parallels Prufrock's (sexualized) dilemmas. Nevertheless, we might observe that the woman sounds a great deal like Prufrock himself. Perhaps they understand each other far better than Prufrock imagines.

In *The Waste Land*, Eliot allows signification to break down altogether in the song of the three Thames daughters, when they chant wordless sounds that nevertheless communicate an onomatopoeic, agonized wailing of a degenerating emotional state, "Weialala leia / Wallala leialala" (lines 277-8 and 290-1). At times we must abandon language altogether in our search for iterability. Eliot argues in his essay on "Dante" – whom he called "the most *universal* of poets in the modern languages" – that Dante's poetry works especially well because "the word is lucid, or rather translucent."[39] In the same essay Eliot even makes the difficult (and some suggest preposterous) assertion that "genuine poetry can communicate before it is understood."[40] In all of this, Eliot is positing a kind of "third space" beyond the unpleasure of language's confines – a space where something like Benjamin's "pure language" could be conveyed without transliteration or translation. Eliot also seems well aware of a suggestion Lacan would later make that "there is no demand that does not in some sense pass through the defiles of the signifier."[41]

HETEROSEXUAL DISPLEASURES

In Eliot's early poems he is obsessively negotiating desire and its limits, frequently finding desire undesirable but nevertheless still, as if compelled, writing out desire and its relations to subjectivity and anteriority. While we find clear desires in "The Love Song of J. Alfred Prufrock" for social decorum, for answers to difficult (and often inarticulable) questions, for language-as-communication, and for time itself, male–female relations are distressingly *undesirable.* Yet, although they are usually more disquieting than attractive, verging on gothic rather than enchanting, Eliot diligently returns to female figures in every single poem in the *Prufrock* volume. That is, as vulgar as these women are in Eliot's portrayal, they, like the very undesirability of desire, represent a troubled figurality in his work that he repeatedly feels called upon to explore.

Through the *Prufrock* volume desire repeatedly meets its limit by confronting a traditional heterosexual desire that cannot thrive because it fails to come to terms with the perceived sordidity of the female body. The extra-linguistic communications of women's flesh – particularly its less appealing smells and imagos – destabilize the culturally sanctioned imaginary order that reads the female body as a desirable end for phallic longing. Women in these poems are chattering, prostituting, diseased, or physically repellent; they suggest the possibility of sexual desire by their presence, but through their shocking physicality they cause revulsion. This is an aspect of Eliot's work that others have noted, including Lyndall Gordon, who observes that "as early as 1910" Eliot already evinced "a ruthless rejection of the body's uncleanness."[42] Despite this horror of the flesh, though, Eliot compulsively writes out this repulsion, as though by returning to the most visceral aspects of the sensual he might, through poetic intellection, "work through" his corporeal disgust. Slavoj Žižek contends that in our interpersonal encounters with Otherness "our sense of reality is always sustained by a minimum of disidentification (for example, when we engage in communication with other people, we 'repress' our awareness of how they sweat, defecate, and urinate)."[43] In Eliot's abhorrence for women, women hold a synecdochic and charged symbolic place for an over-all human physical grotesque, and disgust is called into being with the thought of being asked, under a heteronormative regime, to be attracted to *that.*

In the *Prufrock* volume, ambivalent desires for the female body also conjoin with representations of thwarted longings for the past, as the female body stands in as a metaphor for memory and history in ways that anticipate this figuration in "Gerontion." Eliot's distaste for female sexuality is played out in several poems, including "Rhapsody on a Windy Night," which had originally been published in Lewis's *Blast.* In "Rhapsody" Eliot personifies a street lamp by investing it with what we might think of as a broken mechanical speakerly function. Like

Woolf's broken gramophone in *Between the Acts* to which I will return in chapter 7, the street lamp is barely able to get its words out: standing counter to the alienated, feminized, but ostensibly natural moon that presides over the scene, the lamp "sputtered" (lines 14 and 47), "muttered" (lines 15 and 48), and "hummed" (line 49), issuing imperative commands to "Regard that woman" (line 16), "Remark the cat" (line 35), and "Regard the moon" (line 50). In the first stanza Eliot had written, "Whispering lunar incantations / Dissolve the floors of memory" (lines 4-5), and the poem is just as preoccupied with the inevitable failures and returns of memory along axes of desire as his other work. Indeed, while the lamp reports. "The moon has lost her memory" (line 55), we immediately learn that "her" sexual past remains visible as a disease that has written her body: "A washed-out smallpox cracks her face" (line 56). Then, only six lines after announcing the moon's amnesia, Eliot presents a paratactic list of "reminiscences" that focus on texture, smell, and decay: "sunless dry geraniums," "dust in crevices," "Smells of chestnuts in the streets," "female smells in shuttered rooms," "cigarettes in corridors," "And cocktail smells in bars" (lines 63-8). Moving through dryness ("dry geraniums," and "dust") to the potential seeds for growth ("chestnuts"), Eliot nevertheless recoils from this glimmer of open sensual appreciation to express an oppressive and claustrophobic rendering of the female body whose excretions (smells) threaten to supersede desire.

Burning tobacco, and then the smell of wet cocktails concludes the dialectic between dryness and wetness that this little mini-cycle enacts, and which Eliot will revisit more thoroughly in *The Waste Land*, where the land's drought is echoed in the spiritual dryness of the waste land's inhabitants. Linking memory and the body, each recollection in "Rhapsody on a Windy Night" depends on a sensory association registered in the body at the time of its formation. The list as a whole is also prompted, in a very Proustian way, by isolation and smell: "She is alone / With all the old nocturnal smells / That cross and cross across her brain" (lines 59-61). The speaker is apparently fascinated with the disharmony between disgust and delight, as female corporeality is staged as an excrescence that is both imprisoned and enclosing, experiencing its own scent as a recurrent *crossing* (repeated three times in a single line) that traverses the senses with (and toward) memory. Eliot seems to be partaking of what Françoise Meltzer designates in her important study of literary originality as the "patriarchal system that seeks to objectify all that is feminine and to feminize all that it sees as objectionable."[44] And, as elsewhere in his poems, the feminine does the work of circumscribing and effectively ending desire, as though Eliot "colonizes" the feminine to do the metaphoric labor of representing the dangers and oppressions of being subject to desire.[45]

In "Preludes," another poem from 1915, also published in *Blast*, Eliot continues to link memory with feminized sexual undesirability. In part III we find a woman in a dream-like state, addressed in the second person:

> You tossed a blanket from the bed,
> You lay upon your back, and waited;
> You dozed, and watched the night revealing
> The thousand sordid images
> Of which your soul was constituted;
> They flickered against the ceiling.
> And when all the world came back
> And the light crept up between the shutters
> And you heard the sparrows in the gutters,
> You had such a vision of the street
> As the street hardly understands . . .
> (lines 24-34)

While in a liminal state of near sleep this woman experiences a filmic vision of her soul's mnemonic constitution. As if to illustrate Freud and Bergson's still-developing theories about the tenuous links between the unconscious and conscious aspects of the psyche, the speaker transports us between interiorities and exteriorities to suggest that this woman's soul is so polluted that even the filthy street, with its "newspapers from vacant lots" (line 8) is no objective correlative for its baseness. Her physical lineaments, jaundiced and soiled, provide a perfect corollary for her interior destitution, with her efforts at personal beauty appearing manufactured and even ugly: "Sitting along the bed's edge, where / You curled the papers from your hair, / Or clasped the yellow soles of feet / In the palms of both soiled hands" (lines 35-8). Her yellow feet recall the smog – the "fog" and "smoke" – of the cunning and lascivious cityscape in "Prufrock": "The yellow fog that rubs its back upon the window-panes, / The yellow smoke that rubs its muzzle on the window-panes, / Licked its tongue into the corners of the evening, / Lingered upon the pools that stand in drains" (lines 15-18).

In every one of these instances, Eliot situates women within the discourse of sex – they stand as sexual objects – but their very sexuality is *undesirable*. In "Prufrock" this dialectic of curiosity and disgust, of apprehensiveness and horror, continues. Here the speaker is mesmerized, shocked, and repelled by the hair on women's arms: "And I have known the arms already, known them all – / Arms that are braceleted and white and bare / (But in the lamplight, downed with light brown hair!)" (lines 62-4). As though guile constitutes the feminine – and its alliance with historicity (a suggestion Eliot repeats in "Gerontion," as I have shown) – the suddenly illuminated hair on the women's arms reminds one that the dance of intimacy must negotiate disguise. The half-remembered and half-known corporeality that the artificial "lamplight" betrays is uncanny, and not concordant with eros as purified possession. Eliot's rendering here again comes close to Freud's thinking. In his essay on "The 'Uncanny'" Freud cites Schelling to concur that "'*Unheimlich' is the name for everything that ought to have remained . . . secret and hidden but has come to light.*'"[46] For Freud, what is uncanny is also "nothing new or alien, but something which is familiar and old-established in the mind and which has become alienated from it only through the process of repression."[47] Still, even in the uncanny (*heimlich–unheimlich*) surprise of the physical, we feel a perplexed libidinous excitement (or at least curiosity) that derails the speaker from his train of thought.[48] This unexpected feminine hirsuteness constitutes a trick not unlike the "cunning passages" of women's genitalia in "Gerontion," where Eliot evokes the labyrinthine, swollen contours of history whose geography one cannot repress. In "Prufrock" the speaker is unsettled and then quickly recovers, but not without self-consciously announcing the interruption of the feminine and its sensual accoutrements: "is it perfume from a dress / That makes me so digress?" (lines 65-6).

We might think of Eliot's fascinated mode of attention to the horror of the female corporeal as a kind of inverse fetishism that abhors – rather than invests with desire – substitutions for the phallus. He reads parts and smells (hands, feet, odors, faces, corridors, passages, hair on arms) synecdochally as objects apart from the body as a whole. Then, in "Prufrock," the speaker must literally move through scenes of bodies for sale (Eliot juxtaposes the butcher's sawdust on the sidewalk, used to cover the blood and remains of animal flesh, with the flesh of prostitutes) to reach the refined gatherings of high society, where "women come and go / Talking of Michelangelo" (lines 13-14). The simultaneous infection and incommensurability between cultures of inside/outside, high/low, elite/marginal that operate as animating (and always contested) binaries in Eliot's work emerge here through the contrast of the women prostitutes with the almost bodyless and highly mobile female consumers of art history.

Indeed, in a poet who is noted for his "impersonality," it becomes astonishingly difficult to separate T. S. Eliot himself from Prufrock. Eliot complained to Conrad Aiken shortly after he had arrived in London of "nervous sexual attacks which I suffer from when alone in a city." In the same letter he admitted, with some apparent shame, "I am very dependent upon women (I mean female society)."[49] His language in both cases sounds quintessentially Prufrockian.

At the end of "Prufrock" Eliot describes the confrontation between nature, the linguistic, the social, and the cultural as an occasion for death. Echoing the remark earlier in the poem, "I should have been a pair of ragged claws / Scuttling across the floors of silent seas" (lines 73-4), he openly borrows from John Donne's "Song" in which Donne writes, "Teach me to – hear Mermaides singing":

> I have heard the mermaids singing, each to each.
>
> I do not think that they will sing to me.
>
> I have seen them riding seaward on the waves
> Combing the white hair of the waves blown back
> When the wind blows the water white and black.
>
> We have lingered in the chambers of the sea
> By sea-girls wreathed with seaweed red and brown
> Till human voices wake us, and we drown.
> (lines 124-31)

In contrast to the all-too-human women of the poem, mermaids signify promise (like the old seers they have something to sing, they have answers), a possible destination for Prufrock's desire, and the freedom of riding outward, away from land, the location of culture. At the same time, they are caretakers – they "comb" the "white" (aged?) hair of the rough waves of the sea. With an impersonal and indeterminate "we," the speaker suggests that he and another (or others – he does not specify the gender or number) find this distance from the world satisfying enough to want to prolong the visit: "We have lingered in the chambers of the sea." Unlike the underworld traveler in Dante's *Inferno*, however, Eliot's speaker has no Virgil to guide him back to the surface. Prufrock takes refuge from the world of strained proprieties in the "chambers" of the mythic-natural (as correlatives to the "room" where "women come and go / Talking of Michelangelo") only to "drown" as he awakes from the dream where he finally meets a still-point of desire.

STEALING FROM THE PAST

It is well known that T. S. Eliot was not above borrowing or stealing material from other writers. By 1920 he was able to make fun of this inclination within his criticism, raising intertextual theft to the level of "mature" art. In his essay, "Philip Massinger," he makes the infamous statement, "Immature poets imitate; mature poets steal; bad poets deface what they take, and good poets make it into something better, or at least something different."[50] Unfortunately, this kind of high-art theft was an issue for which others sometimes suffered. Late in 1915 Harriet Monroe, the editor of *Poetry* magazine in Chicago, was attacked by *The Dial* for "allowing Eliot's 'plagiarism' in 'Cousin Nancy' of George Meredith's line, 'The army of unalterable law.'"[51] Eliot wrote to Monroe several months later, in March 1916 with a jocular, unconcerned response: "Thank you for the clippings in regard to the *Dial* [*sic*] episode. Does the battle still go on? I should be glad to participate with a few quotations which the critic would perhaps not identify."[52] Eliot's almost flippant, Wildean humor indicates a sense of entitlement about his right to circulate freely within and among others' texts. Françoise Meltzer argues that such intertextual borrowing pays homage to the dialectical and dialogical nature of literature by enacting the conviction – held, too, by Paul Célan and Martin Buber – that "all art is encounter."[53] In this way, Eliot's "steal[ing]" from others means a refusal to privilege intellectual ownership of literary language, a destabilization of the search for secure and discoverable "origins," and an affirmation of literature as encounter.

Contrary to Eliot's admonition in "Philip Massinger" that "a good poet will usually borrow from authors remote in time, or alien in language, or diverse in interest,"[54] he may also have borrowed, or "stolen," several of his key tropes in *The Waste Land* from modernist contemporaries. In 1919 Richard Aldington published two volumes of poetry, *Images of War* and *Images of Desire*, explicitly linking war and desire by coupling the titles through their repetition. In so doing he suggests that both the tangible historical fact of war and the emotive quality of desire may be approached through "image" – a term that would have resonated with both the recent Imagist movement and with experiments in contemporary visual arts. War and desire are hardly interchangeable with "memory and desire," but by 1919 "war" in some senses meant, urgently and immediately, *memory*, since the Great War was the most recent major shared cultural event.

This is only the beginning of the resonances between Aldington and Eliot's writing of this period. In one of Aldington's short poems from 1919, "Epigrams," published in *The Egoist* while Eliot was assistant editor, he writes,

> Your mouth is fragrant as an orange-grove
> In April, and your lips are hyacinths,
> Dark, dew-wet, folded, petalled hyacinths
> Which my tongue pierces like an amorous bee.[55]

Eliot would not write *The Waste Land* for another two years, but the images of April linked with sexual desire and the symbolic weight of hyacinths must have resonated strongly with his imagination, and he uses both of these figures within the first half of "The Burial of the Dead." Yet the comparison does not stop here. Aldington published another short poem, "Reserve," in the same issue of *The Egoist*, and this time he draws a poignant connection between memory and desire. The full poems reads as follows:

> Though you desire me I will still feign sleep
> And check my eyes from opening to the day,
> For as I lie, thrilled by your gold-dark flesh,
> I think of how the dead, my dead, once lay.[56]

Instead of acceding to the desire of a racialized, dark-skinned beloved, the desired stalls the sexual encounter, choosing to "feign sleep" so that he may ponder the "thrill[]" of the present backed by the past. In the instant of desire, then, Aldington's speaker turns abruptly to memory – which carries the specter of death in its erotic allusiveness – as a mode both of intensification and deferral. Eliot's way of writing the zeugma of memory and desire was to make history everywhere enunciative of itself, even if the historical speaks obliquely, even if its utterances occur in Baudelairean "confusing speech," mingled with approximations of the meaning of desire.

LATER POEMS AND THE REFUSAL OF DESIRE

Hence the soul cannot be possessed of the divine union, until it has divested itself of the love of created beings.

(St. John of the Cross, epigraph to T. S. Eliot's "Sweeney Agonistes: Fragments of an Aristophanic Melodrama")

Eliot is busy modifying, regulating, and displacing desire all through his early verse, but after his conversion in 1927 his poems proclaim that desire has been superseded. By the time of "Ash Wednesday" (1930) he is able to open the poem this way:

> Because I do not hope to turn again
> Because I do not hope
> Because I do not hope to turn
> Desiring this man's gift and that man's scope
> I no longer strive to strive towards such things
> (Why should the agèd eagle stretch its wings?)
> Why should I mourn
> The vanished power of the usual reign?
> (lines 1-8)

Instead of asking questions, as he does in "Prufrock," Eliot begins this long meditation, named for the first day of Lent, by *answering* an unheard question. His vision is apparently more decided, and less ambivalent – instead of asking "Do I dare?" he asserts "I do not hope." A few lines later he affirms, "I rejoice that things are as they are and / I renounce the blessèd face / And renounce the voice" (lines 20-2). Importantly, just as he claims to have renounced desire, we see an accompanying and incontrovertible shift in his representation of women. In contradistinction to their squalid eroticism in his earlier poems, women become virginal, pristine, and goddess-like. It is as though the face of male heterosexual desire's primary object must change to accommodate Eliot's turn away from coding such desire in explicitly erotic terms.

In the second section of "Ash Wednesday," the speaker addresses an unnamed "Lady" to describe, from a kind of afterlife, an animalistic feasting on his body: "Lady, three white leopards sat under a juniper-tree / In the cool of the day, having fed to satiety / On my legs my heart my liver and that which had been contained / In the hollow round of my skull" (lines 42-5). Instead of the nervous, stuttering reaction in "Hysteria" to the threat of incorporation, the speaker conveys a placid acceptance of the scene of his engorgement. Dexterously moving through Old Testament echoes – from Psalm 27:2, "When the wicked, even mine enemies and my foes, came upon me to eat up my flesh, they stumbled and fell," to 1 Kings 19:5, "But he himself went a day's journey into the wilderness, and came and sat down under a juniper tree," to a translation of Ezekiel's cry, "Son of man, can these bones live?" (37:3) – Eliot renders an intertextual pastiche of scriptural quotation much as he had done in a more secular vein in his earlier poetry. The "bones" we are so familiar with from *The Waste Land* are no longer "lost" or "rattled," but they are capable of a speech that judges and venerates the power and "goodness" of the feminine:

> And that which had been contained
> In the bones (which were already dry) said chirping:
> Because of the goodness of this Lady
> And because of her loveliness, and because
> She honours the Virgin in meditation,
> We shine with brightness. (lines 47-52)

Sexuality and the threat of a heterosexual copulative function have been vacated from the feminine, which is now – allied with Mariolatry and virginity – made safe, pristine, and sanitary (dry), as Eliot professes a move past desire via sublimation, displacement, and sheer performative insistence. Further, the faltering iterability that Eliot traces through the *Prufrock* volume seems also to have been overcome, and in its place is a striking clarity of tongues. Disallowing Babel's confusion, God and bones converse freely with both the human and a symbolic Real of the feminine; the search for transcendence has discovered immanence, and death's remainder, as elsewhere, lives on as an archive of bones that testifies to the truth of both present and past.

Concomitantly, by this point in his oeuvre Eliot arrives at a new conception in his treatment of memory. Instead of constantly seeking anamnesis – instances of recollection – and meaning from the past, he more fully embraces a Nietzschean forgetfulness that is nevertheless available only to the dead: "Let the whiteness of bones atone to forgetfulness. / There is no life in them. As I am forgotten / And would be forgotten, so I would forget" (lines 59-61). For a moment we are no longer being called to do the work of remembrance and temporal relativity – "Consider Phlebas, who was once as handsome and tall as you," even as Phlebas himself "forgot the cry of gulls, and the deep sea swell" – but we are entreated to release the residue of time's relics. A few lines later in "Ash Wednesday" Eliot connects beauty, nature, and desire to join them with both memory and forgetting:

> Rose of memory
> Rose of forgetfulness
> Exhausted and life-giving
> Worried reposeful
> The single Rose
> Is now the Garden
> Where all loves end

Terminate torment
Of love unsatisfied
The greater torment
Of love satisfied
(lines 69-79)

Eliot has evidently not ceased to link memory with desire – their binding will agitate his writings to the end – but he is distanced enough from the erotic charge of their pairing to work by way of symbolic singularities: a gardenscape is reduced to "The single Rose," as he contracts desire's register to a surprisingly conventional romantic figure of flowering.

Eliot then returns to the yoking of memory and desire in some of his very latest poetry. To circle back ourselves to one of the epigraphs for this section, we should remember that in "Little Gidding" he writes,

This is the use of memory:
For liberation – not less of love but expanding
Of love beyond desire, and so liberation
From the future as well as the past.
(lines 157-60)

Here, memory is, rather paradoxically, what grants us freedom from time. Memory, in this sense, involves recognition – literally a *re-cognizing* – of the past, whether personal or historical; it grants the subject a freer futurity. Only by revisiting and recognizing our past may we move forward; the way upward and the way downward are the same, and we will always exist at the crux of "the enchainment of past and future" ("Burnt Norton," line 81). Eliot is here repeating a version of his argument from "Tradition and the Individual Talent," where, as I will show, he insists on discovering an infusion from the past in order to produce the new: "the past should be altered by the present as much as the present is directed by the past."[57] Still, in "Little Gidding," the "liberation" that memory offers may only occur by moving "beyond desire." By this stage in his poetic career he is ready to say that desire must undergo a kind of translation for one to discover a greater opening and expansion through the surrender to "love beyond desire" (line 159). This "liberation" is bound up with stepping outside of the strict logic of chronos, causality, and subjective want toward a purity of an "expand[ed]" *love* that entails a "detachment / From self and from things and from persons" (lines 153-4). Desire, that is, must be transmuted and taken by way of a restoration after decay to repair, even partially, the terrible lack in its impossible call: "renewed, transfigured, in another pattern" (line 166).

We might say that by the time of the *Four Quartets* Eliot has moved several degrees away from the painful eroticization of history and memory we find in *Prufrock and Other Observations*, "Gerontion," and *The Waste Land*, toward acceptance, and perhaps even resignation. "History may be servitude, / History may be freedom," he writes ambivalently toward the end of "Little Gidding" (lines 163-4). The uncertain statement tells us that even this late in Eliot's career he could pronounce no definitive answer about history's bondage or release. History fetters us with the desire to retrieve or revisit things past, but *knowing* history opens us to freedom's potential that is intrinsic to knowledge as power. Throughout the *Four Quartets* we feel an almost tangible desire for history – this time in its eternal aspect, discoverable in the expanding historicity of every moment, and touched with the residues of religion, nature, and national identity: "history is a pattern / Of timeless moments. So, while the light fails / On a winter's afternoon, in a secluded chapel / History is now and England" ("Little Gidding," lines 235-8). As Woolf will propose in her own way, the past is bound up for Eliot with its (re)discoverability in place (*topos*) and sensation, while it is written on the body and always open to being reexperienced through its corporeal traces. Eliot's constant looking backward might just represent his most erotically charged longing.

CHAPTER 4

T. S. Eliot: writing time and blasting memory

I sometimes wonder if that is what Krishna meant –
Among other things – or one way of putting the same thing:
That the future is a faded song, a Royal Rose or a lavender spray
Of wistful regret for those who are not yet here to regret,
Pressed between yellow leaves of a book that has never been opened.

T. S. Eliot, "The Dry Salvages"[1]

If Time and Space, as Sages say,
Are things which cannot be,
The sun which does not feel decay
No greater is than we.
So why, Love, should we ever pray
To live a century?
The butterfly that lives a day
Has lived eternity.

T. S. Eliot, "If Time and Space as Sages Say"[2]

But while we looked into the future, we were completely under the power of the past.

Virginia Woolf, "A Sketch of the Past"[3]

It is one of the paradoxes of modernist writing that in its self-conscious efforts at making it "new," writers from across its experiment repeatedly turned to the past. Of course, what is absolutely new is always already historical, and Ezra Pound's rallying cry, "make it new," invokes a repeated adage about the phantasy of leaving behind old orders – outworn words, aesthetics, structures, styles, politics, and psychic dispositions. Jacques Lacan suggests that "Repetition . . . demands the new,"[4] and we might think of the modernist fixation on newness as registering an anxious obsession with the dilemma of their own repetition and belatedness. These writers were pushing boundaries and breaking new aesthetic ground, but next to the call to newness that so many modernist writers emphatically embraced, the past creeps in as one of their primary figures of desire. Alongside my emphasis on modernist modes of remembrance and its intimate reliance on registers of desire and sensuality, then, I also take up questions of what it meant for Eliot and Woolf to write their epoch, by asking how they wrote the *present* of modernism. For Eliot, writing the present often meant mourning the severance (in time) from experiencing the past with the direct apprehension that the present craves, but it also involved asserting that present and past time are simultaneous and interdependent, that repetition denotes change, and that our existence in time marks a constant oscillation between forgetting, remembering, and being conscious of the uniqueness of the present. For Woolf, writing the present often involved stressing the numinosity of the moment through describing what she came to call "moments of being" – instances of particular ontological and epistemological intensity, which I will discuss below – that both contain and (re)make memory's effects. Both writers appreciated the fact that remembered history (whether personal or cultural) denotes, quite literally, a *corpus* (a body *and* its work) that operates in dialogue with the present, which is, in turn, subject to time's corporeal stamp.

Lyndall Gordon, Eliot's preeminent biographer (who has also published a biography of Woolf),[5] claims that "Eliot was most in his element in the act of memory. He chose as his totem the elephant who never forgets."[6] And, while never forgetting, Eliot was intent on writing his time. This involved a combination of mimesis, repetition, and mirroring the present back to itself through a prism of form that acknowledged the past, ambivalently longed for its incorporation, and would come to be known by its dilapidated refinements and revisions of literary modes. For both Eliot and Woolf their efforts in the present all at once involved dismantling *and* preserving literary and cultural ideals, while building on and among shifting cultures, histories, topographies, textualities, and desires. Nietzsche helps us to see this modernist predilection to venerate the past while self-consciously *making* the present and future when he suggests in the mid-1870s, "The voice of the past is always the voice of an oracle; only if you are architects of the future and are familiar with the present will you understand the oracular voice of the past . . . only those who build the future have the right to sit in judgment of the past."[7]

Edwin Muir makes some similar pronouncements in his 1918 essay, "What is Modern." He writes, "If modernism be a vital thing it must needs have roots in the past and be an essential expression of humanity, to be traced, therefore, in the history of humanity: in short, it can only be a tradition . . . Is there a 'modern spirit' not dependent upon time and place, and in all ages modern?"[8] As Eliot would do the following year in "Tradition and the Individual Talent," Muir was elaborating on a particularly urgent dilemma about the value of the past for the avant-garde that, as I have argued, continues to be debated today. By contrast, in his capacity as editor of the short-lived but influential magazine, *Rhythm*, John Middleton Murry outlines rather different aesthetic goals:

To treat what is being done today as something vital in the progress of art, which cannot fix its eyes on yesterday and live; to see that the present is pregnant for the future rather than a revolt against the past; in creation to give expression to an art that seeks out the strong things in life; in criticism to seek out the strong things of that art – such is the aim of *Rhythm*.[9]

The battle for what "modernist" historicity would mean had begun, with John Middleton Murry and, as I will show, Wyndham Lewis, as two of the most vociferous proponents for insisting that the past provided no sustenance for the modernist moment and needed to be relinquished.

At the core of Eliot's sensibilities is a persistent, though often uneasy, gesturing to affiliations with past time – recognizing that the materiality and body of both history and memory would inevitably be found again in the "new." "Past time" frequently presented an agonistic (and even antagonistic) relation to the "modern," whose literary exemplars were anxious about the fragile temporality of their specific moment. Muir continues in "What is Modern" to declare that although contemporary writing requires a historical sense, "The past has certainly lost its mystery for us."[10] Nevertheless, he exclaims, "the future is still ours, and there, at Man's goal, our myths must be planted . . . we who have faith in the Future *must* believe."[11] Anticipating Marinetti's Futurism, Muir's language of possession, myth-making, and even religiosity tells us that writing *of* the present *for* the present always involved a quasi-sacred act of begetting futurity. But this intense compulsion toward the future occurred with an obsessive glancing backward to an anteriority that for Eliot could not simply be inherited, was never taken for granted, and was as troubling as it was inspiring.

In *The Waste Land*, the life-writing that charts Eliot's walk to work at Lloyds' Bank "down King William Street" (line 66), the section of "A Game of Chess" that Ezra Pound marked "photography?," and the voices of the two working-class women at the end of "A Game of Chess," stand as exemplary moments in the poem's status as a snapshot of the contemporary moment. Although it was undervalued as a cultural and historical document for decades – Michael Levenson claims in 1999 that we need to remind ourselves of the cultural and even political valences the poem would have had for its first readers[12] – the poem's function as a comment on the agonies of London *circa* 1921–2 is unparalleled in its pithy evocation of a bleak postwar mood. In a characteristic insistence of the "impersonality" of poetry while nevertheless attesting precisely to the "personal," Eliot denied this had been his intent. He writes to his brother, Henry, confessing he was flattered that some had understood *The Waste Land* as a cultural document, but refusing such status: "Various critics have done me the honour to interpret the poem in terms of criticism of the contemporary world, have considered it, indeed, as an important bit of social criticism. To me it was only the relief of a personal and wholly insignificant grouse against life; it is just a piece of rhythmical grumbling."[13] We cannot, though, take Eliot's protests entirely seriously. As Frank Kermode points out, "the important words in that sentence are *to me*:"[14] to Eliot *The Waste Land* was an "insignificant" emotional "relief" – to his readers it stands as a significant instance of modernist testimony.

In contradiction to Eliot's well-known protest to his brother, many of Eliot's letters disclose an acute sense of his role as cultural witness, deeply committed to the task of *writing time*.[15] In a letter to his mother in April 1918, he expresses frustration that, living in the United States, she did not understand the devastation the Great War was wreaking in Europe:

> Judging from American newspapers, the war seems to have affected the country not very seriously yet. I don't mean that it is not the chief subject of interest, but that it is *simply* the chief subject of interest, and not the obsessing nightmare that it is to Europe. And we can't make you realize three thousand miles away all that that means. Even with all your privations and difficulties. Your papers talk about the "fight for civilisation"; do they realise either what civilisation means or what the fight for it means? We are all immeasurably and irremediably altered over here by the last three years.[16]

Eliot's sense of the nightmarish scarring of contemporary history would find its way into *The Waste Land* within a few years, and, as Samuel Hynes reminds his readers in his seminal study, *The Auden Generation*, "*The Waste Land* was an important factor in the process by which the post-war generation became aware of itself and its situation."[17] That is, *The Waste Land* became a part of the culture from which it sprang – a historical object contemporaneous with its own historicity. Still, Eliot was turning away from mimesis as art's recording mode, offering not only a reflection of his time, but claiming that poetry makes, creates, and tempers its cultural and historical conditions of possibility. These conditions, in turn, are absorbed and refracted back to it, so that poetry functions as source as well as comment.

The interest modernist writers had in defining their writing in terms of its temporal location found particularly vocal expression in Wyndham Lewis's *Blast*, where Lewis insists that the modernist moment is best described as a super-charged "vortex" of temporally loaded experience. In a section called "The Turbine" that Ezra Pound contributed to the first issue of *Blast* – in which Eliot's "Preludes" and "Rhapsody of [*sic*] a Windy Night" were originally published, but for which his Bolo poems were rejected – Pound enunciates the Vorticist credo in explicitly temporal terms:

> All experience rushes into this vortex. All the energized past, all the past that is living and worthy to live. All MOMENTUM, which is the past bearing upon us, RACE, RACE-MEMORY, instinct charging the PLACID, NON-ENERGIZED FUTURE.
>
> The DESIGN of the future in the grip of the human vortex. All the past that is vital, all the past that is capable of living into the future, is pregnant in the vortex, NOW.[18]

Although Eliot did not actually sign the Vorticist manifesto (its circulation, in any case, occurred shortly before he arrived in England in 1914), and we cannot associate him unproblematically with the short-lived movement, Pound's words provide a prescient summing-up of what would become a prevailing literary attitude toward temporality. Pound was affirming that it is the "energ[y]" and "momentum" of the past that are quite literally "charg[ed]" (as electricity, or as ethics) with invigorating the still-inert but potently imagined future. He therefore perceived the phantasmatic future as needing an infusion from nothing less than the phantasm of history. And, Pound affirms, this past was ready to give birth (it is "pregnant in the vortex") in the "now" of the modernist moment at hand.[19]

This schema of modernism's relation to time is both refined and contradicted elsewhere in the same issue of *Blast*. In "Long Live the Vortex!" Lewis expresses a dramatically different position to Pound's, affirming, "We stand for the Reality of the Present – not for the sentimental Future, or the sacripant Past."[20] Valuing the present because it is where we discover "Reality," Lewis places an ahistorical and hypercharged *nowness* at the center of the manifesto's demands, much as writers of the Beat Generation would do forty years later, divulging a phantasy of pure innovation. His call requested that Vorticist writers abandon the burden of history by resituating themselves in a unique beyond of time that could mean beginning again, from the place of a "new" modernity. For Lewis, with his insistence on upper-case letters for "Past," "Present," and "Future," only the "Present" signifies "Reality." The "Future" is bad because it is bonded to sentiment, sensation, and emotion; perhaps already, like Eliot's vision of an anterior of futurity in "Dry Salvages," "the future is a faded song." In contradistinction, Lewis describes the "Past" as "sacripant": that is, "rare," and a "boastful pretender to valour" (*Oxford English Dictionary*). The past is uncommon, though it masquerades with a false heroism, hardly constituting material from which to forge a new aesthetics. By making these calls Lewis is, of course, already implicitly concerned with locating his movement in terms of historical difference. Indeed, his disagreements with Pound continue elsewhere in the same issue, and we might think of *Blast* as one of the central battlegrounds for the crisis of defining modernist temporality and historicity. For his part, Pound critiques Lewis's ahistorical dream of the present by insisting that the present is criss-crossed already with *both* past and future time: the present is the meeting point of the "vital" past and the future, and it is only through embracing and enfolding the rich and strange textures of what has been that modernist writers could build their futures.

In *Blast*'s second issue (of only two) in 1915, Lewis again affirms,

> This paper wishes to stand rigidly opposed, from start to finish, to every form that the Poetry of a former condition of life, no longer existing, has foisted upon us. It seeks to oppose to this inapposite poetry, the intensest aroma of a different humanity (that is Romance) the Poetry which is the as yet unexpressed spirit of the present time, and of new conditions and possibilities of life.[21]

Appealing to writers to discover a kind of spirit of the present age, Lewis repeats and transforms the word "form" to make it "former," thereby linking, with a pun, formalist concerns with the outdated aims of "former" times. His claim for an absolute cleavage between the present of modernist aesthetics and its past was a petition whose logic modernist writers could not easily resist since its disavowal spoke of a revolutionary poetics involving resistance, resituation, and renewal. Lewis's call would gradually become more muted, however, displaced by the praxis of a modernism whose story – in Eliot, Freud, Proust, Woolf, Bergson, Walter Benjamin, Pound, Stein, Faulkner, and so many others – became centrally concerned with not being able to lose memory after all. Nevertheless, Lewis's appeal became one of the defining hermeneutic lenses through which the modernist relation to the past has been understood.

AN ATRADITIONAL RENDERING: "TRADITION AND THE INDIVIDUAL TALENT"

The version of modernism that T. S. Eliot writes certainly agrees with a feeling of being cut off – in a moment of energetic discontinuity – from the ages that had come before, but, as with other modernist writers, the relation to the past that he articulates is inevitably more complicated than this. The past was all at once a never-fully lost favorite object, an ossified poetics of culture and art, and a force of presence that he labored to include in the body of the present – sometimes while foregrounding the woundedness of rupture. In an advertisement that ran in *The Egoist* on 1 March 1915, we find this summation for the Chicago-based *Little Review*, edited by Margaret Anderson:

> [The *Little Review*] Has been called "the most vital thing ever started in America"
> Unacademic, enthusiastic, appreciative and youthful
> Free from propaganda and outworn tradition.[22]

The publicity ad links the "vital" with a break from the past – from "outworn" tradition – but it still leaves room for "tradition" that is not "outworn," or for "tradition" that might contribute to the energy of the present. And, although Eliot did not become assistant editor for *The Egoist* until 1917, it would be within the pages of that magazine that "Tradition and the Individual Talent" would appear in 1919. The modernist consciousness that Eliot wrote was decidedly *not* severed from its past, and in fact relentlessly sought to redraw the concatenating effects of a history that could not be hindered, bound, or restricted in its play within the present. In 1921, when giving Richard Aldington advice about Aldington's forthcoming book of criticism, Eliot urged him to seek a model of "some historical continuity" in a "book of criticisms,"[23] invoking "tradition" as the very condition of possibility for poetry. Nevertheless, as I will show, Eliot understood tradition in atraditional ways, affirming that tradition operates as a trump for temporality, and a foil for time, offering itself to the present by way of an encounter with the eros of the past.

According to "Tradition and the Individual Talent" – Eliot's most explicit inquiry into relations between writing, time, memory, and history – part of the obligation of tradition is to carry the marks of time:

> It involves, in the first place, the historical sense, which we may call nearly indispensable to anyone who would continue to be a poet beyond his twenty-fifth year; and the historical sense involves a perception, not only of the pastness of the past, but of its presence; the historical sense compels a man to write not merely with his own generation in his bones, but with a feeling that the whole of the literature of Europe from Homer and within it the whole of the literature of his own country has a simultaneous existence and composes a simultaneous order. This historical sense, which is a sense of the timeless as well as of the temporal and of the timeless and of the temporal together, is what makes a writer traditional. And it is at the same time what makes a writer most acutely conscious of his place in time, of his own contemporaneity.[24]

Eliot was well aware, years before Michel de Certeau would explicate his theory of historiography, of "the rupture between a past that is its [history's] object, and a present that is the place of its practice," whereby "history endlessly finds the present in its object and the past in its practice."[25] Furthermore, Eliot's understanding of the "historical sense" describes a hermeneutics through which the specificity of present time compares with its eternal aspects. Perhaps invoking the *zeitgeist* of Freud – already present within the modernist culture of 1919 – he describes the modern poet as situated in a "contemporaneity" that is taken to task for being "conscious" of none other than its location, or, its "place in time." In this rather postmodern reading, Homer, Dante, Baudelaire, Gertrude Stein, and Toni Morrison, for example, would not follow consecutively from each other, but they would exist together by virtue of a neo-Barthesian ascendance of the reader.

Eduardo Cadava writes in an essay on Walter Benjamin's theses of history that "Benjamin's historical materialist seeks to delineate the contours of a history whose chance depends on overcoming the idea of history as the mere reproduction of a past."[26] Although writing outside of a Marxist register, Eliot's notion of history seeks a commensurate overcoming of the illusion of history as mere reproduction. The past "should be altered by the present as much as the present is directed by the past" (15). Tradition is not a simple set of cultural artifacts, nor is it invisibly transmitted through the osmosis of the social realm. Rather, tradition signifies anterior textual inscriptions, proper names, written bodies, and the plenitude of ideas that are physically and psychically available to the present that surrenders itself to them. As such, tradition requires both conscious and unconscious "labour" to "obtain" – from the Latin, *obtinēre*, "towards holding" – these effects in and for the present. And what is labored for will inevitably meet change in its present incarnation since tradition murmurs in a quiet speech that enacts both a dialogue and a contestation between then and now.

As Woolf will do later in her autobiographical fragment, "A Sketch of the Past," Eliot thus proposes that the literatures of past times are not only continuous with each other, but *contiguous*. In Woolf's terms, to which I will return, the past is a sensuous archive that always remains open because the past continues to exist *in and with* the present: "I see it – the past – as an avenue lying behind; a long ribbon of scenes, emotions. There at the end of the avenue still, are the garden and the nursery."[27] Rather oddly, though, "Tradition and the Individual Talent" seems to have compelled generations of misreadings. It has been widely interpreted only in its narrowest sense, as valuing an outmoded and hierarchical value of "tradition." Douglas Mao, for example, misses what I argue is Eliot's exceedingly *un*-traditional reading of "tradition," overlooking Eliot's sense, already strongly expressed in 1919, of the difficulty of speaking of and naming tradition. In his essay Eliot asserts, "In English writing we seldom speak of tradition . . . We cannot refer to 'the tradition' or to 'a tradition'" (13). Contrary to Eliot's statements, which stake a claim against a monolithic notion of cultural background as legacy, Mao contends that "Eliot argues for a literary tradition by implying that the idea of such a tradition is itself traditional and, as such, authoritative."[28] Similarly, Elisa K. Sparks states that in "Tradition and the Individual Talent" Eliot conveys an "absolutistic aura of authority," and constructs a system "imaged in figures that stress hierarchy and rigidity."[29] By contrast, in an essay that problematizes Eliot's "Traditional Claims," Elizabeth Beaumont Bissell cites John Paul Riquelme's reading of "Tradition and the Individual Talent" to agree with him that it is nothing less than "revolutionary":

> To read the essay as readily intelligible and under our control is . . . a failure of literary understanding, for such a reading cannot recognise the continuing, permanent character of its radical qualities. "Tradition" is not merely revolutionary in a specific historical situation that has now passed; it is permanently revolutionary because of certain curious and compelling features of its style.[30]

The language of Eliot's early essays and poems reveals not so much a hierarchical logic, but an epistemology that depends upon and proposes dynamic and ever-changing systems of relationality.

One of Eliot's principal points of focus in "Tradition and the Individual Talent" is "the importance of the relation of the poem to other poems by other authors," and he urges his reader to think of poetry as "a living whole of all the poetry that has ever been written" (17). His model of both literary history and cultural memory is, in fact, radically dialogical; there is no order of absolutes, but rather, an ever-changing arrangement of "combinations": "the past should be altered by the present as much as the present is directed by the past. And the poet who is aware of this will be aware of great difficulties and responsibilities. In a peculiar sense he will be aware also that he must inevitably be judged by the standards of the past" (15). Further, as Eliot writes, "No poet, no artist of any art, has his complete meaning alone. His significance, his appreciation is the appreciation of his relation to the dead poets and artists" (15). This approach conceives of time, exchange, influence, and reciprocity through the power of creative texts to shatter their strictest alignments. The past exists *in* the text, and textuality is therefore one of the primary means for the ongoing agitation of a never-resolved history to speak to us. History is a still-living, palpable presence not unlike Eliot's sprouting "corpse" in *The Waste Land* that is always ready to return, modified by the desires of the present.

The other way in which "Tradition and the Individual Talent" has been vastly misunderstood is when critics have claimed that Eliot argues for an anti-emotional, highly intellectual approach to writing poetry that vacates subjectivity in favor of a spurious claim to "male" objectivity. Sandra Gilbert and Susan Gubar insist, for example:

> the Eliotian theory (propounded in "Tradition and the Individual Talent") that poetry involves "an escape from emotion" and "an escape from personality" constructs an implicitly masculine aesthetic of hard, abstract, learned verse that is opposed to the aesthetic of soft, effusive, personal verse supposedly written by women and Romantics. Thus in Eliot's critical writing women are implicitly devalued and the Romantics are in some sense feminized.[31]

Gilbert and Gubar altogether miss the contradictoriness of Eliot's statements on emotions and feeling. His essay is convoluted in this regard, it is true, and we will likely never be able to clarify exactly what he means by "emotion" as distinct from "feeling." But we do have to remember that he describes the activity of writing poetry in terms of nothing less than "emotions and feelings" within the same essay, and that "emotions and feelings" are a marked preoccupation of his other critical writings. In his 1921 "The Metaphysical Poets," Eliot praises Chapman's "direct sensuous appreciation of thought, or a recreation of thought into feeling, which is exactly what we find in Donne,"[32] while I. A. Richards declares in 1926 that *The Waste Land*'s "symbols are not mystical but emotional."[33] In "Tradition and the Individual Talent," Eliot makes an "analogy" between a shred of platinum and "the mind of the poet" since both are necessary to transform material (gases on the one hand, experience on the other) into another form (sulphurous acid and poetry). And then Eliot emphasizes "emotions and feelings" as not merely supplements to poetic generation, but as prime movers in the metamorphosis from life to art:

> the elements which enter the presence of the transforming catalyst, are of two kinds: emotions and feelings. The effect of a work of art upon the person who enjoys it is an experience different in kind from any experience not of art. It may be formed out of one emotion, or may be a combination of several; and various feelings, inhering for the writer in particular words or phrases or images, may be added to compose the final result. Or great poetry may be made without the direct use of any emotion whatever: composed out of feelings solely. (18)

Eliot then tells us that Dante – the poet he admired most – presents a "working up of the emotion" in Canto XV of the *Inferno* (18), and he maintains that "The poet's mind is in fact a receptacle for seizing and storing up numberless feelings, phrases, images, which remain there until all the particles which can unite to form a new compound are present together" (19).

The famous passage about poetry being an "escape from emotion" (21) constitutes only one small part of Eliot's argument, and in no way represents his thesis as a whole.[34] *Othello* and the *Agamemnon*, he further contends, offer a "transmutation of emotion," while Keats's ode "contains a number of feelings" (19); all three are texts he admires unreservedly. In a later essay on Tennyson's *In Memoriam*, he stridently defends Tennyson precisely *because* of his emotional depth: "I do not believe for a moment that Tennyson was a man of mild feelings or weak passions. There is no evidence in his poetry that he knew the experience of violent passion for a woman; but there is plenty of evidence of emotional intensity and violence."[35] Then, in a little-known essay called "Reflections on Contemporary Poetry," published the same year as "Tradition and the Individual Talent" but rarely collected, Eliot praises Herbert Read's book of war poetry, *Naked Warriors*, because it is "honest; because it is neither Romance nor Reporting; because it is unpretentious; and it has emotion as well as a version of things seen."[36] The instances of Eliot's uncompromising attention to the very necessity of emotionality to poetry far outweigh the brief moment he talks about escaping emotion.

(IM)PERSONALITY

What happens in "Tradition and the Individual Talent" is a deconstruction of the illusion of the Cartesian totality of the subject, years before this became fashionable. Eliot makes this argument quite clearly: "The point of view which I am struggling to attack is perhaps related to the metaphysical theory of the substantial unity of the soul: for my meaning is, that the poet has, not a 'personality' to express, but a particular medium, which is only a medium and not a personality" (19-20). His reasoning does not suggest that poetry avoids emotions and personality, but that personality as it is conventionally understood is a fiction. When one writes poetry one's emotions are so finely attenuated and concentrated that they are no longer emotions as they are experienced only by a personal subjectivity; they are transformed in the activity and adaptive *transposition* involved in translating psychic experience (within and outside of language's limits) to the idiom of poetry. Perhaps we can conceive of it in this way: Eliot is not seeking an erasure of subject status, but he does want to displace the phantasy of a unified self; as such, Eliot's rendering of poetic identity points to a destabilization of subjectivity that is one of the hallmarks of modernism. In Eliot's model, emotions are not negated; rather, they are intensely expressed by a singularity that is not reducible to "personality."

Even Eliot's bracketing of "personality" in "Tradition and the Individual Talent" is also only provisional, as we realize again that Eliot's oeuvre does not represent the perfectly closed and cohesive hermeneutic circle that some would believe it does. Eliot actually uses the very term "personality" within his criticism on several important occasions. In a later preface to Simone Weil's *The Need for Roots: Prelude to a Declaration of Duties Towards Mankind* (1952), he even takes steps toward revising his earlier critique of personality to insist on rather different terms:

> After reading *Waiting on God* and the present volume I saw that I must try to understand the personality of the author; and that the reading and re-reading of all of her work was necessary for this slow process of understanding . . . We must simply expose ourselves to the personality of a woman of genius, of a kind of genius akin to that of the saints.[37]

More than thirty years after "Tradition and the Individual Talent," then, he is willing to rehabilitate the worn-out term, "personality," in relation to a book by a major woman writer. Exposing himself to "personality" might equal exposing himself to subjectivity, and even to biography, as he had earlier exposed himself to history, and by 1951 he seemed ready to take on the danger of such an encounter.

In that rarely reprinted essay, "Reflections on Contemporary Poetry," reading the past operates through unexpectedly erotic intimacies.[38] Early in the piece Eliot considers anxieties about literary influence decades before Harold Bloom would make these questions central to *The Anxiety of Influence* in 1973, insisting, "There is a kind of stimulus for a writer which is more important than the stimulus of admiring another writer. Admiration leads most often to imitation; we can seldom remain long unconscious of our imitating another, and the awareness of our debt naturally leads us to a hatred of the object imitated" (39). Mimicry, Homi Bhabha has convincingly shown, cannot fail to objectify the Other, inevitably leading to an ambivalence and even hatred for what was once an object of homage.[39] In place of mimicry, then, Eliot proposes another relation along the spectrum of love and hate, outlining a method of reading the past that urges a passionate connection between the contemporary poet and his precursors. Rather than either merely imitating or resisting our predecessors, Eliot suggests that if we can move past "admiration" of our literary ancestors we might experience a different "relation" altogether. This would involve "a feeling of profound kinship, or rather of a peculiar personal intimacy, with another, probably a dead author" (39), after which we experience a transformative "crisis" that he sees as crucial to poetic maturation.

From here Eliot is intent on taking this erotic encounter – the "peculiar personal intimacy" that leads to a "crisis" – a step further, as he outlines a homoerotic argument for the love affair that arises between the contemporary poet and the writers of the past.

> We are never at ease with people who, to us, are merely great. We are not ourselves great enough for that: probably not one man in each generation is great enough to be intimate with Shakespeare. Admiration for the great is only a sort of discipline to keep us in order, a necessary snobbism to make us mind our places. We may not be great lovers; but if we had a genuine affair with a real poet of any degree we have acquired a monitor to avert us when we are not in love. Indirectly there are other acquisitions: our friendship gives us an introduction into the society in which our friend moved; we learn its origins and its endings;

we are broadened. We do not imitate, we are changed; and our work is the work of the changed man; we have not borrowed, we have been quickened, and we become bearers of a tradition. (39)

Anticipating "Tradition and the Individual Talent" Eliot describes something apropos the "labour" necessary to acquiring a "historical sense." The labor in this instance is precisely that of erotic appreciation, of loving both the letter of the past and those from whom the writing comes, and then of "bear[ing]" the lessons of that love into the future. A poet thus approaches the alterity of the past by bringing its Otherness into proximity through nothing less than an erotic openness to the incorporation that history both promises and threatens. This intimacy then brings one into relation with the dead as though into a relation with an ideal love object. We incorporate the dead by loving their words, and though we "may not be great lovers," we make love to the poets by allowing the traces of our relation to them to exist in our poetry. In effect, Eliot is arguing that the literary past is an erotic body to which we must by necessity exist in a relation of intimacy if we are to know it at all. Nor is the metamorphosis simply of the writer, but of the human being, as the shock of intimacy transforms him or her from "a bundle of second-hand sentiments into a person" (39). Laboring for tradition, then, is a labor of and for love. It also requires the labor of translation, since, as Eliot suggests, the terms of the past speak differently to each person and each generation. Implicit in his writing of desire is a refusal of the *pastness* of the past, a longing to make the past again present, and a concomitant desire for its (altered) repetition and cyclical renewal. Time in this way does not signify linear abstraction; instead, nearly a decade before his conversion to Christianity, Eliot calls for a quasi-religious offering to and bowing down before the vastness of time, tradition, and the erotic effects of the dead within the present poetic.

This erotic and affective attachment to the past is something Paul Ricoeur describes in one of his discussions on the philosophy of history. Ricoeur suggests that "the encounter with history is never a dialogue, for the first condition of dialogue is that the other *answer*; history is this sector of communication without reciprocity. But granting this limitation, it is a kind of unilateral friendship, like unrequited love."[40] In Eliot's terms the exchange between the present and the past is somewhat more dialogic: a love affair with poetic language changes one, but the works of the past themselves are *also* altered by the singular pressure of each encounter in the present. In "Tradition and the Individual Talent" Eliot puts it this way:

> The existing monuments form an ideal order among themselves, which is modified by the introduction of the new (the really new) work of art among them. The existing order is complete before the new work arrives; for order to persist after the supervention of novelty, the *whole* existing order must be, if ever so slightly, altered; and so the relations, proportions, values of each work of art toward the whole are readjusted. (15)

Eliot's erotic expressionism departs from the ostensible repulsion from desire that we find in so much of Eliot's canonical poetry, and points to the never-resolved conflicts Eliot had in writing desire. On the one hand, when he writes of the past, desire is the tropological figure that is always already invited into the discussion; on the other hand, writing of desire risks invoking a male–female eroticism that Eliot most often frames as repulsive. To write of the past through a homoerotic lens circumvents the horror about heterosexuality that Eliot's poetry so palpably betrays, and allows Eliot greater free play. Indeed, it begins to seem that Eliot only recoils from the gesture of writing desire alongside memory when he finds himself up against the need to figure history and femininity together. As long as the past can be evoked by its more desirable male representatives then the problem of writing both anteriority and desire is resolved. We might think of this dynamic in the context of one of Eliot's more revealing comments in his essay on "Dante" about the simultaneous concentration of time involved in reading a poem, and time's astonishing expansion found in the gift of reading:

> The experience of a poem is the experience both of a moment and of a lifetime. It is very much like our intenser experiences of other human beings. There is a first, or an early moment which is unique, of shock and surprise, even of terror (*Ego dominus tuus*); a moment which can never be forgotten, but which is never repeated integrally; and yet which would become destitute of significance if it did not survive in a larger whole of experience.[41]

The difficulty of facing the "intenser" encounters with alterity involves a dialectic of attraction and horror similar to the problem of facing memory and history, which are, for Eliot, some of the "intenser" experiences of life. It is as though the past, in and of itself, as a category, reminds Eliot of the dangers that arise in human intimacy.

Part of what Eliot's writing announces is a version of history and memory that mourns while it makes new, and which therefore includes not only the residue of the past within the present, but which insists that the inscription and impress of the present makes itself felt in every rendition of the past. In contrast to a sometimes fearful anxiety about the past's unruliness that we find in Eliot's poems, his criticism discloses an intense desire for the presentness (and presence) of the past, and a striking desire to collapse time as a means of lessening the distance between then and now. Even so, Eliot recognizes the impossibility of what Linda Hutcheon (in turn referencing David Carroll) has called "any attempt to reflect or reconstruct the 'present-in-the-past' as unproblematic presence";[42] the past is always, in fact, a problem in his texts, but one which demands an ongoing reapproach. In reading Eliot's oeuvre, one often feels a palpable desire for another age, or another time, and then these very desires are intensified by the impossibility of their realization. At the end of *The Waste Land* we find the phrase, "These fragments I have shored against my ruins" (line 430). We might understand this as a self-conscious reference to the composition of the poem: the "fragments" of intertextual quotations, and the tissues from others' words, help to fortify the "ruins" of Eliot's poetic and personal attempts at both survival and recuperation. The buttressing material of culture, memory, and history, however, appear too weak for the task. Yet, the momentous orchestration of such bathos in conjunction with the poem's powerful metaphysical, theological, and mythical reach generate nothing less than one of the greatest poems of the century – a work that is perfected through its very ruination.

We might also say that these "fragments" denote the remains of both past and present desire that are attached to their history by the tenuous threads of an eros scarcely diminished by time. As such, in order to build the new, Eliot relies on ruination. Acknowledging the ongoing play – and even *jouissance* – of the past's structures within the now is a prerequisite to inducing anything like a flowering. Eliot is interested, therefore, in a broken anamnesis: a recalling to mind whose process stutters and founders as it moves between unconscious and conscious remembrance, always pressing toward healing and unbrokenness, but foregrounding the shattering and ruination that time's passage means.

This attachment to the past of course involves a degree of mourning, or even melancholia, but this is not simply a story of longing for the object of lost time. There is always more than this at stake in Eliot. We find in his essays an almost *tangible* desire to take on the difficult labor of encountering history – a wish to affirm a vital connection with what is ostensibly dead and finished as a still-living order of things and ideas. In Freud's much debated analysis, "Mourning is regularly the reaction to the loss of a loved person, or to the loss of some abstraction which has taken the place of one, such as one's country, liberty, an ideal, and so on. In some people the same influences produce melancholia instead of mourning and we consequently suspect them of a pathological disposition."[43] In the healthy psyche, trauma's effects "will be overcome" after a certain amount of time elapses, and a de-cathection can occur, but melancholia extends itself when the grief-work is indefinitely suspended and unresolved. Eliot's poems chart puzzling desires to revisit the past in many guises – from the distant past of Greek myth and of Eastern and Western theological mysteries, to the more immediate personal and cultural histories of shifting subjectivities, cityscapes, and aesthetic experimentation. This certainly entails a refusal to withdraw eros from the equation of knowing the Otherness of the past, but the libidinal bind to these ideas and ideations is attenuated, stretched, and, finally becomes not only acceptable, but positively animating and life-affirming. Melancholy, yes, mournful, yes, but his work pushes at such designations to approach a more plural ethics of creative affect where losing becomes part of (a non-masochistic) gain. Eliot's conception of the past is not so attached to the dead letter and the dead object of the past that it cannot creatively transform these in the body of the new, apprehending their absence, but effectively making ruins live again – under a determinately new set of conditions.

Rather than expressing a reminiscent nostalgia for the past that would see history as discrete, static, and sealed off from the present, Eliot pays homage to his antecedents by recycling and revivifying their work and ideas in the context of the present. Indeed, *The Waste Land* may testify more profoundly than almost any other poem in the English language to a willingness to *approach* and to *know* the Otherness of the language of one's ancestors. At the same time, part of the modernist rendering of history and memory involves a call to a newness that is itself replete with the ruination of what someone like Faulkner might call the *un*-new. Rather than a simple story of decline, Eliot's narrative of the past proffers a redemptive attempt to incur upon the present both the fullness and the fragmentation of a past to which one could never fully expose oneself. To use the language of the *Four Quartets*, Eliot's poetry renews and transfigures history and memory, "in another pattern" – a "pattern" that endlessly repeats, but that still remains "new in every moment" ("Little Gidding," line 166, and "East Coker," line 86).

Eliot's focus on the past betrays a strong desire to *incorporate* it into the current moment – literally to enfold the material effects of language into the body of the new and the now by invoking and even re-using its significations. We might say that this desire for a labor of incorporation is part of what Eliot spells out in "Tradition and the Individual Talent" when he repudiates the prospect of "inherit[ing]" tradition (14). Tradition, unlike property or a proper name (which can be inherited), may only be known through a struggle that internalizes it through a nuanced embrace. In "Tradition and the Individual Talent" Eliot positions himself as a riddled and confused laborer, and not as an entitled heir – a gesture that, some might argue, disingenuously evokes humble origins to which Eliot could lay no claim, coming from one of the most respected families of New England. Nevertheless, I prefer to read Eliot's statement in a more generous light, perhaps suggesting – as he does in "Reflections on Contemporary Poetry" – that to incorporate history means to make oneself subject to the past through the difficult labor of loving it.

CHAPTER 5

Virginia Woolf, (auto)biography, and the eros of memory: reading Orlando

> And I find myself again in the old driving whirlwind of writing against time. Have I ever written with it? But I vow I won't spend longer at Orlando, which is a freak; it shall come out in September, though the perfect artist would revoke & rewrite & polish – infinitely. But hours remain over to be filled with reading something or other – I'm not sure what . . . And yet the only exciting life is the imaginary one.
>
> Virginia Woolf, *Diary*, 21 April 1928[1]

> That would be a glorious life, to addict oneself to perfection; to follow the curve of the sentence wherever it might lead, into deserts, under drifts of sand, regardless of lures, of seductions; to be poor always and unkempt; to be ridiculous in Piccadilly.
>
> Virginia Woolf, Neville in *The Waves*[2]

Virginia Woolf begins the biographic meditation that is *Orlando* with a fascinating claim for our pairing of memory and desire: after the narrator rejoices in Orlando's beauty, remarking that his "face, as he threw the window open, was lit solely by the sun itself," he continues, "Happy the mother who bears, happier still the biographer who records the life of such a one!"[3] In a text that is more than half a flirtatious homage to the "real-life" Vita Sackville-West,[4] Woolf here draws analogies between herself and Orlando/Vita's mother, between birthing and writing a life, and between biological labor and the eros of the letter. In writing *Orlando*, Woolf claims to give birth to Orlando/Vita by writing his/her life as a fictional tale of androgyny across the centuries, loves her as her own child, and finds that in the eros of scripting her fictional-historical bios the alternately male and female biographer discovers a kind of Aristotelian happiness – where happiness is an activity expressing virtue, in this case the virtue of love. Biography, as such, is not simply life writing, but it is also life giving, as Woolf proposes that writing breeds life, and that the two gerunds of writing and living coexist in a dialectical relationship of necessity and self-sustainability. Under this rubric the biographer breathes life into his subject as the deus ex machina who sculpts him/her, while he simultaneously sustains himself as *scriptor* by bearing – a term that includes the valences of a difficult weight, while marking degree zero of the psychoanalytic maternal – and loving his subject. In this formulation, writing, and especially "life writing" as a mode of writing memory, is inherently a language of desire since biography shapes its subject precisely as it testifies to the longings of its producer/mother.

In *Orlando* – which we ought to remember is subtitled *A Biography* – Woolf reinforces this playful coextensiveness between writing and desire only one sentence later: "Never need she [Orlando's mother] vex herself, nor he [the biographer] invoke the help of novelist or poet. From deed to deed, from glory to glory, from office to office he [Orlando] must go, his scribe following after, till they reach whatever seat it may be that is the height of their desire" (12). In the first of many equations that spell out the task of the biographer for the terms of the text, the mother very quickly drops out of the biographic formula to leave only the biographer and his subject, who *together* "reach . . . the height of their desire" – suggesting both that a mutuality of desire is discoverable for biographer and subject, and that the climax point of desire is attainable only inseparably, in common. The happiness of the proud mother is thus superseded by a more overtly sexualized mode of desire, as Woolf implies that to write the life of her aristocratic lover, who "descends from Dorset, Buckingham, Sir Philip Sidney, and the whole of English history, which she keeps, stretched in coffins, one after another, from 1300 to the present day, under her dining room floor,"[5] she will inevitably mix memory and desire, history and sex, anteriority and eros. Punning on the valences of gay sex to unite the biographer and his love object, the climax of the biographer's and Orlando's desire occurs at nothing less than "whatever *seat* it may be" (my emphasis), as the gendering of the biographer in most instances as male (e.g. the biographer "must fly as fast as he can," 32) allows and invites a homoerotic dimension in the early parts of the novel when Orlando is male. This queering then androgynously inverts female–female erotic desire onto a male–male dyad – a move that resists effacing the homoeroticism of Woolf and Sackville-West's relation but which nevertheless displaces lesbian desire.

Despite the turn to the homoerotic over the maternal, Woolf is not quite ready to dispense with the mother figure altogether. She gestures to her again a few lines later, when we are told that the young Orlando is especially impressionable to sensation and peculiarly unsettled by the "sight" of his mother: "Sights disturbed him, like that of his mother, a very beautiful lady in green walking out to feed the peacocks with Twitchett, her maid, behind her; sights exalted him – the birds and the trees; and made him in love with death – the evening sky, the homing rooks" (12-13). Turning away from the maternal to a Keatsian worship of nature that is, in its own experience of self, half-in-love with death[6] – a trope that will repeat itself through the novel – the maternal occupies a point of displacement and lack, even as the biographer claims to be already standing in for that absence. It is as though the narrator, in the act of constructing the narrative, is making room for himself as poietic mother *and* lover by claiming an omniscient access to Orlando's emotions and sensations that will both invent and decipher the portrait of Orlando for the novel.

This homoerotic and quasi-incestuous affiliation rings true to life, since Woolf and Sackville-West themselves felt involved at times in a kind of mother–daughter love affair. In December 1925 Woolf writes in her diary that Sackville-West "lavishes on me the maternal protection which, for some reason, is what I have always most wished from everyone."[7] The young Virginia Stephen had lost her own mother very suddenly when she was just thirteen, and the desire to seek out such "protection" may have been related to this early loss. For her part, Sackville-West also claims an anaclitic relation to Woolf in various letters to her husband, Harold Nicolson, where Sackville-West dismisses the erotic dimension of their friendship, writing in 1926,

> She makes me feel protective. Also she loves me, which flatters and pleases me . . . I am scared to death of arousing physical feelings in her, because of the madness. I don't know what effect it would have, you see: it is a fire with which I have no wish to play. I have too much real affection and respect for her.[8]

Two years later Sackville-West repeated another version of this: "I feel extraordinarily protective towards her . . . she has a sweet and childlike nature."[9]

After the initial rustle of the disturbance of the mother, the maternal almost entirely drops out of *Orlando*, and we hear very little more about either Orlando's mother, or, later, of Orlando's own motherhood when the narrative reaches the late nineteenth century and she chooses to obey "the spirit of her age," take a husband, and give birth to a child who would then be a sibling to the eighteenth-century male Orlando's "three sons" whom he fathered with the "gypsy," Rosina Pepita (119). Toward the end of the novel Orlando gives birth to another son without the reader even knowing she has been expecting (204), and we learn of the event in just two isolated, functionally parenthetical sentences: "'It's a very fine boy, M'Lady,' said Mrs. Banting, the midwife, putting her first-born child into Orlando's arms. In other words Orlando was safely delivered of a son on Thursday, March the 20th, at three o'clock in the morning."[10] We then hear almost nothing further of the relationship between mother and child. Woolf may have been offering a portrait of what she perceived to be Sackville-West's attitudes on motherhood, who, in the words of her son, Nigel Nicolson, only "felt a distant affection" towards her children: "Babies," he writes, "were an interruption, a reminder of duty, of her place in the home, a reminder of their innocence compared with her guilt, a reminder, even, of maternity, which by then, under Violet's influence, she found distasteful".[11]

The number of subject-positions and substitutions in the cycle of desire and longing for Orlando/Vita becomes dizzying very early on in the novel, as Woolf presents us with an almost infinite regress of erotic positions (fictional and "real") from whose vantage point to appreciate Orlando/Vita. First, there is the author, Woolf – who, we are to understand through convention, exists outside of the text as its maker – who carried on a real-life love affair with the subject of her fiction. Second, the text's narrator doubles as Woolf-as-narrator since the novel asks to be read (auto)biographically as well as fictionally – as about Sackville-West and Woolf's connection *and* as about Orlando. Third, the fictional, male narrator/biographer – whom we must distinguish from Woolf – is enamored with his subject, and, as both lover and mother he androgynously desires and bears Orlando as his son, daughter, lover, and historical subject.

Because Orlando scarcely ages, and passes through the centuries as easily as s/he changes genders, the text presents Orlando's story as expressly lodged in both the fantastic and the phantasmatic. Importantly, though, these fantastic and phantasmatic dimensions break down because they consistently meet the historical real of a remembered and ongoing affair: through blending the author with the fictional phantasy she constructs, and through occluding the distance between the writer and the subject of her text (the object of her desire), Woolf is proposing that the near-fairy-tale dimension of the novel and the real of our psychic fantasies disclose mutually discernible truths about the character of desire and memory. Mark Hussey argues that Woolf's 1925 collection of essays, *The Common Reader*, shows a clear thematic interest in reading literary histories and with bridging contemporary reality with the past,[12] while Alex Zwerdling proposes that Woolf had a "sharp sense that our memory perpetually revises the past."[13] It is this dialogue between recollection, revision, imagination, and desire that Woolf seemed especially keen to explore in writing *Orlando.* Orlando/Vita is borne from Woolf's pen (as the text's writer) *and* body (as the text's mother) as the perfect, narcissistically satisfying, love object: she is both that radical Other one seeks to know in the encounter of loving, and a more fully knowable facet of the self. Woolf has thus brought Sackville-West near to the fold of the same by claiming the power to write her life as a form of textual seduction.

Daniel Albright has suggested that Woolf had an "abiding obsession with autobiography."[14] It might, though, be more accurate to say her "abiding obsession" was with life writing more generally, including biography, memoirs, letters, diaries, and fiction. "As everybody knows, the fascination of reading biographies is irresistible," she writes in a 1930 essay entitled "I am Christina Rossetti."[15] *Writing* biographies proved irresistible for Woolf as well, even though she was extraordinarily skeptical about the task of squeezing any life into a discursive or narrative frame, and throughout her oeuvre she stresses the hazards of life writing. In her unfinished autobiography, "A Sketch of the Past," which I will discuss more extensively in chapter 6, she criticizes the biographic method at length, beginning the piece by enumerating several of "the memoir writer's difficulties." First among the "difficulties" is that "they leave out the person to whom things happened";[16] that is, memoir writers traditionally narrate events, but perpetuate the fallacy that events define a person. In *Orlando* Woolf highlights the presence of the biographer in extended parenthetical interjections that offer embedded self-referential critiques of his/her aims, methods, and limits. This emphasis on the biographer as a subject of his own rendition again argues for his presence as both extrinsic and intrinsic to the text, proposing that in constructing an object of Otherness every biographer is working at the boundaries of the strange intimacies of historical and mnemonic interpretation.

The tenor and reason for the biographer's interjections most often involve a playful yet anxious desire to pursue the correct method of biography – to operate by rules of the genre-game that are elaborated to his audience through a critique of method. He interjects fairly regularly in the narrative flow to comment on his own approach, suggesting, for example, that biographers have the right to "lay bare rudely" "curious trait[s]" about their subject (20); that "though we must pause not a moment in the narrative we may here hastily note that all his images at this time were simple in the extreme" (26); that he strives "to fulfil the first duty of the biographer, which is to plod, without looking to right or left, in the indelible footprints of truth" (47); and, "To give a truthful account of London society at that or indeed at any other time is beyond the powers of the biographer or the historian" (135).

Woolf's experiment with blending fictionality with the residues of the historical was not entirely new for her. As early as 1908, in "The Memoirs of Sarah Bernhardt," she was already asserting a dynamic interpenetration between life and fictionality. Here, when discussing performance and role playing, she takes it as a given that "each part [that an actress] plays deposits its own small contribution upon her unseen shape, until it is complete and distinct from its creations at the same time that it inspires them with life."[17] Despite the confusing proliferation of the possessive "its" here, by the actress's "unseen shape" Woolf seems to mean a combination of character and soul, forged in relation to the fictional roles an actress adopts on the stage: an actress's identity is prior to and distinct from the characters she portrays, but is nevertheless necessary to recall in order to bring "life" to her roles. Both the actress's personality and the roles she adopts create the Other of theatrical character: an actress, as an artist, is thus a combination of her own being and the being she expresses when she becomes another character. Both the person and the adaptation become lost in each other, exposing a radical interpenetration of subjectivities that would be hard to untangle. This is a complicated model of identity that Woolf proposes at the age of twenty-six, seven years before she would publish her first novel, *The Voyage Out*. Already she is arguing for a fundamental instability of self and cogito that she will pursue in almost all of her later fictional texts, and that will become a hallmark of modernist writing.

BIOGRAPHIC TIME COLLAPSED

Shortly after he has waxed elegantly on the bind between memory and desire, which are together inextricably tied up with the eros of writing and with the perturbing figure of the mother whom we already understand the biographer will replace, Woolf's narrator interjects and momentarily disrupts the emerging symbiotic relation between the narrator and his (beloved) subject. In this text Woolf is always ready to undo what she has begun, and inevitably seeks to complicate what we think we understand. The narrator steps in, as he will often do, to comment self-reflexively on the biographic method, and to announce an ostensible desire for emotional distance between the biographer and his subject: "riot and confusion of the passions and emotions," he asserts, are things that "every good biographer detests" (13). Only a moment earlier the narrator was interested in sexing his subject, and here he wants to distance himself from Orlando's "passions." Is the narrator already so involved in the romance of his project that he needs to seek the defense of distancing? The gesture is certainly parodic, as Woolf extends her life-long critique of biography's spurious claims to objectivity by showing up the paradoxical doubling that emerges in such attempts at distancing: biography, she insists, involves the knowledge of *being subjected to* the demands of one's subject in his most intimate modes of being even as one claims to be abstracted from the "passions." We might also borrow the words of Roland Barthes to underline the eros Woolf delineates as part of this life writing: echoing Lord Alfred Douglas's famous euphemism for homosexuality he claims "any biography is a novel that dares not speak its name."[18] *Orlando* is both a historically encrypted biography of desire and a novel that dared to speak its name; it dared to inhabit and critique several genres at once as part of its strategy of writing out bisexual desire and Woolf's own particular history of love.

The question then arises: is Woolf's narrator (or Woolf-as-narrator) a "good" biographer? Does the biographer in this instance disrupt that traditional paradigm of objective distance from the subject/object of the study to participate more deeply in the eros involved in the sustained study of a life? The answer is yes to both questions because the narrator/biographer performs a sustained, full-blown romantic *blason* for over 200 pages as testimony to his enchantment/enchainment with his subject, devoting extensive attention to Orlando's beauty, elegance, physical attributes, sensitivity, and cleverness. This tribute to Orlando's synecdochic "parts" has the effect of both satirizing the male tradition of worshiping a woman's body by way of the catalogue, and of tropologically invoking Woolf's own appreciation for Sackville-West's physical charms: early on we hear that Orlando "had eyes like drenched violets" (12), and in the context of the novel's time line, the narrator reports that as late as the twentieth century Orlando "scarcely looked a day older" than s/he had in the Renaissance: "She looked just as pouting, as sulky, as handsome, as rosy (like a million-candled Christmas tree, Sasha had said) as she had done that day on the ice, when the Thames was frozen" (209). In effect, the novel-as-*blason* produces the biography of Orlando as a body as well as a text, offering a sustained catalogue of the physical as a necessary complement to the portrait of a life.

In "The Art of Biography" Woolf describes the sea-change that overcame biographic writing with the publication of Lytton Strachey's "three famous books, *Eminent Victorians*, *Queen Victoria*, and *Elizabeth and Essex*" (1918–28):

> at last it was possible to tell the truth about the dead; and the Victorian age was rich in remarkable figures many of whom had been grossly deformed by the effigies that had been plastered over them. To recreate them, to show them as they really were, was a task that called for gifts analogous to the poet's or the novelist's.[19]

Part of her "task" in 1927–8 while she was composing the novel was to give Orlando's body and history a poetry and a physicality with her novelist's "gifts." Such an endeavor confirms what I will explore as Woolf's more general understanding of past experience as a materiality that demands the translation of inscription.

Orlando's body moves through and makes history, while Woolf borrows from geography and architecture to relate the passage of time, and to materialize history as both the lived-through and the marker of what *has been*, and of what *remains* of the past. As Sandra Gilbert forcefully argues in her introduction to *Orlando*,

> Orlando *is* history, if only because the light of her mind is the lamp that lights up time for Woolf's readers, and her stately mansion, with its allegorically resonant 365 bedrooms and 52 staircases, is the house whose endurance-through-change is the metaphor that Woolf gives us for human duration . . . the terms of history become Orlando's terms, and finally even history itself becomes Orlando's story, the tale of a body now male, now female. (xxvii)

Pierre Bourdieu insists that the body "does not represent what it performs, it does not memorize the past, it *enacts* the past, bringing it back to life. What is 'learned by the body' is not something that one has, like knowledge that can be brandished, but something that one is."[20] In the instance of Orlando, the human body is as enduring as a "stately mansion," though it carries the residue of the past more effectively than stone and mortar. Orlando can and does speak of the centuries in a decipherable language, and we are led to understand that part of the phantasy Woolf was indulging while writing the novel was to claim an indestructible historical thread that was capable of narrating itself and of reiterating the real of the past through conjoining discourse with the body.

After following the letter of the biographic mandate with diligence, toward the end of the narration *Orlando*'s biographer condemns the incompleteness of his method, juxtaposing a theoretical statement about the indeterminacy of temporality with an assertion about an equally mathematically dizzying multitude of selves. Noting that "there are (at a venture) seventy-six different times all ticking in the mind at once," the narrator entreats the reader:

> how many different people are there not – Heaven help us – all having lodgment at one time or another in the human spirit? Some say two thousand and fifty-two . . . [Orlando] had a great variety of selves to call upon, far more than we have been able to find room for, since a biography is considered complete if it merely accounts for six or seven selves, whereas a person may well have as many thousand. (212–13)

In *Jacob's Room* (1922), Woolf's narrator makes a similar comment, claiming, "It is no use trying to sum people up. One must follow hints, not exactly what is said, nor yet entirely what is done."[21] Time, consciousness, and identity, she contends, are commensurately unknowable and unrepresentable since *writing time* and *writing a life* can each only be stabs at the problem of representation.

Woolf's biographic method in writing *Orlando* is ironic to say the least, particularly coming from the daughter of the "eminent Victorian," Sir Leslie Stephen, to use Lytton Strachey's phrase from his 1918 biographic study, *Eminent Victorians.* Leslie Stephen founded and was the first editor of the *Dictionary of National Biography,* and Woolf playfully alludes to her father's compendium near the end of *Orlando.* Only with a few people, she asserts, can we

> justly say that they live precisely the sixty-eight or seventy-two years allotted them on the tombstone. Of the rest some we know to be dead though they walk among us; some are not yet born though they go through the forms of life; others are hundreds of years old though they call themselves thirty-six. The true length of a person's life, whatever the *Dictionary of National Biography* may say, is always a matter of dispute. For it is a difficult business – this time-keeping; nothing more quickly disorders it than contact with any of the arts. (211)

Woolf's biographical experiment challenges the artificiality of confining a lifetime to its calendrical span as she maps a confluence of multiple temporalities *and* multiple identities, critiquing the Western cultural fallacy that consciousness is reducible to a discernible singularity framed neatly by diachronic time.

In her 1937 novel, *The Years,* Woolf again approaches this twin unknowability of identity and time. Riding in a carriage with her aunt, Eleanor, Peggy wonders:

> Where does she begin, and where do I end? . . . On they drove. They were two living people, driving across London; two sparks of life enclosed in two separate bodies; and those sparks of life enclosed in two separate bodies are at this

moment, she thought, driving past a picture palace. But what is this moment; and what are we? The puzzle was too difficult for her to solve it. She sighed.[22]

In this instance the limits of the flesh become the markers for the hypostatization of an idea of the self that cannot be mapped onto the specious literality of the body. The singleness of the body seems to promise containability through its very site-ability, visibility, and locatability. But while Woolf writes out the dyadic contingency of these "two living people," "two sparks of life," and "two separate bodies" (repeated twice) with a stuttering repetition that betrays some anxiousness about juxtaposing these doublings with the ostensible singularity of the time of "this moment" (also repeated twice), she also affirms that the bodies work merely to "enclose[ ]" "sparks of life" that are themselves irreducible to identity.

Turning back to *Orlando*, perhaps the most striking moment of all the biographer's interpolations comes when he first cites the "real" date of the novel's composition within the text-body of the fictional biography. This happens when the biographer-narrator is musing about the randomness of our actions and our lack of awareness about our own motivations, when suddenly Woolf-as-biographer interjects, parenthetically, with the present date:

Nature, who has played so many queer tricks upon us, making us so unequally of clay and diamonds, of rainbow and granite,[23] and stuffed them into a case, often of the most incongruous, for the poet has a butcher's face and the butcher a poet's; nature, who delights in muddle and mystery, so that even now (the first of November 1927) we know not why we go upstairs, or why we come down again, our most daily movements are like the passage of a ship on an unknown sea. (55)

In keeping with Freud's stress on the force of the unconscious on more than one level, and thus providing one of the many instances where Woolf indicates more knowledge of Freud than she admitted to having, Woolf's punctuation of the text with this historical, autobiographical detail about the chronology of its composition both highlights the self-referential nature of biography-as-autobiography while affirming a sudden overflow of synchronic time within the novel's parameters. Quite strikingly, it is nothing less than a temporal marker that arrests the narration in order to highlight its non-fictionality. Such a gesture asks us to pause in our own understanding of temporal flux, the time of writing, and the time of reading; it blurs the lines of an ostensible "fiction" with those of "historical" time, mixing the "inside" of the text with its "outside."

In "The New Biography," published originally in the *New York Herald Tribune* while Woolf was composing *Orlando*, Woolf lays the stakes for what appears to be a deliberate rebuttal to Eliot's 1919 delineations of the "impersonality" of the writer by affirming that the best way to know a biographic subject is through the intimacies of individual character, or "personality."[24] The Victorian biography, she claims, "was a parti-coloured, hybrid, monstrous birth. For though truth of fact was observed as scrupulously as Boswell observed it, the personality which Boswell's genius set free was hampered and distorted."[25] Contending that alongside "truth at its hardest," with its "almost mystic power," biography "demands" the supplement of "personality": "All the draperies and decencies of biography fall to the ground. We can no longer maintain that life consists in actions only or in works. It consists in personality."[26] In order to render the "truth" of "personality" Woolf emphasizes that "facts must be manipulated; some must be brightened; others shaded; yet, in the process, they must never lose their integrity."[27] This statement brings us very close to her claims a year or two later in *A Room of One's Own*, where Woolf warns her reader, "Fiction here is likely to contain more truth than fact . . . Lies will flow from my lips, but there may perhaps be some truth mixed up with them; it is for you to seek out this truth and to decide whether any part of it is worth keeping."[28]

Michel de Certeau makes a similar proposal about historiography when he reminds us that "if the narrative of facts takes on the allure of a 'fiction' belonging to a given type of discourse, we cannot conclude that the reference to the real is obliterated."[29] Fictionality, historicity, and truth alternately bespeak the real – a real which Woolf is showing us needs to be articulated under varying guises, genres, and discursive tools to be true to the memory of its own nuances. In this way *Orlando* performs a self-conscious critique about the vagaries of life writing from within a fictional context. Offering itself as an eminently readable tale – as though neither the degree of its fictionality, its historical record, nor its fantastic dimensions urgently require separate decoding – the novel's tone is blithe and uninhibited. That is to say, while the text straddles the boundary between historical writing and fictional phantasy, it does so with a delightful contentment about its method since the degree to which the book is and is not a fiction or a game of historically real desire is not meant to trouble us terribly much at all.

Other theorists of life writing have considered biography a lesser version of traditional historical exposition. Claude Lévi-Strauss, for example, insists that "Biographical and anecdotal history, which is the lowest on the ladder [in a hierarchy between 'strong' and 'weak' histories], is *weak* history that does not contain . . . its own intelligibility, which it only gets when transported wholly into a history stronger than itself."[30] The "history stronger than itself," or, the historical supplement to Woolf's life writing, would, though, be at least twofold: it is both the cultural history of the English aristocracy from roughly 1600–1928 that Woolf charts in her novel, nestled like a glimmer of everyday "truth" amid the fictionality of her story, and it is also the historical reception of Woolf's texts that has made them, in themselves, symbolic markers of the now-historical high literary modernism. Notwithstanding his above arguments, Lévi-Strauss does grant that "biographical history" is "richer from the point of view of information" than either a "strong" or a "total" history, "because it considers individuals in terms of what is special to them and goes into details" that are missing from "stronger history."[31] What Woolf gives us, then, is a self-consciously imperfect shadow of larger English history, conveyed through the lens of life writing preoccupied with the task of scripting and exposing desire.

Later in "The New Biography" Woolf expressly alerts us to the necessary imposition of an author's character on the biography he or she creates: "He is as much the subject of his own irony and observation as they [his subjects] are. He lies in wait for his own absurdities as artfully as for theirs. Indeed, by the end of the book we realize that the figure which has been most completely and most subtly displayed is that of the author."[32] When Woolf startles us by coordinating her dates of composition with the events of Orlando's life, she alerts us to biography's self-reflexivity by temporally arresting the narration to highlight its non-fictionality. Henry James insisted in 1884 that

> The only reason for the existence of a novel is that it does attempt to represent life. When it relinquishes this attempt, the same attempt that we see on the canvas of the painter, it will have arrived at a pretty strange pass . . . [We need] to insist on the fact that as the picture is reality, *so the novel is history*.[33]

Orlando straddles the "queer amalgamation of dream and reality, that perpetual marriage of granite and rainbow,"[34] with Woolf refusing to sit neatly outside the boundaries of the text as she is writing Vita/Orlando's life. Instead, Woolf interjects to relate details from her own life that are more properly factual than any of those she narrates in telling the "truth" of Vita/Orlando's story, and in this way she urges us to consider again the blurred territories between fiction, truth, history, and biography. There is something extraordinarily truthful about fiction, and utterly candid about phantasy.[35]

With Woolf's palpable romantic desire for Sackville-West driving the project of writing her history and genealogy, *Orlando* testifies to Woolf's attachment to Sackville-West in a public (albeit coded) way, performing the act of erotic devotion by writing a whimsical history of her lover's heritage. This also tells us that Woolf thought of memorialization as the language of courtship, and as a major constituent in the discourse of love. Woolf had once written to Sackville-West, "Thinking about copulation, I now remember a whole chapter of my past that I forgot, I think, to tell you."[36] Nigel Nicolson calls *Orlando* "the longest and most charming love letter in literature," arguing eloquently that in *Orlando* Woolf "explores Vita, weaves her in and out of the centuries, tosses her from one sex to the other, plays with her, dresses her in furs, lace and emeralds, teases her, flirts with her, drops a veil of mist around her, and ends by photographing her in the mud at Long Barn, with dogs, awaiting Virginia's arrival next day."[37] T. S. Eliot proposes in "The Dry Salvages," "the past experience revived in the meaning / Is not the experience of one life only / But of many generations—not forgetting / Something that is probably quite ineffable."[38] Part of Woolf's commitment involves precisely this "not forgetting," and her sustained encounter with the play of Sackville-West's imagined ancestry insists that writing the past is a sensuous act, while recording revisitation here works as erotic homage.

Despite the narrator's occasional pleas for objectivity – not wishing to be embroiled in the passions of his subject, and hence hoping to follow the correct rules of the biographical method – Woolf shows that such distancing is yet another impossibility. Instead, her narratology parodies the intense identification and mimetic attachment to Orlando. In describing the way Orlando's "mind worked . . . in violent see-saws from life to death, stopping at nothing in between" (32), Woolf insists that the biographer is, in fact, riveted to the "violent see-saws" of his subject's psyche, and compelled to "keep pace" with the vagaries of mood, action, and speech to come close to a real portrait: "the biographer must not stop either, but must fly as fast as he can and so keep pace with the unthinking passionate foolish actions and sudden extravagant words in which, it is impossible to deny, Orlando at this time of his life indulged" (32). As such, the writerly mode of *Orlando*'s omniscient narration is defined for us as a concatenation of passionate strivings that play slave to the intimate caprices of its subject as the master of its method.

ORLANDO AND THE TRUTH OF HISTORY

When Woolf first recorded the idea for *Orlando*, she conceived of it as part of a project that would be

> like a grand historical picture, the outlines of all my friends. I was thinking of this in bed last night . . . It might be a way of writing the memoirs of one's own times during peoples [*sic*][39] lifetimes. It might be a most amusing book. The question is how to do it. Vita should be Orlando, a young nobleman. There should be Lytton. & it should be *truthful*; but *fantastic*.[40]

The truth-content of the story was at issue from the first instance, as Woolf sought to write a blend of fiction and history that would be more truthful in its psychological value than traditional histories are in their impersonal records of events and battles. Her fiction would bear on similitude by repeating "the real" in its fictional form as the most honest testimony to desire. Around the same time, Woolf wrote to Sackville-West, asking her permission of sorts:

> But listen; suppose Orlando turns out to be Vita; and its all about you and the lusts of your flesh and the lure of your mind (heart you have none, who go gallivanting down the lanes with Campbell) – suppose there's the kind of shimmer of reality which sometimes attaches to my people, as the lustre on an oyster shell (and that recalls another Mary) suppose, I say, that Sibyl next October says "Theres Virginia gone and written a book about Vita" and Ozzie [Dickinson] chaws with his great chaps and Byard [of Heinemann] guffaws, Shall you mind? . . . it sprung upon me how I could revolutionise biography in a night: and so if agreeable to you I would like to toss this up in the air and see what happens. Yet, of course, I may not write another line. [*sic*][41]

Sackville-West agreed to the portrait, and though Woolf's revolutionizing of biography took six months rather than "a night," her transgendered revisioning of the genre of life writing, and her critique of what it means to write and think history vis-à-vis the present of modernism, broke with conventional biographic modes more than has been properly appreciated.

A few months later, when she was already halfway through the composition of *Orlando*, Woolf wrote to Clive Bell about the endeavor of writing history, offering an uncanny echo of the language she had used to imagine the project: "Does it strike you that history is one of the most *fantastic* concoctions of the human brain? That it bears the remotest likeness to *truth* seems to me unthinkable . . . Ought it not all to be rewritten instantly?"[42] In the startlingly repetitious rendition of her earlier claim that she had wanted her own historical-biographical experiment to be at once "truthful" and "fantastic,"[43] she reaffirms that in writing *Orlando* she is rewriting history – both as phantasy and as truth. It is as though Woolf was making the case that to write Sackville-West's personal past was also to write national memory, with Sackville-West's aristocratic genealogy insisting on her imbrication in the cultural past. Quite amazingly, Woolf found that the British upper classes read *Orlando* with just this kind of an acute literality, interpreting it as a faithful and worthy portrait of themselves. Five years after the novel was published, during the unusually cold winter of 1933, a group of English aristocrats – Lord Riddell, Lady Newnes, and Lady Burney – undertook to (re-)enact the 1604 ice-carnival dance on the Thames Woolf had dramatized in her novel. Woolf missed the event herself, but she reports to Sackville-West in a letter of January 1933: "Oh and tonight theyre dancing Orlando on the ice, and I shant be there. Its a remarkable fact – the whole British peerage says they descend from the Courtiers I invented, and still have the snow boots which they wore on the frost which I invented too" [*sic*].[44] That Woolf chooses to write history in the case of *Orlando* as it is experienced by a single, undying, nearly unaging body asks us to think the possibility that genealogies might be more corporeal than we imagine, and that the contours of personal history might be physically traceable, as though they were both material and retrievable. History, as such, endlessly inscribes the body and the body carries this residue in the form of memory.

EMBEDDING HISTORY: *ORLANDO* AND THE BODY OF THE PAST

These were two of the adventures of my professional life. The first – killing the Angel in the House – I think I solved. She died. But the second, telling the truth about my own experiences as a body, I do not think I solved.

(Virginia Woolf, "Professions for Women"[45])

We begin to discover that the boundary between memory and history is slight in Woolf's writings, and as she does with Sackville-West in *Orlando*, Woolf persistently conflates her own personal past with the cultural and public domain of capital "H" History. That is, she seems to understand herself as continuous not simply with her own family heritage, but with English history and cultural memory. Part of how she accomplishes this is by proposing in certain texts that her body – like Orlando's body – is genealogically embedded in the history of England and its literature. Elena Gualtieri draws our attention to an instance in

Woolf's 1919 essay, "Reading," unpublished during her lifetime, where she "weaves together different temporal planes, from the passage of time within a day to the course of human life from childhood to maturity and old age, interlacing these different stages with the history of English literature."[46] In a little-known and posthumously published essay called "Byron and Mr. Briggs" that was originally planned as a first chapter to a book on "Reading" (which likely became *The Common Reader*), Woolf locates her cultural antecedents not in her immediate precursors, the Victorians – to whom she felt too "close" to be able to read properly – but in the Romantics. Here she insists that her own background is traceable to a fictional early nineteenth-century critic named Briggs, who "knew Coleridge": "[T]he genealogists <may> dispute this claim; but if one has waited <impatiently> for three weeks to get Byrons letters from the library <& swallowed them whole> then, according to my <definition> one is a grandchild of Briggs [*sic*]."[47] As in *Orlando*, Woolf's logic playfully disturbs conventional rules of biology, genealogy, and inheritance, while she nevertheless insists on a familial connection to the past of English literary history. In *A Room of One's Own*, while she is criticizing the sustained historiographical exclusion of women in accounts of the past, Woolf insists that part of her feminist call is that "the book has somehow to be adapted to the body."[48] We might say that she is also speaking of the book and the text of history, proposing that we need to learn how to conjoin so-called objective history with the interiority of bodily experience and desire.

To extend the relation between Orlando-as-fiction, Orlando-as-history, and Orlando-as-testimony to homoerotic devotion, Woolf sent Sackville-West a leather-bound copy of the novel on 11 October 1928, the day of its publication, the day on which the novel's last chapter takes place, and the day that marks the end of its status as a private manuscript. With this act, Woolf superimposes her fictional rendition of personal history and biography with a real-life love token, allowing her fanciful testimony to both the passage of time and to the flowering of a sexual infatuation to push toward the presentness of an erotic gift. For when are we more fully "present" than when we are giving a token of love? If we want to read beyond the margins of the novel, then, we can say that Sackville-West resumed Orlando's story when the last page left off, and the rest of Sackville-West's life, from 11 October 1928 onward, is her "sequel" to Orlando's passage through time. Woolf thus again creates a double temporality: one that will forever remain frozen as the present historic of the novel's tense, and one in which two October elevenths, and two

Vitas, co-existed for a single day more than three-quarters of a century ago. By the end of the novel, that is, the novel's temporality has caught up with the time of writing, so that Orlando, Woolf, and Sackville-West share a synchronous temporality in the final pages.

As if to highlight the encroaching temporal confluence with the time of the real, Woolf dates her heroine's adventures more frequently and more exactly in the final section, until she notes 11 October 1928, the day on which the novel closes, no fewer than three times in the last twenty-five pages (206, 211, 228). The past actually catches up with the act of writing time and creates the effect of time pressing at the limits of the present. We experience the sensation that the temporality of the novel could overtake "real" time in a fantastic rush of unstoppability if the novel's end did not arrest it by imposing the artificial finality and framing that a book's last page still announces. All of Woolf's novels – as any novel is, by necessity, whether it is about the past or not – are, of course, historically contained, always-already artifacts once they are published. With *Orlando*, though, Woolf tricks time, however briefly, by offering a novel whose protagonist is fully contemporaneous with its real-life counterpart for a single day on the day of its publication, insisting that fictional and historical time slip into each other's purview. This gesture also anticipates Woolf's concluding fictional comment on writing time in *Between the Acts*, when the players in the village pageant prompt their audience to realize and inhabit "the present time. Ourselves."[49] As she does in *Between the Acts*, in *Orlando* Woolf forces her characters to pick up the burden of understanding themselves in relation to the continuum that we know as "English history," while she simultaneously seeks to broaden notions of what that historical might include.

Historical awareness in this way becomes infinitely expandable, as Woolf proposes a model of time-as-history that is brought home to Orlando in the final section of the novel. Here Orlando exhibits an awareness of her location in time with respect to the novel's teleology, suddenly knowing herself as a figure of her biographer's narration. In the book's last pages the narrator conveys Orlando's agony over the fact that the present time has been reached:

> It was the eleventh of October. It was 1928. It was the present moment.
>
> No one need wonder that Orlando started, pressed her hand to her heart, and turned pale. For what more terrifying revelation can there be than that it is the present moment? That we survive the shock at all is only possible because the past shelters us on one side and the future on another. (206)

Past and future are where safety lies, protecting us with the "shelter" of an architectural support from the intensity of the present, as Woolf renders the present as more traumatic than the worst of the past. The present is a "narrow plank" that one crosses, and it "fell from her like drops of scalding water" (207). Unless one belongs to the few who "somehow contrive to synchronise the sixty or seventy different times which beat simultaneously in every normal human system," one is always vulnerable to the "violent" force of the present: "as she stood with her hand on the door of her motor-car, the present again struck her on her head. Eleven times she was violently assaulted" (211). The present is terrifying because it is where all time perpetually conjoins, and with it all possibility; it is where we experience what Woolf calls in her unfinished memoir our "shock-receiving capacity,"[50] and it is where epiphanies burst upon us. Part of the disdain we find for the "narrow plank" of the present also occurs because of Woolf's sense that it constrains and reduces us; its temporality is too relentlessly *single.* Characterized by its extreme and eternal brevity – a *too-shortness,* we might say – the present strikes, but strikes within a confining temporal and symbolic parameter. The present means too forcefully, leaving insufficient room for the multiple and endlessly proliferating turnings of memory that Woolf wants to celebrate.

When Orlando is giving up her ancestral home – as Sackville-West had to do herself the year the book was published, when on her father's death the property passed to the nearest male relative rather than to her – she feels "Braced and strung up by the present moment," as time takes on an urgency and a materiality that have only been implicit before (223). The present exists as an unstable ground of assault between the unknowable and the knowable, its unraveling is always uncertain, and it represents a frightening domain of immediate experience. In these last pages the present literally batters her down. Orlando is only occasionally

> relieved of the pressure of the present. There was something strange in the shadow that the flicker of her eyes cast, something which (as anyone can test for himself by looking now at the sky) is *always absent from the present* – whence its terror, its nondescript character – something one trembles to pin through the body with a name and call beauty, for it has no body, is as a shadow without substance or quality of its own, yet has the power to change whatever it adds itself to. (223, my emphasis)

A few pages later, when "some church clock chimed in the valley . . . The present showered down upon her head once more" (226). Unlike the full *bodiliness* of memory and history, the present is a spectral, not – yet – narratable, disembodied place of *absence.* The present of *Orlando* also means the end of the future, since reaching the present equals reaching the end of the story and the end of the possibility of existing in narration. The novel's present thus denotes the death of the novel's subject – both the closing point of its subject matter, and the expiration of its subject's existence: a literary-mimetic correspondent to biological death through narrative closure.

THAT "HUSSY," MEMORY

In a text that is already about the interweavings of national histories (the aristocratic Orlando holds power as an ambassador to Turkey in the sixteenth century; he meets eminent poets throughout his life; and his aristocratic lineage lends him an aura of minor historical importance), personal memory and heritage (both Woolf and Sackville West's), as well as Woolf's own erotic desires, Woolf in no way sets up memory as either inviolable or especially reliable. As T. S. Eliot will do elsewhere with history, when he writes in "Gerontion" that "History has many cunning passages, contrived corridors / And issues" (lines 33-4), Woolf explicitly feminizes and sexualizes memory in *Orlando.* In an early section of the book Woolf offers a two-page disquisition on capitalized "Memory," claiming that "she" is what holds together the randomness of our experience, albeit in unpredictable ways:

> Memory is the seamstress, and a capricious one at that. Memory runs her needle in and out, up and down, hither and thither. We know not what comes next, or what follows after. Thus, the most ordinary movement in the world, such as sitting down at a table and pulling the inkstand towards one, may agitate a thousand odd, disconnected fragments, now bright, now dim, hanging and bobbing and dipping and flaunting, like the underlinen of a family of fourteen on a line in a gale of wind. Instead of being a single, downright, bluff piece of work of which no man need feel ashamed, our commonest deeds are set about with a fluttering and flickering of wings, a rising and falling of lights. Thus it was that Orlando, dipping his pen in the ink, saw the mocking face of the lost Princess and asked himself a million questions instantly which were as arrows dipped in gall. Where was she; and why had she left him? Was the Ambassador her uncle or her lover? Had they plotted? Was she forced? Was she married? Was she dead? (55–6)

Orlando's act of "dipping" his quill into the ink, and thereby into the past through the contemplation that accompanies inscription, recalls Lily

Briscoe's "dip[ping] into the past" via the inscription of painting in *To the Lighthouse*.[51] Memory, under both guises, functions as a quasi-tangible order of things that is stimulated by physical touch. "Memory is inexplicable" (56), but in Woolf's allegorisis "she" is charged with arranging past experience into a discernible symbolic order that the psyche can both carry and understand. Memory is the mistress of our experiences, she undertakes repair and restoration, but she stitches a bit too wantonly, with embarrassing combinations, disturbing the already fragile equilibrium of the present with the further unpredictability of the presence of the past. In this way, Woolf suggests, along with Henri Bergson, that "there is no perception which is not full of memories."[52] Memory is always present to experience, and it creates a dizzyingly uneven patchwork liable to throw up "disconnected fragments." Memory – the one who sews together past time – is, in other words, replete with a passionate jouissance.

In signaling memory's operations like this Woolf again links memory with eros, coming very close to her description of desire in her essay, "Phases of Fiction," published in installments in the American journal, *Bookman*, less than a year after *Orlando* appeared. In "Phases of Fiction" Woolf exposes her own intertextual mnemonic archive by undertaking to "record the impressions made upon the mind by reading a certain number of novels in succession," noting that "Desires, appetites, however we may come by them, fill it [the design] in, *scoring now in this direction, now in that*."[53] Desire, appetite, and memory are the whimsical organizers of existence to whose vicissitudes we are always subject. Memory is "capricious," straddling a dialectic between order and chaos, and unsettlingly out of full conscious control. In this very unpredictability, however, Woolf seems to find at least some delight. Memory's "fluttering and flickering of wings . . . rising and falling of lights"[54] offers, in any case, a counterpoint to the artificially ordered realism of Edwardian novels – the "series of gig lamps" – that Woolf famously warns against in "Modern Fiction" (1919).[55] Memory's unruliness, as such, might be read as a positive contribution to Woolf's revision of conventional biographic modes, offering a welcome disarrangement of fact, history, and narrative sequence.

Explicitly aligning memory with sexual promiscuity, Woolf asserts (again parenthetically) that memory can, nevertheless, be disciplined, punished, and controlled: "(For we can, if we have the resolution, turn the hussy, Memory, and all her ragtag and bobtail out of the house)" (56). In Woolf's oddly classist and misogynistic portrayal here, memory is a domestic trouble – a female servant ("seamstress") who transforms with astonishing agility into a figure of uncontrollable sexual license ("hussy"). As in the case of Woolf's own troubled relation with her servants, whom she would occasionally dismiss and then re-hire, the temptation is to turn the "hussy" of memory "out of the house" and disallow her effects. Memory in this sense signifies an excess; she is too much (sexual) trouble. Ironically, in a novel that is driven by Woolf's own desires to explore Sackville-West's personal heritage, the claim about memory's erotic excesses persists, with Woolf later referring to "him" (memory, as Orlando and the narrator, is transgendered) as a recalcitrant figure, "whose habits have already been described" (71).[56] Turning memory "out of the house," however, is clearly an impossible task for the narrator or for Orlando, and this exhortation represents only a temporary phantasy of displacement. Memory's link with licentiousness will persist, but with a marked pleasure in the dangerous play between erotic homage and fictional remembrance.

MEMORY'S REPAIR

Orlando is not the only place in which Woolf renders time and memory as fragments of cloth. In her diary she repeatedly ponders her motivations for keeping a journal, and more often than not comes up with the answer that she writes in order to capture time and memory – in order not to forget. In September 1921, after describing "the loveliest of evenings" she worries whether even her careful attention will preserve the memory of the evening: "Will this recall anything? I am so anxious to keep every scrap, you see."[57] Time, at this point, is a torn tissue, made of fissures and tears, and Woolf is the careful hoarder. With her pen she stores the scraps, hoping, perhaps, one day to piece them together to make a kind of restored patchwork that would heal the fractured relation between fragments and wholes that haunted Woolf through her life. In this instance, Woolf is in need of memory as the seamstress, yet she also wants a more predictable worker than the wanton "hussy" we find in *Orlando*, whose weavings are too unruly to bring the comfort in recollection that Woolf expresses elsewhere.

Immediately after the section of *Orlando* where Woolf delineates memory as a "hussy," Orlando begins to reflect on his own immortality, wondering how he will be registered in the future memory of others. This pause leads him to want to be a writer as a means of preserving something of himself for posterity. Looking at a "page of Sir Thomas Browne," the words rose "Like an incantation . . . not dead, embalmed, rather, so fresh is their colour, so sound their breathing – and Orlando, comparing that achievement with those of his ancestors, cried out that they and their deeds were dust and ashes, but this man and his words were immortal" (57). Like Eliot's insistence in *The Waste Land* that the archive of the past may always bloom again, and in the vein of Shakespeare's sonnets where language works as a preservative, Woolf insists on the vitality of poetry's "embalmed" meaning. In so doing, Woolf creates another circular *mise en abîme* structure around the bond between memory, desire, and writing: Woolf is writing a historical-fictional biography of a figure who decides to become a writer out of the desire to be remembered, and who has, from our historical vantage point, already achieved this aim, while Woolf writes partly in order to render both her beloved Sackville-West and her desire for Sackville-West for posterity.[58]

This naming of memory as sexually available is not the only place in Woolf's oeuvre where she aligns memory with promiscuity. In *To the Lighthouse*, when the heroic Mrs. McNab is cleaning the abandoned Ramsay home on the "Isles of Skye" [*sic*],[59] Mrs. McNab is obsessed with memory, the passage of time, and the haunting presence of Mrs. Ramsay, while her ruminations anticipate the nostalgic ambivalences of James, Cam, Lily, and Mr. Ramsay in the final section of the book. Woolf writes:

> Slowly and painfully, with broom and pail, mopping, scouring, Mrs. McNab, Mrs. Bast, stayed the corruption and the rot; rescued from the pool of Time that was fast closing over them now a basin, now a cupboard; fetched up from oblivion all the Waverley novels and a tea-set one morning; in the afternoon restored to sun and air a brass fender and a set of steel fire-irons.[60]

As she works, Mrs. McNab – as Lily, especially, will do later – imagines Mrs. Ramsay not merely as belonging to the past, but as a Stetson-like apparition that continues to inhabit the present as a palimpsestic ghost of memory: "Yes, she could see Mrs. Ramsay as she came up the drive with the washing."[61] She muses that the Ramsay family "lived well in those days. They had everything they wanted (glibly, jovially, with the tea hot in her, she unwound her ball of memories, sitting in the wicker arm-chair by the nursery fender)." Then, as Mrs. McNab continues cleaning, the narrator describes her as "*wantoning* on with her memories."[62] Mrs. McNab's diligent restoration of the domestic architectural space that had earlier seemed, from the outside, to enfold them in a cohesive family unit, thus performs memory as a co-mingling of recollection, desire, and erotic pleasure. The body and the ruins of the past, Woolf posits, attach themselves to the subject, provoking memorial while simultaneously eliciting new and febrile emotions within the singularity of each desiring "I."

MODERNIST MEMORY *AS* DESIRE

In Adam Phillips's reading of Freud in *On Flirtation*, he elucidates some similar proposals to the ones I have been making here about the astonishing links between memory and desire in modernist writing. In "Freud and the Uses of Forgetting" Phillips emphasizes the bind between symptoms, desire, and memory: "A form of involuntary and disguised memory, symptoms are mnemonics of desire; and desire, for Freud – what he referred to as 'instinctual life' – is unforgettable."[63] Symptoms as such are a mode of archival expressivity that unconsciously reveal the ineffaceability of both desire and memory through their belated trace effects. Without specifically naming it, Phillips is undoubtedly referring to a moment in *Civilization and Its Discontents* when Freud stakes a claim against one of his earlier positions, in which he had posited that memory-traces are in fact *effaceable*:

> Since we overcame the error of supposing that the forgetting we are familiar with signified a destruction of the memory-trace – that is, its annihilation – we have been inclined to take the opposite view, that in mental life nothing which has once been formed can perish – that everything is somehow preserved and that in suitable circumstances (when, for instance, regression goes back far enough) it can once more be brought to light.[64]

Freud's argument, like Woolf's, contends that any experience which has taken form within the psyche is, strictly speaking, retrievable. Bergson, too, confirms this modernist rendition of memory as involuntarily and indelibly recorded in the psyche: "In reality, the past is preserved by itself, automatically. In its entirety, probably, it follows us at every instant; all that we have felt, thought and willed from our earliest infancy is there, leaning over the present which is about to join it, pressing against the portals of consciousness."[65]

Phillips's analysis extends this general rule about the preservation of experience to the specific case of desire, as he pushes his argument to assert that "memory, Freud had begun to believe, was *of* desire."[66] Phillips then presents us with a paradox at the crux of his own thesis, proposing that in the course of psychoanalytic treatment the indestructibility of the memory-trace needs to be overcome, since for Freud, "the aim of analysis was not to remember, but to establish sufficient states of forgetting."[67]

As such, the desire of the subject to "heal" him- or herself by "dealing with" the past – the past as the ostensible object of scrutiny for both patient and analyst, who uncover and unravel it in order to learn how better to live with one's inheritance (the history that happened to one by chance) – also involves the demand of coming to terms with desire by facilitating a needful forgetting. Only in so doing is one able to relinquish the pressure of the past's desires – to "let it go," or to "just forget about it," as the common phrases go, whose simple wisdom could cure the melancholic.

Since Freud and Phillips both propose that memory and desire are *indestructible*, though, what are we to make of Phillips's position when he insists that the aim of Freud's method was to "establish sufficient states of forgetting"? Phillips's commentary exposes a marked point of ambivalence in Freud's thinking about memory. Phillips's appeal to a necessary "forgetting" contradicts Freud's stipulations about the radical indestructibility of memory, and the call for an abreactive "remembering, repeating, and working through"[68] at the core of the analytic process. As it turns out, in *Civilization and Its Discontents* Freud remains ambivalent about how the past stores itself in the psyche. Only a few pages after he asserts that "everything is somehow preserved," he hesitates, claiming, "Perhaps we are going too far in this. Perhaps we ought to content ourselves with asserting that what is past in mental life *may* be preserved and is not *necessarily* destroyed."[69] Shortly thereafter he contends, "We can only hold fast to the fact that it is rather the rule than the exception for the past to be preserved in mental life."[70]

In Phillips's reading, Freud's call to memory is an opening to the past that seeks to dispense with it – either through projection ("spitting it out") or repression ("like eating something").[71] Phillips, in effect, brings Freud quite close to a Nietzschean model where, because "all of us suffer from a debilitating historical fever," one must "learn to forget," without clinging "to what was past"; "an excess of history is harmful to life."[72] Phillips's emphasis first on memory as "*of* desire," and second on an idealized psyche that would exist in having forgotten, pushes us to pressure points in Freud's argument, and to questions about the extent of the desire for memory and the desire for forgetting in modernist texts. I would claim that Eliot and Woolf's versions of memory hold fast to something like Freud's initial proposal: they render previous experience as fundamentally retrievable *in some form*. Neither Woolf nor Eliot proposes a sustained, discernible will to forget – in "Ash Wednesday" Eliot even writes, "Let the whiteness of bones atone to forgetfulness" (line 59), as though even a post-mortem amnesia requires expiation – and instead they figure memory and history as a compelling ground and body that invite perpetual re-exploration. Forgetting sometimes happens, by accident or by chance, but forgetting is fundamentally perceived as a kind of unchosen mistake. Memory, on the other hand, is conscientiously and consciously foregrounded, and we find what amounts to a persistent – even obsessive – drive to investigate the conditions of recollection, remembrance, and the past's return.

We might say that Freud's argument is typically modernist in its concerns to articulate a standpoint on memory in relation to a no longer fully coherent subjectivity. In addition to citing Nietzsche's call to amnesia (even if only obliquely), Freud's argument recalls Proust's contentions in *A la recherche du temps perdu*, where he offers another mnemonic schema in which memory is centrally present to every "new" experience. Like Eliot in "Tradition and the Individual Talent," Proust employs the term "labor" to express the efforts involved in consciously recuperating memory:

> It is a labor in vain to attempt to recapture it ["our own past"]: all the efforts of our intellect must prove futile. The past is hidden somewhere outside the realm, beyond the reach of the intellect, in some material object (in the sensation which that material object will give us) of which we have no inkling. And it depends on chance whether or not we come upon this object before we ourselves must die.[73]

Unlike Eliot's contentions that one must study and "labour" to revisit, intimately, the vitality that remains embedded in texts of the past, Proust stresses the labor necessary to recalling *personal* experience – which also involves one's experience in culture – as a task the "intellect" may not perform. Instead, the past returns to us most authentically through involuntary recollection of certain *moments privilégiés.*[74] This "chance" presents another version of Freud's claim about the need for "suitable circumstances" to arise for the past to be "once more be brought to light."[75] Indeed, even the metaphors Proust and Freud choose are remarkably close: for Proust "[t]he past is *hidden* . . . beyond the reach of the intellect" until an emotionally or sensually driven reopening to the past reanimates it; for Freud what is "preserved" must be "*brought to light*" through language and address (my emphasis). In both instances an obscured experience is again made available. At the same time, memory for Proust is infinitely desirable. Memory is longed for with a limitless thirst, and might even be said to be the primary object of desire of *A la recherche du temps perdu.*

Woolf writes in 1923, "I am perhaps encouraged by Proust to search out & identify my feelings,"[76] and Proust proffers another modernist exemplum which places the burden of remembering on a sensuous triptych comprised of the body, the senses, and the materiality of objects. In the (re)tasting of the madeleine, the contours and depths of the past emerge through the mysterious workings of sensation, and in his marvel at his recaptured childhood memory Proust finds effects that demand a sustained delineation long after the initial memory-event. Proust here participates in a twofold sensualization of time and experience: he wishes to know and possess the present memory event itself (the moment of recollection in which one turns back to the past), as well as to recover the always mutable memory content from the past. We might think of Woolf's writing of memory as an approach to a tangible order to which we may again *connect* ourselves, if we may only discover the aleatory condition or the technology proper to such an endeavor – as I will explore in chapter 6 – while Proust figures the senses as containing an always-fecund opportunity for *retaking* the past, making it again present to ourselves as an object of our self-possession: "taste and smell alone, more fragile but more enduring, more unsubstantial, more persistent, more faithful, remain poised a long time, like souls, remembering, waiting, hoping, amid the ruins of all the rest; and bear unflinchingly, in the tiny and almost impalpable drop of their essence, the vast structure of recollection."[77] In the geometry of the senses of "taste and smell" that Proust charts, involuntary bodily functions are the most faithful conduits of the past. They are responsible for supporting the entire apparatus of remembrance, while they are at once untrainable and unsupersedable.

The "rest" – Proust's unrediscoverable past – lies in ruins, as Proust invokes another modernist formula for the past that is central to our discussion: the evidence of the past may crumble, but the past itself will still always exist, and ruins can be undone. Woolf writes in *Mrs. Dalloway* of Clarissa's contemplation of her unsatisfactory meeting with Peter Walsh in terms of the lost ruins of both the senses and the emotions:

> Looking back over that long friendship of almost thirty years her theory worked to this extent. Brief, broken, often painful as their actual meetings had been, what with his absences and interruptions . . . the effect of them on his life was immeasurable. There was a mystery about it. You were given a sharp, acute, uncomfortable grain – the actual meeting; horribly painful as often not; yet in absence, in the most unlikely places, it would flower out, open, shed its scent, let you touch, taste, look about you, get the whole feel of it and understanding, after years of lying lost.[78]

Then, in *The Waves* (1931), when Louis has left school and is working in London, he remembers the unexpectedness and violence of his first kiss, and likens this anamnestic moment to a mythic scene of ruins: "I woke in a garden, with a blow on the nape of my neck, a hot kiss, Jinny's; remembering all this as one remembers confused cries and toppling pillars and shafts of red and black in some nocturnal conflagration."[79] He doesn't actually *remember* "toppling pillars," but he links the sudden intensity of his first kiss with the power of such ancient, archetypal images. Myth and personal memory stand on equal footing: myth can be as real as fact if we have incorporated it as analogous to personal memory. We might say that it is the task of the modernist writer to restore, to acknowledge, and to affirm the vitality of the deathly pallor of the ruined. Woolf plays this out again in *To the Lighthouse* when it becomes Mrs. McNab's task to restore the "ruined" interior space of the abandoned Ramsay household in the Hebrides so that it may again shelter the dreams and dramas of the living, with all their unresolved memories of death, desire, and longing.[80]

For each of these writers – Woolf, Eliot, Freud, and Proust – when the past leaves its traces in our bodies and on our psyches, it inscribes memory with the indelible ink of desire. Just as in Freud's topographic model of the psyche in *Civilization and Its Discontents*, the body holds memory's imprint, while this writing is simultaneously bound to a logic of place, architecture, and the palimpsest. In a kind of postmodern imagining of a three-dimensional holograph of the psyche, Freud uses the "analogy" of "the Eternal City" to propound his theory of the preservation of "the memory-trace": as in Rome, the "ruins" of memory are never fully destroyed but only built among by later buildings/memories that in turn will become open to restoration.[81] The psyche from this perspective is a continually encrypted tablet with an unlimited space to welcome the language of memory.

The analogy is highly imperfect, Freud concedes, because it attempts to render temporality and history through a spatiality that cannot signal more than one meaning-content at once. Still, he insists on the merit in realizing that, unlike the body and the city, where maturation and damage cause the original entity to be finally unrecognizable, "only in the mind is such a preservation of all the earlier stages alongside of the final form possible."[82] Freud's vision of the history of the psyche navigates both backward and forward along something resembling the two-way street that Woolf conjures in "A Sketch of the Past": an "avenue lying behind; a long ribbon of scenes, emotions" that may always again be walked.[83] For Woolf, memory supplements and complements the past by reordering it with infinitely enigmatic combinations. In her topography of the self she maps a subjectivity that wishes to be firmly bound to the traces of the past, as if by invisible filaments that are felt but not seen. Neville phrases it this way in *The Waves*: "the person is always changing, though not the desire";[84] desire as such is a fixed impulse that perennially greets the present, loaded with its complement of memories.

CHAPTER 6

Other kinds of autobiographies: sketching the past, forgetting Freud, and reaching the lighthouse

> I read some history: it is suddenly all alive, branching forwards & backwards & connected with every kind of thing that seemed entirely remote before. I seem to feel Napoleons influence on our quiet evening in the garden for instance – I think I see for a moment how our minds are all threaded together – how any live mind today is of the very same stuff of Plato's & Euripides. It is only a continuation & development of the same thing. It is this common mind that binds the whole world together; & all the world is mind. Then I read a poem say – & the same thing is repeated. I feel as though I had grasped the central meaning of the world, & all these poets & historians & philosophers were only following out paths branching from that centre in which I stand. And then – some speck of dust gets into my machine I suppose, & the whole thing goes wrong again.
>
> Virginia Woolf, 1 July 1903[1]

> She held her hands hollowed; she felt that she wanted to enclose the present moment; to make it stay; to fill it fuller and fuller, with the past, the present and the future, until it shone, whole, bright, deep with understanding.
>
> Virginia Woolf, Eleanor in *The Years*[2]

If we look at Virginia Woolf's autobiographical fragment, "A Sketch of the Past," that she left unfinished at the time of her suicide in 1941, we see a sustained fascination with the past and its links to sexuality, sensuality, and desire. Throughout the memoir Woolf records an emotional, intellectual, and physical pleasure in *writing* about past time: like Proust she both revels in the intense and almost total return to particularly sensual moments of the past – a return that collapses time to revisit prior instantiations of what she calls "moments of being"[3] – while she affirms the gratification in the present achieved through (re)membering and inscribing the bodily effects of the past. In her enchantment with the past, and in her recurrent recourse to registers of sensual desire and delight in writing and thinking of memory, her language evinces a residual libidinal charge in the still-becoming materiality and real of the past. In so doing she implicitly agrees with Freud's notion that the "sexual instinct," eros, is "the preserver of all things," and we might think of her writing as a kind of eros-laden "self-preservative" life instinct.[4] Woolf, however, claims not to have read Freud until the very year, 1939, in which she both meets Freud and begins drafting her memoir. I want to argue, though, that this date represents a belated confession of her familiarity with his work, since she had directly encountered Freud as early as 1924 when she set the type for the Hogarth Press's *International Psychoanalytic Library*.

In "A Sketch of the Past" Woolf's expressed desire is to return to the "free page" (115) of remembrance – a phrase she uses both in her memoir and in her diary of the time[5] – particularly to instances of recollection that occurred either before or after what she calls "the seven unhappy years" (136) of 1897–1904. She writes, "I could fill pages remembering one thing after another. All together made the summer at St Ives the best beginning to life conceivable. When they took Talland House father and mother gave us – me at any rate – what has been perennial, invaluable" (128). As we have seen with *Orlando*, for Woolf writing of the past in some sense stays time. To write of private remembrance for Woolf involved disclosing a cathected relation to an order of things that is still undergoing a kind of *becoming*. In inscribing memory, Woolf announces a kind of archival embalming of the past as a charged object that can, through textuality, always be re-encountered (by oneself or by an Other). In a letter to Violet Dickinson in December 1936, thanking her for binding some 350 letters Woolf had written to her in her youth, Woolf writes, "Letters seem more than anything to keep the past – out it comes, when one opens the box."[6] The past is both the material object of the actual letter and a thriving presence contained within its words.

"A Sketch of the Past" is hardly a simple rendering of a linear personal history, and at stake in its opening pages is the very status and value of the genre. Quite tellingly its title puns in important ways: in addition to outlining the formal aims of the fragment in terms of an aesthetically arranged artistic evocation of the past (a "sketch"), the text diagrammatically and provisionally delineates ("sketches") a poetics of memory. When Woolf began to write the piece, she had in fact already participated, twenty years earlier, in another only partially realized attempt at writing autobiography through the Bloomsbury Memoir Club. Woolf's niece, Anne Olivier Bell, explains that this club

> was invented by Molly MacCarthy in the hope of inducing Desmond MacCarthy to write something other than journalism. The members – about a dozen old friends – were expected every month, after dining together, to foregather in one or another of the member's houses and each read a chapter of what was to become a full-length autobiography. This proved too ambitious, and the contributions and the frequency of the meetings were reduced.[7]

The club, though it met erratically, had an impressive longevity: begun in 1920, it continued in various incarnations through 1956, with its original members including E. M. Forster, Duncan Grant, David Garnett, Maynard Keynes, Roger Fry, Saxon-Sydney Turner, Lytton Strachey, Vanessa and Clive Bell, Molly and Desmond MacCarthy, Adrian Stephen, and Leonard and Virginia Woolf.[8] The group's conspicuous failure to script the past in a produced form performatively attests to the difficult labor of writing time and memory.

Woolf initially experienced the Memoir Club meetings as unwanted and even painful instances of self-exposure. After the second gathering she writes in her diary,

> Leonard was objective & triumphant; I subjective & most unpleasantly discomfited. I dont [*sic*] know when I've felt so chastened & out of humour with myself – a partner I generally respect & admire. "Oh but why did I read this egotistic sentimental trash!" That was my cry, & the result of my sharp sense of the silence succeeding my chapter. It started with loud laughter; this was soon quenched; & then I couldn't help figuring a kind of uncomfortable boredom on the part of the males; to whose genial cheerful sense my revelations were at once mawkish & distasteful. What possessed me to lay bare my soul![9]

The whole passage announces a recoil from the dangers of giving testimony to the intimate revelations of memory. In her response to the shock of the unsought "loud laughter" and gendered (male) "boredom," Woolf internalizes these external critiques to chastise herself for sentimentality, self-absorption, and having bared too much. Our modes of remembrance, Woolf shows, attest both to our inmost patterns of intellection as well as to one's attachment to experience; they are modes of a profound vulnerability, and Woolf understandably hesitates when entering the terrain of this limited "public" disclosure. Within a few months, though, she becomes accustomed to the shock of disclosure, light-heartedly congratulating herself on her performance – probably of her piece, "22 Hyde Park Gate" – at a meeting in November 1920: "The Memoir Club was fearfully brilliant – I mean I was; & Leonard so much more impressive with so much less pains; & Morgan [Forster] very professional; & Mary [Hutchinson] never laughed once at my jokes."[10] The meetings continued, and in 1922 Woolf was asked by the Club to write an autobiographical account of Bloomsbury.

Woolf agreed to the task, but the piece that emerged, "Old Bloomsbury," begins with a stuttering, dash-ridden protest and an plea for exculpation: "At Molly's command I have had to write a memoir of Old Bloomsbury – of Bloomsbury from 1904 to 1914. Naturally I see Bloomsbury only from my own angle – not from yours. For this I must ask you to make allowances."[11] Asserting that she writes her recollections because of an insistence from without, and from within a necessarily limited personal frame, she anticipates the charges of egotism and sentimentality for which she admonished herself after the Memoir Club's second meeting, displaying and displacing these anxieties by registering her writing as a call to duty. In strikingly parallel fashion, Woolf only begins writing "A Sketch of the Past" seventeen years later at the behest of her sister, the painter Vanessa Bell, who urged her to record her life's story. Again Woolf's prose is replete with caesuras and dashes: "Two days ago – Sunday 16th April 1939 to be precise – Nessa said that if I did not start writing my memoirs I should soon be too old. I should be eighty-five, and should have forgotten – witness the unhappy case of Lady Strachey" (64). Woolf had been keeping journals assiduously since childhood, and had thought on several occasions that she would eventually "write my memoirs out of them."[12] But despite her fame as a woman of letters, she still had never attempted a sustained "autobiography," even as late as 1939. It turns out that despite her willingness and propensity to record the past in fictional autobiography (I am thinking of *To the Lighthouse* especially), biography (*Orlando: A Biography*, *Flush: A Biography*, and *Roger Fry: A Biography* – each highlighting its genre through a subtitle), and in diaries and letters, she needed a demand from without to be pushed to transpose her life to the memoir form.

Why would this be so? Alex Zwerdling points out that Woolf came from a long line of memoirists: "The Stephens had written memoirs for generations and had made sure to preserve the family legacy for posterity."[13] Just as Woolf understood Vita Sackville-West to be a part of "the whole of English history," Woolf belonged to the tradition of life writing in Britain.[14] Nevertheless, formalized "autobiography" was not her most comfortable mode, and she dramatically leaves "A Sketch of the Past" unfinished (and undestroyed), as though to illustrate performatively her resistance to joining her patriarchal forefathers by writing out her life as a "whole." In terms that look forward to her comments in *Orlando* about the multiplicity of selves contained within any ostensibly singularity, in 1924 she had written, "we're splinters & mosaics; not, as they used to hold, immaculate, monolithic, consistent wholes. How I scribble; & what use will this be for my great memoir writing age?"[15] As I discuss in chapter 5, she had also expressed criticisms of both biography and autobiography throughout her life, considering them primarily as forums for men to boast about their achievements. In *Jacob's Room* the narrator refers to an essay Jacob is composing called "'Does History consist of the Biographies of Great Men?'"[16] Jacob's paper is very likely a critical response to Thomas Carlyle's lecture on "The Hero as Divinity," which, as Kate Flint points out in her notes to the novel, argues that "The History of the World is but the Biography of great men"[17] – precisely the attitude to historiography that Woolf condemned throughout her life.

At the beginning of "A Sketch of the Past" Woolf is apprehensive about the "failures" of autobiography as a genre because of its inability to relate the nuances of personality and subjectivity: memoirs relate "events" and "what happened" but they "leave out the person to whom things happened" (65). More than ten years earlier, in *A Room of One's Own*, she remarks with discernible sarcasm that we live in a self-obsessed (male) "age of biography,"[18] noting later in the piece, with a repetitive series of additive "ands" that is surely meant to be mocking, "There were the biographies: Johnson and Goethe and Carlyle and Sterne and Cowper and Shelley and Voltaire and Browning and many others."[19] Of women she notes, "All these infinitely obscure lives remain to be recorded, I said, addressing Mary Carmichael as if she were present; and went on in thought through the streets of London feeling in imagination the pressure of dumbness, the accumulation of unrecorded life."[20] In similar terms in the draft of *A Room of One's Own*, "Women and Fiction," she laments women's historic exclusion from the domain of inscription: "We know nothing of them except their names and the dates of their marriages and the number of children they bore."[21] Then, in *Three Guineas*, which she finished the year before she began "A Sketch of the Past," she continues her critique of conventional life writing by linking such an endeavor with the politics and history of war: "almost every biography we read of professional men in the nineteenth century, to limit ourselves to that not distant and fully documented age, is largely concerned with war."[22]

Rather poignantly, given her ambivalence to life writing, Woolf also happens to begin writing her "Sketch" while she is drafting the biography of her deceased friend, the painter Roger Fry. Like Woolf, Fry, too, left not a complete memoir behind, but, as she tells us on the first page of his biography, "a fragment of autobiography."[23] On the first page of her own personal account Woolf justifies her readiness to respond to her sister's request that she write her memoirs by explaining, "As it happens that I am sick of writing Roger's life, perhaps I will spend two or three mornings making a sketch" (64). Once she embarked on the task, she relished the process, referring to it as a "holiday" from the exertion of writing Roger's life: "The drudgery of making a coherent life of Roger has once more become intolerable, and so I turn for a few days respite to May 1895" (75, 85). Writing her own narrative of remembrance, in effect, provided solace for having to (re)construct another person's past. Later, after she had put the piece away for nearly a year – between July 1939 and June 1940 she "forgets" about it, and had even thrown her "sheaf of notes" into the "waste-paper basket" with "all my life of Roger" in a curiously ambivalent accident – she again proposes that "it was to refresh myself from that antlike meticulous labour [of writing Fry's biography] that I determined to look for these pages" (100). Then, toward what became her memoir's end she writes, "My book [Fry's biography] is out; and jaded and distracted I return to this free page" (115). She had written in "The Art of Biography" that "the novelist is free; the biographer is tied,"[24] but her own *auto*biography, although insisted upon from without, functions as a component of freedom and as a means to "refresh." Her turn from writing *Roger Fry: A Biography* to composing her own life's history seems to enact a response, finally, to the frustration she felt about so few memoirs being written by or about women. It would have been sadly ironic, to say the least, if Woolf had left behind three "biographies," but no equivalent contribution about herself.

May 1895 indicates the very month that Woolf's mother died, when Virginia Stephen was a girl of thirteen. Why, then, would such a date provide "respite"? Part of what we find in considering Woolf's writing of the past is a persistent return to what we might call a *positivity in the midst of trauma* – a (re)discovery of a plenitude of being precisely at the moments when one seems most divested of being. Cathy Caruth's influential and provocative work on trauma that in turn is deeply engaged with a reading of Freud's notion of trauma situates the traumatic instance as one involving a break in temporality: "What causes, trauma, then, is a shock that appears to work very much like a bodily threat but is in fact a break in the mind's experience of time."[25] There is an epistemological abyss, or gap, however, that imposes itself on the experience so that one fails to bear witness to one's traumas at the moment in which they occur: "The shock of the mind's relation to the threat of death is thus not the direct experience of the threat, but precisely the *missing* of this experience, the fact that, not being experienced *in time*, it has not yet been fully known."[26] It is this failure to participate – this being absent at the most crucial of moments – that then leads to a potentially never-ending need to repeat and return to the traumatic scene in order to find a way in to its testimony and then, perhaps, dispersal. Scholars have paid significant attention to Woolf's perspectives on personal trauma, but what I am hoping to do here, at least in part, is to point to her insistence that memory – even memory linked with trauma – can also provide openings, apertures, and even salves that are directly implicated with drives to inscription. In 1940 she turns, in her diary, to soothing recollections about her brother, Thoby, who died suddenly at the age of twenty-six from typhoid fever: "Scraps of memoirs come so coolingly to my mind. Wound up by those 3 little articles (one sent today) I unwound a page about Thoby."[27] In turning to writing about her long-lost loved ones as solace from the tensions and "drudgery" of the present, Woolf reveals a certain resolution (worked-throughness) in relation to the traumas of that past. Hermione Lee argues that Julia Stephen was for almost all who knew her "the object of idealised memories,"[28] and in "A Sketch of the Past" Woolf describes her mother as "of course 'a vision' " (87). She borrows here the language of her final sentence of *To the Lighthouse* where the narrator reports Lily Briscoe's inner monologue: "I have had my vision."[29] But there is more than just idealization at work here, and Woolf very importantly records the effects of death on her adolescent perception as producing, along with trauma, a witnessing that involved a kind of wonder and "a certain silence" ("Sketch," 88).

When Woolf comes to describe the days immediately following her mother's death, she recollects an experience of "rapture." Juxtaposing the terrible trauma of the loss with "one memory of great beauty," she describes going to Paddington station to pick up Thoby:

> It was sunset, and the great glass dome at the end of the station was blazing with light. It was glowing yellow and red and the iron girders made a pattern across it. I walked along the platform gazing with rapture at this magnificent blaze of colour, and the train slowly steamed into the station. It impressed and exalted me. It was so vast and so fiery red. The contrast of that blaze of magnificent light with the shrouded and curtained rooms at Hyde Park Gate was so intense.

Also it was partly that my mother's death unveiled and intensified; made me suddenly develop perceptions, as if a burning glass had been laid over what was shaded and dormant. (93)

One can hardly refrain from reading this as a barely atheistic allusion to First Corinthians 13:11-12: "When I was a child, I spake as a child, I understood as a child, I thought as a child: but when I became a man, I put away childish things. / For now we see through a glass darkly; but then face to face: now I know in part, but then shall I know even as also I am known." In the sudden catapult to an unsought maturation, Woolf relates both the matter and the *mater* of memory – the *mother* matter and the *maternal material* of memory that arrives unbidden as a postmortem gift of sight, giving the young Virginia Stephen a sudden access to vision akin to the revelation of a profound exposure.

Consonant with Barthes's *punctum* – where an unexpected disturbance arises in viewing a photograph – and Benjamin's stress on the link between shock and photography, Woolf suddenly finds perception to be like seeing through "burning glass."[30] Immediately after the above description Woolf links that flash of experience to a newfound, post-traumatic ability to move past "words" in reading poetry. This transcendence of textuality led her as a girl of thirteen to discover an almost Blakean "correspondence" between the ostensible Otherness of language and the realm of inner "feeling":

I had a feeling of transparency in words when they cease to be words and become so intensified that one seems to experience them; to foretell them as if they developed what one is already feeling. I was so astonished that I tried to explain the feeling. "One seems to understand what it's about," I said awkwardly. I suppose Nessa has forgotten; no one could have understood from what I said the queer feeling I had in the hot grass, that poetry was coming true. Nor does that give the feeling. It matches what I have sometimes felt when I write. The pen gets on the scent. ("Sketch," 93)

Her mother's death thus engenders a kind of life, bringing a new vitality to the language of others – and, in turn, to her own experience of writing in pursuit of that "scent" – that further inflects the yoking of memory and desire by showing it to be a crucial nexus of both readerly perception and textual production. Her memory of death is embedded with a memory of first grasping a transcendent experience of language (dare we say of *logos*?). This remembrance also helps her to map the history of her writer's consciousness. Her drive to write in a vein that could approach such "transparency," where words are *felt* and "experience[d]" in the body and through the emotions, finds part of its genealogy in the awakening to meaning Woolf traces in her testimony about loss. We might also here recall T. S. Eliot's comment in "The Metaphysical Poets" (1921) when he disparages Tennyson and Browning because "they do not feel their thoughts as immediately as the odour of a rose."[31] Indeed, the mnemonic potency of Woolf's transformative (almost photographic) exposure, when she began to *feel* language, would remain with her for a lifetime, to be eventually transcribed forty-four years later in the context of her memoir.

In one of the most erotically charged moments in all of Virginia Woolf's writing (people are always complaining that Woolf never writes about sex in her novels, but they haven't read between the lines in her memoirs), when she is recalling her earliest childhood memories she describes them in sensual and sexual terms that evoke a naturalistic space of primordial desire. Until the death of her mother she and her family had spent what Woolf remembers as idyllic summers at Talland House in St. Ives, Cornwall. In "A Sketch of the Past" she describes a childhood scene of stopping to look at some apples and flowers on the way to the beach:

> The gardens gave off a murmur of bees; the apples were red and gold; there were also pink flowers; and grey and silver leaves. The buzz, the croon, the smell, all seemed to press voluptuously against some membrane; not to burst it; but to hum round one such a complete rapture of pleasure that I stopped, smelt, looked. But again I cannot describe that rapture. It was rapture rather than ecstasy. (66)

After she records what she calls her "colour-and-sound memories," she feels compelled to pause in her narration:

> The strength of these pictures – but sight was always then so much mixed with sound that picture is not the right word – the strength anyhow of these impressions makes me again digress. Those moments – in the nursery, on the road to the beach – *can still be more real than the present moment.* This I have just tested. For I got up and crossed the garden. Percy was digging the asparagus bed; Louie was shaking a mat in front of the bedroom door. But I was seeing them through the sight I saw here – the nursery and the road to the beach. At times I can go back to St Ives more completely than I can this morning. I can reach a state where I seem to be watching things happen as if I were there. (67, my emphasis)[32]

The past is "more real than the present" because it is available both to experience and re-experience – to understanding and to the enhanced re-cognition involved in *knowing again.* As Henri Bergson proposes in his 1911 lectures at Oxford, "We tend to represent the past as if it were non-existent"; while this is an "illusion," he claims, that is essential for life, it is "dangerous in the highest degree."[33] Further, "the past makes a body with the present and continually creates with it."[34] One's position toward the past is open both to the ongoing *becoming* of the past, and to a stabilization of previous experience that the present cannot yet offer. For Woolf – as for Bergson and Freud – the intenser moments of the past leave palpable psychic and sensual remains, while memorialization itself, and especially writing of the past, becomes a way of approaching a temporality deepened by the past's enduring becoming.

Woolf's insistence on distinguishing between rapture and ecstasy in her experience of the Cornwall gardens underscores the intensely physical quality of the pleasure she describes. Rapture, the *Oxford English Dictionary* tells us, is partly derived from the Latin *rapere*, to seize, to rape. Rapture, that is, is linked etymologically with somatic seizure, and it has been used theologically and secularly to mean an overwhelmingly physical and pleasurable overtaking. Only secondarily does the *OED* list it as "mental exaltation, specifically as a result of religious feeling or inspiration." Ecstasy, on the other hand, comes from the Greek verb, *existanai*, "to put out of place," suggesting that its experience involves almost a kind of exile – a being transported to a position of *elsewhere*. In recent years the two terms appear to be edging closer in meaning, and in three of its eight current definitions the *Oxford English Dictionary* has taken recourse to a tautological slippage in defining ecstasy as a kind of "rapture" (e.g. ecstasy is "The state of being distracted by some emotion; a frenzy, a stupor; an exalted state of feeling, *rapture*," my emphasis). Ecstasy and rapture collude, and their boundaries are difficult to describe. Ecstasy, though, properly speaking, has more to do with the sensation of being psychologically or spiritually moved than it does with a feeling of a physical seizure. Both were important to Woolf, and in *Orlando* she asserts, "it's ecstasy that matters,"[35] while in her autumnal childhood memory, Woolf recalls being seized and *taken* by the force of the bloom and the bodily humming she perceived. Memory in this way also comes to delineate an aesthetic category – it stands as the sensual relic of a materialized empiricism that has made a mark on consciousness and that matters so much because of its still-emerging beauty.

If we are in doubt at all about the deep connection between rapture and memory, Woolf spells it out for us again in *A Room of One's Own*:

> The very reason why the poetry [of Tennyson and Christina Rossetti] excites one to such abandonment, such rapture, is that it celebrates some feeling that one

used to have (at luncheon parties before the war perhaps), so that one responds easily, familiarly, without troubling to check the feeling, or to compare it with any that one has now. But the living poets express a feeling that is actually being made and torn out of us at the moment. One does not recognize it in the first place; often for some reason one fears it.[36]

The contemporary writer does not "excite[ ]" to rapture because her work only manifests the incompleteness of present "feeling." The present, which so often signifies a lack in Woolf, can only produce a "feeling" still in its basic stages of development. Such a feeling is taken from the writer almost too hastily – or, one has not enough temporal distance from the object to find the "abandonmnent" and "rapture" of remembering an emotional timbre of the past. The present is much more difficult to write; its still-unformed fluidity (insufficiently informed by memory's crucial supplement) gave Woolf fearful pause in more places than just in her expostulations on the present's violence within *Orlando.* As she exclaims to Ethel Smyth while praising her for her life writing in *Impressions that Remained* (1919), which Woolf was rereading: "how then do all these people stand and live in their own element with the life of their own time rushing past, as might be fish caught in a net of water: living, breathing and about to shoot on – the whole torrent pouring past, nothing frozen and final as happens with the usual skilled hack?"[37]

The "voluptuous[ ]" "press" "against some membrane" at the center of Woolf's childhood memory also asserts that what she remembers is, more often than not, associated with the body, sensuality, and eroticism. Quite astonishingly, however, most critics grant Woolf a sexual and sensual body primarily when discussing her childhood sexual abuse.[38] Woolf's relationship with her body was undoubtedly ambivalent and even vexed. Although she mentions "ecstasy" and "rapture" with astonishing frequency in her memoir – one of the two terms appears on all but one of the first five pages – she also adds one caveat: she could feel "ecstasies and raptures spontaneously and intensely and without any shame or the least sense of guilt, so long as they were disconnected from my own body" (66). From here she links this need to disconnect intense pleasure from the corporeal to her shame and fear about her body that she traces in the sexual abuse she suffered at the hands of her half-brother, Gerald Duckworth.[39] She learned, she explains, "a feeling about certain parts of the body; how they must not be touched; how it is wrong to allow them to be touched" (69). Just five lines further on in "A Sketch of the Past," however, she writes, rather provocatively, that her memory of sexual abuse "throws light not merely on my own case, but upon the problem that I *touched* on the first page; why it is so difficult to give any account of the person to whom things happened" (69, my emphasis). In writing her memoir Woolf is *touching* on the project of remembrance as it is related through text. With her slippage and echoing of terms – from Gerald's *touching* of her body to her *touching* on the problem of writing a life – I want to suggest that she is already undertaking to recuperate and re-own *touch* within the context of her recollections. Woolf's palpable pleasure in the "rapture" and "ecstasy" she so frequently describes betrays a deeply corporeal delight that Gerald apparently could not quite take away from her. That is, the disconnection she affirms from her body seems also to be overridden (and overwritten) by the pleasures of remembrance, which she felt as intensely and tenderly as if they worked precisely through the tactile and the sensual. When Woolf first starts composing *Orlando* she tells Sackville-West that as soon as she had conceived of the work, "my body was flooded with rapture."[40] She was writing of history, memory, and desire together, and the effects of this undertaking were not simply written on, but became intrinsic to her body. And the body has its way of speaking history.

Elsewhere in "A Sketch of the Past," in terms remarkably akin to Freud's emphasis on the primacy of childhood memories in shaping the psyche, Woolf stresses one foundational and deeply sensual memory that functioned as a wellspring for all her subsequent experiences. She writes:

> If life has a base that it stands upon, if it is a bowl that one fills and fills and fills – then my bowl without a doubt stands upon this memory. It is of lying half asleep, half awake, in bed at the nursery at St Ives. It is of overhearing the waves breaking, one, two, one, two, and sending a splash of water over the beach; and then breaking, one, two, one, two, behind a yellow blind. It is of hearing the blind draw its little acorn across the floor as the wind blew the blind out. It is of lying and hearing this splash and seeing this light, and feeling, it is almost impossible that I should be here; of feeling the purest ecstasy I can conceive. (64–5)[41]

Again invoking "ecstasy," and the pleasures of the past, the memory Woolf describes here is scarcely of an "event," and her concern is neither acting nor participating. Instead, she remembers passively experiencing sounds by noting the rhythmic splash of the waves, which she counted in her earliest way of counting – by ones only, not even making it to three or four, simply "one, two, one, two" (we can imagine a musical score in two-two time). She remembers divisions and structures: the waves crashed out of reach, beyond her room, as her early logic negotiates a separation between "outside" and "inside," where the exterior is immensely pleasurable from the vantage point of the inner sanctum of her childhood bed.

What stands between her and the natural scene beyond her window (for she is supplementing what she can perceive visually with what she hears) is no more than a "yellow blind" – a kind of insubstantial film that is still tangible enough to mark, both aurally and visually, the discreteness between her womb-like interior space and the beyond of the sea. She herself is a somnolent receptacle of sensations and impressions, and she describes her role in the memory in terms of the gerund ("lying and hearing . . . seeing . . . feeling") – a present that testifies to its own continuation. She is writing of memory as a study of consciousness, where, as Avrom Fleishman argues, "an overflow from sensation into self-consciousness is recorded."[42] Her consciousness, she affirms, was formed and then continually replenished and sustained by the earliest memories of the light, sound, rhythms, and pleasures that worked upon it. This imprint of memory occurred through experiencing an unforgettably intense corporeal witnessing of the "impossible" perfection of her physical surroundings. While she was finishing *Orlando*, and after one of her minor illnesses, she again affirms her understanding that subjectivity depends on the often involuntary and unconscious effects registered in the body: "Never was anyone so tossed up & down by the body as I am."[43]

Part of the sense of the freedom Woolf found in both private remembrance and in fictional biography – in contrast to the restriction of remaining bound to the facts of other people's lives—comes from the eros of her memories, and the satisfaction she finds in writing them down. Just as Roland Barthes reports that ideas give him a "flush of pleasure,"[44] Woolf discloses a "flush of pleasure" in the act of remembering her ideations of the past. The past is all at once representative of pleasure, a discoverable and retrievable materiality, and a satisfying erotically charged object. This posture toward the past also holds true in Woolf's novels, and during the climactic party scene of *Mrs. Dalloway* Clarissa cries out and then is ignited into bodily heat and excitement when she unexpectedly finds that the friend and near-lover of her youth, Sally Seton, is in attendance: " 'I can't believe it!' she cried, kindling all over with pleasure at the thought of the past."[45] In his early essay, "Screen Memories," which some critics have taken to be a "screen" for Freud's own self-analysis, Freud, too, describes a deeply pleasurable component in recalling distant memories: "It seems, moreover, as though the recollection of the remote past is in itself facilitated by some pleasurable motive: *forsan et haec olim meminisse juvabit* ['Some day, perhaps, it will be a joy to remember even these things.']"[46] Like T. S. Eliot's comments in "Reflections on Contemporary Poetry" about the pleasures of "intimacy" required to commune with the past of literary history (brought into the fold of the personal through the labor of erotic cathection), Woolf turns to memory's reification of past delight as a crucial component for experiencing the plenitude of the present. This is not done merely to repress or displace the past's painful elements, but because Woolf, like Eliot, perceived the past as a still-living body and materiality which one was charged – ethically and even politically – with avowing and remaking in order to find the new.

CITATION AND FORGETTING: THE CASE OF WOOLF AND FREUD

If we turn for a moment to Freud's formulations of memory, which are some of the most central to our period, and with which I argue that Woolf had more familiarity than is generally assumed, we see that Woolf and Freud shared several preoccupations. Both writers had what Freud has termed a "special interest" in discerning the "content" of the "earliest memories of childhood," and in finding a typology for them as a means to decipher the relations between unconscious and conscious experiences, dispositions, fantasies, and motivations.[47] Both Woolf and Freud privilege early childhood memory as the blueprint of our later psychic life, while they concur that what often makes its way into memory are ostensibly minor experiences whose content comes to be charged with the metaphorics and fantasies that come to structure the psyche. While Freud does argue that "the most frequent content of the first memories of childhood are on the one hand occasions of fear, shame, physical pain, etc., and on the other hand important events such as illnesses, deaths, fires, births of brothers and sisters, etc,"[48] he goes on to delineate a theory about the major significance of ostensibly minor experiences from childhood, which operate as essential keys to unraveling the workings of the psyche. He suggests that most childhood memories are merely "screens" for what actually happened: "It may indeed be questioned whether we have any memories at all *from* our childhood: memories *relating* to our childhood may be all that we possess. Our childhood memories show us our earliest years not as they were but as they appeared at the later periods when the memories were aroused."[49] In a later essay of 1910, "Leonardo da Vinci and a Memory of his Childhood," he takes this even further to propose that "generally speaking they [childhood memories] cannot be sharply distinguished from phantasies."[50]

In "A Sketch of the Past," which might be understood as Woolf's manual for reading memory, Woolf remembers mostly episodes that Freud would have categorized as "inessential," but which nevertheless work as foundational and formative indices of psychic development. Instead of recollecting her brother Adrian's birth when she was nearly two, for example, when pinpointing her "first memory" she remembers

> red and purple flowers on a black ground – my mother's dress; and she was sitting either in a train or in an omnibus, and I was on her lap. I therefore saw the flowers she was wearing very close; and can still see purple and red and blue, I think, against the black; they must have been anemones, I suppose. Perhaps we were going to St Ives. (64)

Even in this simple description, she dramatizes the layers of anamnesis that so intrigued Freud. Her mother is first evoked through a double metonymic distancing and imaging (of the pattern of "flowers," and then of her "dress"); the memory is of transit and a certain liminality; she qualifies her memory with phrases like "I think," "perhaps," and "suppose," indicating an awareness of the instability of early memory; and she adds a supplemental name to the flowers which she clearly appended after the memory's formation, perhaps in the act of writing it down: "they must have been anemones."

In Woolf's fiction we find Freud everywhere, and her texts are full of both direct and indirect references to his ideas. To give only a few examples, we might think of the Oedipal concerns of *To the Lighthouse*, with James's recurring phantasies about killing his father – "had there been an axe handy, or a poker, any weapon that would have gashed a hole in his father's breast and killed him, there and then, James would have seized it";[51] we might also consider the ways in which Woolf borrows psychoanalytic language in *A Room of One's Own* in phrases like "subconscious intelligence" and "emotional light," as she playfully suggests she will "adopt the Freudian theory" to solve the question of "Professor von X's" violence;[52] in *Mrs. Dalloway* she gives a scathing portrait of the psychiatrist, Sir William Bradshaw – the "ghostly helper, the priest of science" who charges a "very large fee" for his advice[53] – who dramatically fails in "curing" Septimus Smith of what ails him, whether this is shell shock or his repressed homosexuality. However, despite such invocations of contemporary psychoanalytic practice and theory, and despite the resonances between her approaches to childhood memory and Freud's, Woolf was deeply ambivalent about Freud, and until the last two years of her life she claimed she had had no exposure to his writings.

Woolf insists in both her diary and "A Sketch of the Past" that she read Freud for the first time in late 1939 – quite strikingly just two months after his death in London, and nearly a year after she had met him in Vienna where he had given her "a narcissus" and they had had a "difficult talk" that she records in her journal. It was about "Hitler. Generation before the poison will be worked out. About his books. Fame? I was infamous rather than famous. didn't [*sic*] make £50 by his first book."[54] In December of that year she writes, "Began reading Freud last night; to enlarge the circumference. to [*sic*] give my brain a wider scope: to make it objective; to get outside. Thus defeat the shrinkage of age. Always take on new things. Break the rhythm &c."[55] Then, six months later, while composing "A Sketch of the Past" in June 1940, she *again* states that she had just read Freud "for the first time":

> when Nessa for instance revives the memory of Wednesday and its weekly books, I still feel come over me that old frustrated fury.
>
> But in me, though not in her, rage alternated with love. It was only the other day when I read Freud for the first time, that I discovered that this violently disturbing conflict of love and hate is a common feeling; and is called ambivalence. (108)

Can a December evening six months earlier be "the other day"? Why does she write twice that she is reading Freud for the first time?

Most critics still operate on the assumption that Woolf had virtually no knowledge of Freud before she met him in 1939. Even Elizabeth Abel's incisive book, *Virginia Woolf and the Fictions of Psychoanalysis*, sidesteps the issue of Woolf's knowledge of Freud, and merely points out that Woolf was in close contact with the psychoanalytic movement, at least by the mid 1920s: "Klein delivered her 1925 lectures at 50 Gordon Square, the home of Woolf's brother and sister-in-law, Adrian and Karin Stephen, who were both approaching the completion of their psychoanalytic training . . . 'Next door' (by her own account) in Tavistock Square, Virginia was 'making up' *To the Lighthouse*." Woolf had frequent contact with her brother and her sister-in-law, and, as Abel suggests, "it seems extremely likely that the lectures were discussed."[56] We might also note that by November 1936 Woolf even had a personal shorthand for psychoanalysis, "p.a.", which she represents as a respite from the more usual conversations about politics: "A good deal of p[sycho].a[nalysis]. talked; & I liked it. A mercy not always to talk politics."[57]

Woolf, though, was not merely "exposed" to psychoanalytic ideas. As early as 1920 she was confident enough in her understanding of Freud to write a review essay for the *Times Literary Supplement* on John

Davys Bereford's new novel, *An Imperfect Mother*, that she chose to entitle "Freudian Fiction." In the piece we find rather learned critiques of Freud's "new psychology" in relation to the contemporary novel, with Woolf employing terms and phrases like "unconsciously," "conscious," "unacknowledged passion," "diagnosis," and "cases" to allusively convey Freud's basic apparatus. She does admit to Freud's major cultural influence on the early twentieth-century psyche, noting that "we . . . are conscious of a division of mind which twenty or even ten years ago could hardly have afflicted our predecessors," but she goes on with an accompanying protest: "Yes, says the scientific side of the brain, that is interesting; that explains a great deal. No, says the artistic side of the brain, that is dull and has no human significance whatsoever."[58] Her rejection of his method, we might observe, nevertheless invokes the Freudian notions of a "division of mind" which she has just recognized. Ultimately she finds fault with both Freud and Beresford by deeming the novel an aesthetic "failure" precisely because "all the characters have become cases . . . In becoming cases they have ceased to be individuals."[59]

Woolf also tells Molly MacCarthy in 1924 – shortly before Melanie Klein gave her lectures at Gordon Square – that she read Freud while typesetting the *International Psychoanalytic Library*, published by her Hogarth Press:

> I shall be plunged in publishing affairs at once; we are publishing all Dr Freud, and I glance at the proof and read how Mr A. B. threw a bottle of red ink on to the sheets of his marriage bed to excuse his impotence to the housemaid, but threw it in the wrong place, which unhinged his wife's mind, – and to this day she pours claret on the dinner table. We could all go on like that for hours; and yet these Germans think it proves something – besides their own gull-like imbecility.[60]

Are we to imagine that Woolf somehow managed *not* to read Freud while she was typesetting his writings? What then is called reading? Are we to think that she worked at her own press with the same degree of attentiveness to the meaning of the script as the illiterate typesetters for Shakespeare's quartos and folio? Not at all. In this piece of correspondence – that is left out of the discussions of Woolf and Freud that I have seen – she discloses that she had "read" Freud fifteen years before she claims such knowledge in 1939.

Woolf's rendition of the Freudian story of sexual impotence that she was typesetting diverges in telling ways from the scene Freud recounts.

Freud analyzes the episode in "Obsessive Actions and Religious Practices," where he describes an "obsessive action" of a married woman:

> She would run out of her room into another room in the middle of which there was a table. She would straighten the table-cloth on it in a particular manner and ring for the housemaid. The latter had to come up to the table, and the patient would then dismiss her on some indifferent errand. In the attempts to explain this compulsion, it occurred to her that at one place on the table-cloth there was a stain, and that she always arranged the cloth in such a way that the housemaid was bound to see the stain. The whole scene proved to be a reproduction of an experience in her married life which had later on given her thoughts a problem to solve. On the wedding-night her husband had met with a not unusual mishap. He found himself impotent, and "many times in the course of the night he came hurrying from his room into hers" to try once more whether he could succeed. In the morning he said he would feel ashamed in front of the hotel housemaid who made the beds, and he took a bottle of red ink and poured its contents over the sheet; but he did it so clumsily that the red stain came in a place that was very unsuitable for his purpose.[61]

In Freud's version the husband has no name (Woolf's "A. B." could possibly signify a minor stab at Arnold Bennett – a contemporary realist writer whom Woolf disdained in "Mr. Bennett and Mrs. Brown"), there is no claret, and Freud gives his description in an inverse: he describes the woman's obsessive action first, and only explains its rootedness in the failed consummation after he has established her irregular behavior. Woolf, on the contrary, begins by relating the cause, and ends by describing the symptoms. It seems that Woolf had sufficient ambivalence for Freud that she wished first to revise him, and then to forget that she had even read him. Entirely forgetting the act, though, not to mention obliterating the content of what she read, is unlikely for Woolf, who was deeply concerned with the indestructibility of the past.

It turns out that Woolf's ambivalence to psychoanalysis was so intense that she was willing to deny her knowledge of Freud's writings openly. When she finally attests to reading him, she only does so after his death, as though she needed him to be of the past before she could grapple freely with his ideas. And, in another intriguing turn, by the time Woolf admits to encountering his work, her reading becomes absolutely ravenous, and her reading notebooks are filled with observations on his texts through 1939 and 1940. In the "first" week of reading him she describes the undertaking by way of a metaphor of incorporation: "(I'm gulping up Freud)."[62] The phrase echoes – with rhyme, assonance, and a tinge of onomatopoeia – her critical 1924 comment about the "gull-like imbecility" of "these Germans." In her 1924 comment Freud is likened to a stupid nuisance of a bird that cannot get enough of its own croaking, though in (re)reading him Woolf silently and greedily imbibes a rather palatable Freud.

Uncannily enough, by the time she writes "A Sketch of the Past" Woolf is ready to make an analogy between her writing process and that of psychoanalytic treatment. I have drawn attention to the ways in which Woolf so often figures recollection, even of what she once found painful, as a vehicle of solace. In one of the few instances in her oeuvre where Woolf writes of finding relief from memory, she situates this sensibility of relief within the context of the overriding "respite," "holiday," and "refresh[ment]" of writing memory. That is, she performatively encodes the ambivalent, dialectical bind between the pleasures of returning to past time (May 1895, for example), and the freedom she discovers in the concomitant unleashing of long-held mnemonic pressures (involving unmet desire). Remembrance in this way is doubly pleasurable: it allows a needful revisitation to the scene of the past and simultaneously releases the need to return again. In "A Sketch of the Past" she describes the freeing-up process she discovered in fictionally writing out the trauma of losing her parents. While composing *To the Lighthouse* she ceased to be "obsessed" by her mother: "I no longer hear her voice; I do not see her. I suppose that I did for myself what psycho-analysts do for their patients. I expressed some very long felt and deeply felt emotion. And in expressing it I explained it and then laid it to rest" (81). More than a decade earlier, she had written in her diary, "I was obsessed by them both [father and mother] unhealthily; & writing of them was a necessary act."[63] In "A Sketch of the Past" Woolf – seeking to understand this purging effect – also proposes that

> just as I rubbed out a good deal of the force of my mother's memory by writing about her in *To the Lighthouse*, so I rubbed out much of his [father's] memory there too. Yet he obsessed me for years. Until I wrote it out, I would find my lips moving; I would be arguing with him; raging against him; saying to myself all that I never said to him. (108)

These instances give rather good descriptions of Freud's "talking cure." Woolf may not have literally talked to an analyst, but by verbalizing her feelings for her mother and father – allowing them to meet poetic language and creative expression – and therefore taking away the "force" of their memory, she is implicitly agreeing with Freud's insistence on abreaction, and on the primacy of "remembering, repeating, and working through" for processing the hurt of the past.

"MOMENTS OF BEING"/HERMENEUTICS

Virginia Woolf's fictional and autobiographical writings attest to her conviction that modernist avant-garde literary efforts required a mnemonic awareness precisely because writing depends on and is constituted by recalling "moments of being" which delineate the most ponderous traces of the past. Besides highlighting the therapeutic aspect of writing out the past, in her memoir Woolf is keen to diagnose her reading methods vis-à-vis past time. And, as she queries especially what types of experience become the material of memory, she comes closer to piecing together a "philosophy" about time in relation to writing and ontology than she does anywhere else. She resolves that memory stems from what she calls "moments of being" – instances of heightened consciousness not unlike Joyce's "epiphanies," or Wordsworth's "spots of time." Woolf's description of "moments of being" follows in a tradition of separating what is exceptional in terms of being and experience from that which is only habitual or unconscious. In the 1805 version of *The Prelude* Wordsworth explores the influence of "spots of time" on his memory. Here, like Woolf, he uses the term "trace" to refer to history and memory:

> How shall I trace the history, where seek
> The origin of what I then have felt?
> Oft in those moments such a holy calm
> Did overspread my soul, that I forgot
> That I had bodily eyes, and what I saw
> Appeared like something in myself, a dream,
> A prospect in my mind.[64]

Asking what method he should employ to rediscover the fleeting feeling of "the visionary power"[65] of defining moments in youth, Wordsworth's "spots of time" – or "moments" of "such a holy calm" – offer a spiritual, mystic glimpse into the nature of things. Simultaneously, though, he affirms that his own mind is central in creating these moods and perceptions: our consciousness creates our experience.

Joyce's epiphanies just as clearly link epistemology with ontology by marking a distinction between a kind of unilluminated, everyday reality, and experience that is infused with heightened perception. In *Stephen Hero*, the original manuscript version of what would later evolve into *A Portrait of the Artist as a Young Man* (1916), Stephen Daedalus (changed to Dedalus in *Portrait*) overhears a conversation between a "drawling" "Young Lady," and a "Young Gentleman," barely able to utter a repeated

"I" in response to her stuttering statement, "I was . . . at the . . . cha . . . pel . . ."[66] Stephen thinks of "collecting many such moments together in a book of epiphanies. By an epiphany he meant a sudden spiritual manifestation, whether in the vulgarity of speech or of gesture or in a memorable phase of the mind itself."[67] Further associating epiphany with a desire to write out memory he continues: "He believed that it was for the man of letters to record these epiphanies with extreme care, seeing that they themselves are the most delicate and evanescent of moments."[68] In *Portrait* Joyce omits this detailed delineation of epiphany and uses the device without naming it as such. When Stephen has his most famous epiphany that is predicated on hearing the sound of his name conjugated in Greek, "Stephanos Dedalos!," and on the arresting apparition of a young "seabird" woman standing in midstream, Joyce writes,

> Her image had passed into his soul for ever and no word had broken the holy silence of his ecstasy . . . A wild angel had appeared to him, the angel of mortal youth and beauty, an envoy from the fair courts of life, to throw open before him in an instant of ecstasy the gates of all the ways of error and glory.[69]

As with Woolf's "moments of being," a feeling of extreme pleasure – even "ecstasy" – often accompanies epiphanies, and they grant intensified knowledge about one's state of being in the world. Each of the three writers describes what we might call visionary experience, insisting on the fleetingness of these intense feelings, and on a concomitant desire to preserve some essential truth about these moments through textuality.

Woolf's "moments of being" occur when one receives an emotional blow analogous to a physical "shock" that disrupts the ordinary flow of perception. This "shock" pierces through the "cotton wool" of everyday "non-being" ("Sketch," 72) to offer a brief moment of illumination in which we are suddenly conscious of our ontology – and, as Wordsworth phrases it – "see into the life of things"[70]: a moment in which we know that we are. What is more, in a fascinating turn, Woolf claims that "the shock-receiving capacity is what makes me a writer. I hazard the explanation that a shock is at once in my case followed by the desire to explain it" (72). Such a crashing, such a rupture, asks to be put "into words" – both "to make it real," and to "make it whole" (72). The material of memory and the material of writing are thus spun from the same thread. These "shocks" make a mark on time and memory, asking to be explained and even contained via writing and narration to ease their unexpected disturbance. Writing therefore occurs as a response to being, while being itself is experienced most fiercely in the fleetingness of epiphanic time.

In "A Sketch of the Past" Woolf also paints a poignant picture of how writing the past constitutes both the possibility for healing and the source of what she calls the "real." Her idea of the "real" has a great deal to do with the letter, and with its relationship to being, and we might consider it in relation to Lacan's notoriously enigmatic notion of the Real as, in Anthony Wilden's terms, "not synonymous with external reality, but rather with what is real for the subject."[71] After explaining the "sledgehammer force of the blow" of "exceptional moments" involving, at two extremes, either "horror," or a positive, aesthetic, sensual intensity, Woolf writes that the "blow" she receives during "moments of being"

> is or will become a revelation of some order; it is a token of some *real* thing behind appearances; and I make it *real* by putting it into words. It is only by putting it into words that I make it *whole*; this wholeness means that it has lost its power to hurt me; it gives me, perhaps because by doing so I take away the pain, a great delight to put the severed parts together. Perhaps this is the strongest pleasure known to me. It is the rapture I get when in writing I seem to be discovering what belongs to what. (72, my emphasis)

The "real" exists both "behind appearances," as though it were a secret, hidden from everyday view, empirically inaccessible in all but the most intense moments, and it is simultaneously what Woolf fashions for herself with language. In this formulation, transcribing or translating experience into words is the means through which a trace of the "real" becomes actualized and "whole," as Woolf articulates a theory of experience where the written word not only marks but makes reality. The word thus repeats what has been indistinctly perceived, and it is precisely this repetition that brings existence, proper, to prior experience. No mere echo, transcription, or train of signifiers, language in this way is necessary to the very condition of being and knowing. For Woolf, a "real" exists, always, somewhere, as though it were associated with place, but for the most part we are unable to access or perceive it, unless it is through memory: certain moments from the past "can still be more real than the present" (67).

Still later in "A Sketch of the Past," Woolf extends her argument to propose that memories, or, as she sometimes prefers to term them, "scenes" from the past, "would not survive so many ruinous years unless they were made of something permanent; that is a proof of their 'reality' " (142). As before, she attempts to give materiality to the intangibility of events, and memory is what enables this transformation of events to the permanent. She even pushes her theory of the tangibility, touchability, and physicality of the past to imagine, in 1939, that technology will one day help one to access the still-existing past:

> is it not possible – I often wonder – that things we have felt with great intensity have an existence independent of our minds; are in fact still in existence? And if so, will it not be possible, in time, that some device will be invented by which we can tap them? I see it – the past – as an avenue lying behind; a long ribbon of scenes, emotions. There at the end of the avenue still, are the garden and the nursery. Instead of remembering here a scene and there a sound, I shall fit a plug into the wall; and listen in to the past. I shall turn up August 1890. I feel that strong emotion must leave its trace; and it is only a question of discovering how we can get ourselves again attached to it, so that we shall be able to live our lives through from the start. (67)

The past is physical in Woolf; it is a materiality that persists. And she wants to probe even further, to find out, "made of what?"[72] The past in this respect is all at once tangible, accessible, and infinitely desirable – a never-quite-lost object that lends itself to celebration rather than mourning because it exists eternally on the brink of an infinite (perhaps phantasmatic) promise of a retrievability that would confer pure presence.

Past time itself does not fade and flicker – as memory does – but, like the atomic substructure of everything, is made of substantial matter that can neither be created nor destroyed. To retrieve the matter of memory, we must simply (re)discover the correct "trace" of emotion to reconnect ourselves to the past and make it again conscious to the present. In its spatial sense the past is outstretched behind us in a logical sequence: it is an "avenue" along which we have traveled. A little more than a decade earlier Woolf had used a similar metaphor in *Orlando*: "she reviewed, as if it were an avenue of great edifices, the progress of her own self along her own past."[73] Part of memory's function for Woolf, then, is to create an order of things by imposing a sequential and linear quality to the movement of what has been. But this is not all. In her technological dream in "A Sketch of the Past" Woolf envisions a future utopian technology through which we will be able to shorten the distance not only between *places* – as the automobile, the airplane, the telephone, and the radio had done during her lifetime – but also between *times*.

Ann Banfield proposes that Woolf turned to philosophers like Russell, Whitehead, Moore, and Hume to help her wrestle with her own queries about ontology – " 'Subject and object and the nature of reality' " is the exemplary quotation Banfield chooses from *To the Lighthouse* – arguing that Woolf shared a wish with these male philosophers to understand epistemology and ontology through logic.[74] We might also add that

Woolf placed faith in a certain logic of scientific and technological progress to imagine a future in which the "new" technology might, paradoxically, help take us back to the past. Our future could give us the gift of knowing history. Woolf's technological phantasy in some senses echoes a more general modernist obsession with the dialectic and dialogue between the new and its histories that I have been exploring. Just as modernism was writing for its future, insisting repeatedly on its radical newness, pushing styles and signatures to their futurity – and distilling this inclination into the dazzling simplicity of Pound's rallying cry, "make it new" – it did so while ceaselessly looking backward to cultural and personal memory as the material of its poetic and fictional inscriptions.

Writing memory is not only a pleasurable and healing turn to "the real," but Woolf also claims an ethical dimension to such mnemonic testimony. Rather than "learning to do something that will be useful if war comes" she feels that "by writing [her memoir] I am doing what is far more necessary than anything else" (73). Her insistent return to writing as *necessity* (akin to Freud's *ananke*) means that her modernist vision of writing time held an awareness of itself in which the moment of the modern – the "new" – was broadened, enlarged, and even brought to life through the confrontation with anteriority and immediacy. She is not alone in this gesture. Modernist writers persistently wrote out a sense of their time as located at an interstice of labored and cherished remembering, meeting with desire-as-the-future, as they wrote equally for the present and the future, wanting to incorporate the past's bodiliness into the different malleability of the present.

Woolf's memoir and her novels are full of the "voluptuous[ ]" press of the past on the present. In July 1939, just when rumblings of another major war were beginning to be heard, she writes of the "peace" necessary to appreciate the fullness of past and present time together:

> The past only comes back when the present runs so smoothly that it is like the sliding surface of a deep river. Then one sees through the surface to the depths. In those moments I find one of my greatest satisfactions, not that I am thinking of the past; but that it is then that I am living most fully in the present. For the present when backed by the past is a thousand times deeper than the present when it presses so close that you can feel nothing else, when the film on the camera reaches only the eye. But to feel the present sliding over the depths of the past, peace is necessary. The present must be smooth, habitual. ("Sketch" 98)

This passage shows that for Woolf the past and the present are both *continuous and contiguous* with each other. The past runs into and beyond the present like a deep Heraclitan stream of time – which never repeats itself because, to phrase it sylleptically, neither we nor the river are ever the same – but the past is always present in the present. One "feels" the present as it "presses so close," though it requires the "back[ing]" of the past to experience most fully the depths of the moment at hand. As Avrom Fleishman suggests, her "awareness" of the "current of the past . . . creates not an estrangement from the present but a heightened sense of its reality."[75] Or, we might say that for Woolf the still-present plenitude of the past is *life-giving.*

In its materiality memory is no mere lapidary object whose inscriptions elegantly attest to its fixability. Neither memory nor time is ever fixable. Given *moments* are certainly identifiable and locatable by virtue of their pure existential facticity, but the ways in which we think about such instances always lie open to revisions and retellings. For Woolf, memory thus consists of a potent mixture of the objective and the subjective. Memory is impressed first on the body and the psyche, leaving its tint and trace, and only second as script and text, to aid in its preservation. The mind and its written artifacts become living members of a fully vital archive whose ethics involve an ongoing instauration of the past so that it may communicate to and with a future. We might say with Paul Veyne that the " 'museum piece' is a complex notion bringing together beauty, authenticity, and rarity; neither an aesthete, nor an archaeologist, nor a collector will in his raw state make a good curator . . . the historian, by contrast, is neither a collector nor an aesthete; beauty does not interest him, nor does rarity. Only the truth does."[76]

In her writings of the past Virginia Woolf presents us with a version of Bergson's modernist "matter of memory," proposing, like Bergson, a radical interpenetration of the subject with the object she or he recalls. Memory for Bergson, as I have suggested, is "the intersection of mind and matter," where matter is "*the aggregate of images,*" and mind is the vehicle of perception.[77] Memory is both formed and (re)activated where perception and the exterior world meet. Bergson asks, "does not the fiction of an isolated material object imply a kind of absurdity, since this object borrows its physical properties from the relations which it maintains with all others?"[78] Objects and subjects do not merely coexist, but blend together through the codependency of their quantum mechanics: the "two acts, perception and recollection, always interpenetrate each other, are always exchanging something of their substance as by a process of endosmosis."[79]

TO THE LIGHTHOUSE: HEALING TRAUMA/WRITING THE PAST

In her 1927 novel, *To the Lighthouse*, Woolf again proposes in a number of ways that memory and desire are inextricably bound together. First, in the novel's movement, which follows the unraveling, over a period of more than a decade, of a failed promise to go "to the lighthouse," Woolf avers that even in the literalization of a desire for futurity as place, telos, and destination, desire discloses the deep influence of memory. Such a desire involves moving backward and forward at once, remembering while one is driven to meet a long-delayed future act. In the novel's progression James's initial desire to travel to the lighthouse dissipates by the last section, only to be taken over by Mr. Ramsay in a redemptive effort to address, and perhaps fix, failures of the past. The voyage thus enacts a (re)turn to a childhood object of phantasy as place (the lighthouse), as Woolf constructs an allegory of love, repetition, and revisitation that proposes every voyage is a return, every going is a coming, and that we may only arrive when we recognize the fact of our return. Eliot offers a similar message in "Little Gidding" when he writes, "We shall not cease from exploration /And the end of all our exploring / Will be to arrive where we started /And know the place for the first time."[80]

As with *Orlando*, Woolf blends fiction with life writing in *To the Lighthouse* to create an autobiographical portrait. This time she worries that she relies so greatly on her personal experiences that the book's correspondences with "real life" would be too obvious. She confesses in her diary that she "felt rather queer, to think how much of this [her parents] there is in To the Lighthouse [*sic*], & how all these people will read it & recognise poor Leslie Stephen & beautiful Mrs Stephen in it."[81] Hermione Lee claims that "Any display of naked autobiography is carefully suppressed" in Woolf's writing, noting that Woolf frequently remarked on her discomfort with personal exposure.[82] It is true that when *Three Guineas* was about to appear in 1938 Woolf writes in her diary, "I'm uneasy at taking this role in the public eye – afraid of autobiography in public."[83] Even still, she admits in the same entry (in terms that sound strikingly similar to her comments about the healing effects of writing about her mother in *To the Lighthouse*) that such self-referential writing provides a useful discharge of emotion: "the fears are entirely outbalanced (this is honest) by the immense relief & peace I have gained, & enjoy this moment. Now I am quit of that poison & excitement."[84] Despite her occasional protestations, then, Woolf constantly wrote a kind of modernist autobiography that concealed the personal with highly recognizable masks.

To the Lighthouse explores what it means to wish for the presence – a *re-presentation* that involves both *re-presencing* and *representing* presence – of the irretrievable by rigorously and attentively mapping the longing friends and family feel for the dead, thereby opening an archive of both melancholia and healing. In this way the novel functions as an "elegy" for Mrs. Ramsay and her real-life correlative, Woolf's mother, Julia Stephen – both mourning and honoring the psychic evolution that ensues in the wake of an absent maternal. Of course "elegy" was the term Woolf herself had applied to the project. In 1925, just before she began composing *To the Lighthouse*, Woolf invited her half-sister's widower, Jack Hills, to dinner, and they spoke about the general subject of "biography," as well as about the "autobiography" that she claimed she wanted to write. Recording the conversation in her diary, Woolf muses, "(But while I try to write, I am making up 'To the Lighthouse' – the sea is to be heard all through it. I have an idea that I will invent a new name for my books to supplant 'novel.' A new – by Virginia Woolf. But what? Elegy?"[85] She abruptly ends her diary entry for the day there, though her frustration with the limits of the term "novel" persisted. Nearly three years later she writes, "I doubt I shall ever write another novel after O[*rlando*]. I shall invent a new name for them."[86] Then in the following year, when she was beginning to draft *The Waves*, she writes in her diary, "Autobiography it might be called."[87] These questions about the limits of genre return us to her dream that she might "revolutionise biography in a night" during the composition of *Orlando*.[88] Her experimental stylistics demanded "the new," but this new was mediated by frequent turns to the elegiac.

To the Lighthouse opens with a quick shift from the mother's affirmative (" 'Yes, of course' ") to a subjunctive (" 'if it's fine tomorrow' "), followed by a future qualifier (" 'But you'll have to be up with the lark' ").[89] Mrs. Ramsay's shifts of mood and voice reflect the tension between her maternal desire to fulfill James's wish to go to the lighthouse, and her knowledge that this desire will be frustrated in the case of inclement weather, or in the case of the father's "No." Through its three sections the text then explores the psychic effects of such a promise, the (male) resistance to the promise, and the aftereffects of its failed actualization. James's intense desire for the trip makes itself felt through the novel as a muffled drama of desire interrupted. On the first page, when his mother endows the trip with real possibility – the mother's authorization for what would remain stuck, for ten years, as a childhood phantasy – her words cause even the most ordinary objects (a cut-out "picture of a refrigerator") to be "fringed with joy" (3). Such "heavenly bliss" at the prospect of desire realized is then indefinitely suspended and the narrative sequence never arrives at the next day. The promise is unachieved first because of a paternal halt caused by Mr. Ramsay's devastating " 'But' " (4) that dashes James's "bliss" (3) when Mr. Ramsay claims he can foretell the future: " 'it won't be fine' " (4). Mr. Ramsay's younger protegé, Charles Tansley, "the atheist," then mimics the father's language of negation with what seems to be a compulsive delight, enacted in the context of a suggestively homosocial bond between him and Mr. Tansley: " 'There'll be no landing at the Lighthouse tomorrow,' said Charles Tansley, clapping his hands together as he stood at the window with her husband" (7). While we never learn whether it was "fine" on the next day, Mrs. Ramsay's final utterance that we are privy to before her death enacts an echolalic reversal of her attempted promise to her son. This time she speaks the phrase to her husband, and it is still framed with an affirmative: " 'Yes, you were right. It's going to be wet tomorrow. You won't be able to go' " (124). The promise is then more irrevocably broken by Mrs. Ramsay's unforeseeable death – the mother who had been the condition of possibility for the promise in the first place.

Though the text is initially structured and set in motion with a spoken promise about the future, we soon realize that this teleological structure will dismantle itself. The titles of the novel's three parts, "The Window," "Time Passes," and "The Lighthouse," propel and support the novel's chronological sequence by dividing time roughly into three aspects of a continuous present. I'd like to think of the first section, "The Window," as signifying the aperture to the future, while it becomes what is remembered in the retrospective context of the book's trajectory; the second part, "Time Passes," works as a pure present, rendered with an acceleration of narrative time alongside a condensation of intensely lyrical prose; while we might think of the last section, "The Lighthouse," as the pure, realized and realizable, future. This seems simple, but what is interesting is that in this text the present is always anticipating its future while registering the materiality of the past, while the future finds its meaning in enacting a similar return. We end up with a tripartite template of temporality, with each aspect of past, present, and future often synchronically evoked as Woolf approaches a near-cubist depiction of time.[90]

After Part One – which already through its title, "The Window," proposes a kind of vantage outlook to both space and time – the text changes its focus from futurity to anteriority, from hoping for a trip to the lighthouse, to alternately remembering and repressing the past and its originary mother figure. The novel as a whole bears the pressure of answering to the intensely pure, willed, desiring "I" of James as a six-year-old boy. From the moment when James's desire – with all the profound metaphorical significance this yearning implies (we wonder if James does not want to go to the root of symbol or to the heart of metaphor itself in wanting to go "to the lighthouse") – is refused, his delighted fervor is transformed into a memory of thwarted desire. This initial desire becomes an emotive expression whose signification James will resist when his father tries to thrust its realization upon him belatedly, a decade later. Again, Woolf's project finds an echo in Eliot's *Four Quartets*:

> There is no end, but addition: the trailing
> Consequence of further days and hours,
> While emotion takes to itself the emotionless
> Years of living among the breakage
> Of what was believed in as the most reliable –
> And therefore the fittest for renunciation.[91]

The "years of living among the breakage," the decade in between the family's visits to Skye, take James to a place where he is ready to renounce his boyhood *want*: "He had made them come. He had forced them to come. In their anger they hoped that the breeze would never rise, that he might be thwarted in every possible way, since he had forced them to come against their wills . . . They hoped the whole expedition would fail" (163). Mr. Ramsay, though, apparently, remembers that the initial literality of James's longing was as material as the lighthouse, and as traversable as a short stretch of sea. In Slavoj Žižek's terms Mr. Ramsay's approach would be that of the melancholic: "Mourning is a kind of betrayal, the second killing of the (lost) object, while the melancholic subject remains faithful to the lost object, refusing to renounce his or her attachment to it."[92] Instead, though, I want to propose that we might think of James as having successfully undergone the work of mourning while still maintaining a sufficient loyalty to the lost ideation of his mother's lighthouse promise. He resists the paternal attempt to superimpose a reinvented passageway to his childhood dream, but the confrontation they undergo during the journey moves them, literally, to the new territory of a maturer relationality (both spatially and psychically).

As she proposes in *Orlando* and in "A Sketch of the Past," Woolf thus figures memory as reifiable and materializable – an always potent effect whose conscious and unconscious residues are re-ignited especially when faced with the intensity of approaching a long-held symbol bound up with the maternal, the ethics of the promise, and with the fabric of desire itself. When he is sailing to the lighthouse in the final section of the book, the now sixteen-year-old James recognizes in his seventeen-year-old sister's face a "look he remembered" of his mother when she had "surrendered" to Mr. Ramsay; this recollection of his parents' dialectic of domination and submission incites him to begin "to search among the infinite series of impressions which time had laid down, leaf upon leaf, fold upon fold softly, incessantly upon his brain; among scents, sounds; voices" (168-9). This depiction of memory as *leaves* persists, and nearly twenty pages later we find James ruminating on his ambivalent enchainment and enchantment with his father:

> there were two pairs of footprints only; his own and his father's. They alone knew each other. What then was this terror, this hatred? Turning back among the many leaves which the past had folded in him, peering into the heart of that forest where light and shade so chequer each other that all shape is distorted, and one blunders, now with the sun in one's eyes, now with a dark shadow, he sought an image to cool and detach and round off his feeling in a concrete shape. (184-5)

Time makes an imprint upon our minds; it operates palimpsestically to forge the matter of memory, "leaf upon leaf." And we might say that memory, concretized, does appear to James just as they enter into a strange proximity with the lighthouse that has lain for so long in imagination only. The lighthouse that comes into view as they approach in the boat – "He could see the white-washed rocks; the tower, stark and straight; he could see that it was barred with black and white; he could see windows in it; he could even see washing spread on the rocks to dry. So that was the Lighthouse, was it?" (186) – emerges as a solid, material object in contrast to the "silvery, misty-looking tower with a yellow eye" that had sat nestled among "leaves and flowers" of "that happy world" of his past (186). Both are the lighthouse, he quickly decides, as Woolf insists on leaving open the ethics of memory and immediate experience to their inherent pluralisms: "For nothing was simply one thing. The other Lighthouse was true too" (186).

Not only may memory be traced as a physical impression "folded" within, returned to as a material object, but in the middle of the novel Mrs. Ramsay imagines the past as something "sealed up" that one might return to through volition. During the climactic dinner party that occupies the exact center of the novel, Mrs. Ramsay takes brief moments out of her demanding role as orchestrator and unifier of the diverse needs of her guests to take respite in the past: "that dream land, that unreal but fascinating place, the Mannings' drawing-room at Marlow twenty years ago; where one moved about without haste or anxiety, for there was no future to worry about" (93). Paradoxically, when there was quantitatively the *most* future to think or worry about, the young would-be Mrs. Ramsay remembers no anxiety about what lay ahead. The suggestion repeats Woolf's romanticized sense that the past is an easier, happier time. In contrast, though, to Woolf's other claims about memory, Mrs. Ramsay momentarily qualifies the past as "unreal." It is, nevertheless, infinitely accessible, like "reading a good book again, for she knew the end of that story, since it had happened twenty years ago, and life, which shot down even from this dining-room table in cascades, heaven knows where, was sealed up there, and lay, like a lake, placidly between its banks" (93). Reminiscent of the violence of the present Woolf articulates most fully in *Orlando*, and of her phantasy in "A Sketch of the Past" of reconnecting to the still-existing plenitude of the past, Mrs. Ramsay designates anteriority as a placid and stable embalming of "life" that can be approached again without trepidation.

Lily Briscoe, the painter of the text, who might be read as a conflation of Woolf herself as a childless artist, and as a version of Woolf's sister, the painter Vanessa Bell, offers another sustained elegy for Mrs. Ramsay that complements Mr. Ramsay and the children's elegy-as-sea-voyage. In her relative geographic staticity, painting on the shore while the others travel, Lily recalls a moment of positivity when Mr. Tansley was less acerbic than usual: "this scene on the beach for example, this moment of friendship and liking – which survived, after all these years complete, so that she dipped into it to re-fashion her memory of him, and there it stayed in the mind affecting one almost like a work of art" (160). These "scene[s]" from the past – one of Woolf's preferred terms, as we recall – exist in the same sealed-off way that Mrs. Ramsay describes, and without what Eliot has called "breakage" in "The Dry Salvages," and they may be "dipped into" to re-inform memory. That is, the past exists for Lily as a pure historicity, "complete," whole, and entire, unlike the fragmentation and chaos of the yet-unremembered ongoing present, or the "splinters & mosaic" of identity that Woolf describes in her diary in September 1924.[93] Memory, then, is apropos art in its call to be revisioned. Memory can "re-fashion" the past by bringing new revelations to bear on the old material of what was, and, in the process, add the supplement of what we might call a *new truth of the present* that had not been accessible in the earlier context. Charles Tansley in this remaking is less brutal than we find him in the first section, as Woolf manages to convey that the passage of time means a shift in both the hermeneutics and poetics of experience. Indeed, the statement about the very active artistry of memory compels Lily to reiterate her analogy: " 'Like a work of art,' she repeated, looking from her canvas to the drawing-room steps and back again" (161). And, in a further mnemonic layering, while she contemplates the workings of memory she happens to be painting a scene from memory on her canvas – the very scene she already had to recall to mind at the dinner party, ten years earlier, moving the salt cellar to "remind herself to move the tree" (84-5). She thus ruminates on recollection as she paints while remembering already having remembered to score her canvas in a certain way. Lily has the same architecture and landscape before her, and even the position of her easel is identical, but she and the family members and visitors have either changed or vanished. Still, like Eliot's speaker in *The Waste Land*, who calls out to the shade of Stetson, she reinvokes the animation and presence of the dead by supplementing memory with a vocal appellation, calling to Mrs. Ramsay aloud: " 'Mrs. Ramsay! Mrs. Ramsay!' she repeated. She owed it all to her" (161).

The mixing of memory and desire is what finally prompts Mr. Ramsay to undertake his voyage to the lighthouse, years after his wife's death. It is his very physical demonstration of his love for Mrs. Ramsay – by finally being the one to surrender, to follow the letter of her " 'Yes,' " that opens the novel, her " 'of course, if it's fine tomorrow' " – that is the novel's most surprising elegy. Physically, he must travel to a place he had marked as forbidden in the past. Only in this passage across the water, which he undertakes calmly, almost passively, "reading with his legs curled under him" (183) while he allows James to do the sailing, is he able to realize his deceased wife's optimistic wish for her son's happiness. Elizabeth Abel rightly calls the ten-year interlude between visits to the Hebrides "the decade of suspended desire,"[94] and in the final segment desire returns. Initially in the final section, though, desire and memory have lost their organic link for James, who is the agent at the center of their coupling. But even James eventually comes around, as obedient to the dictates of love and remembrance as the sailboat is to his careful hand, so that in her outcome Woolf offers an intensely redemptive "vision" of familial healing, commensurate with Lily's revelation through painting.

By taking the trip to the lighthouse that was initially sanctioned by the mother, Mr. Ramsay, James, and Cam memorialize Mrs. Ramsay through action. In so doing, Woolf suggests that within the structure of repetition and fixation within which we inexorably exist there is a possibility (and even a promise) of redemption under which we live and under which our lives are endurable. It is by returning to the original *telos* of the mother's promise – the lighthouse as reified symbol, as physical landmark – albeit under changed conditions of experience, that not only James, but the entire family, are enabled to psychic progress. This also suggests that the logic of remembering consists in part of a desire to revisit the past as place: the lighthouse is the place that Mrs. Ramsay knew as the future, as promise, and as an object of comfort for her son. For Mr. Ramsay and the children to return there years later is to return to an object of Mrs. Ramsay's anticipation. It is thus to beget a future from the dead.

CHAPTER 7

Remembering what has "almost already been forgotten": where memory touches history

> It is, if you like, the unrolling of a spool, for there is no living being who does not feel himself coming little by little to the end of his span; and living consists in growing old. But it is just as much a continual winding, like that of thread into a ball, for our past follows us, becoming larger and larger with the present it picks up on its way; and consciousness means memory.
>
> Henri Bergson, "Introduction to Metaphysics"[1]

> [T]he past is beautiful because one never realises an emotion at the time. It expands later, & thus we don't have complete emotions about the present, only about the past. This struck me on Reading platform, watching Nessa & Quentin kiss, he coming up shyly, yet with some emotion. This I shall remember.
>
> Virginia Woolf, *Diary*, 18 March 1925[2]

> The past is literally blasted into consciousness with the Blitz in London.
>
> H.D., *Tribute to Freud*[3]

While Woolf argues for a fundamental indestructibility of the past, she also feared the powers and the contagion of cultural amnesia. As the First World War was coming to an end, and peace looked almost certain, she worried that "people will soon forget all about the war, & the fruits of our victory will grow as dusty as ornaments under glass cases in lodging house drawing rooms."[4] The specificity of her phrase, which moves from anticipating a loss and failure of memory about traumatic events to a simile about the generative – rather than expressly economic – "product" of war, tells us a good deal about Woolf's concerns with memory and forgetting that run through her work. Her simile tropes from the vitality of an event to the death of memory: she imagines that the still-fresh "fruits of victory" will transform into dusty, lifeless, frozen "ornaments," on display for travelers. Rather strikingly, Woolf's logic here laments a prospective death of memory even *before* the war has reached the closure that demands its remembrance. She worries the limits of memory *before* the armistice, attesting to her anxiety about a generalized cultural amnesia.[5] Life – what little life is left in a Europe devastated by millions of dead and permanently wounded, a Europe whose young "fruit" have been prematurely taken – will be transformed all too quickly into the banal showpieces of an embalmed, but not vital, capital "H" History. Bodies as such will cease to matter. Resembling instead the "wax figures" Woolf describes in "The Art of Biography," the signs of war's triumphant ending will only ever be paling substitutions that cannot properly attest to the sublimity of death: "the majority of Victorian biographies are like the wax figures now preserved in Westminster Abbey, that were carried in funeral processions through the street – effigies that have only a smooth superficial likeness to the body in the coffin."[6]

Nearly two months later, and still only one month after the armistice, Woolf confirms her earlier suspicion by observing that "The war is already almost forgotten."[7] From her point of view, the war's presence had ceased to be felt; its devastation, although only a few weeks old, had ceased properly to signify. The war would not be "already almost forgotten" if the populace felt connected to the war, not as history, but as memory – as an event intimately bound up with their own desires, aspirations, and subjectivities. This is a point Woolf will repeat in *Mrs. Dalloway* several years later, when Richard Dalloway moves through the London cityscape with a rare gift for Clarissa, "grasping his red and white roses together": "Really it was a miracle thinking of the war, and thousands of poor chaps, with all their lives before them, shovelled together, already half forgotten."[8] Fighting against cultural amnesia (like Eliot in *The Waste Land*, with his many appeals to memory's multiple guises) Woolf was already diagnosing a failure to incorporate the Great War into existing structures of cultural cognition.

This failure of memory has much to do with failures of language, representation, and knowability. In a diary entry just before the armistice, she claims "the mind doesn't do very much with it," asking herself, "was the whole thing too remote & meaningless to come home to one, either in action or in ceasing to act? Katherine Murry, whom I saw on Wednesday, inclines to think that most people have grasped neither war nor peace."[9] While Jean-François Lyotard names a loss of metanarratives as one of the hallmarks of *postmodernism*, we might also push this disjunction between intellection about culture and one's experience *in* that culture (which counts on a certain repression of the ungraspability of that culture's enigmas) at least to the modernist period.[10] Paul Fussell diagnoses a pervasive sense of cultural "loss" – as well as a loss of culture – after the First World War, and he even locates the origin of a number of ostensibly postmodern ailments in the war: "It might even be said that the current [late twentieth-century] devaluation of letterpress and even of language itself dates from the Great War."[11] Fussell's readiness to find a source for a narrative of decline is a bit suspect, but it does illustrate the ways in which the First World War has been understood to inaugurate a collapse in various codes of meaning.

While Woolf was noting the struggle in thinking the traumatic memory of a major international tragedy – a cognitive dissonance that would characterize much of the world's subsequent relation to a "global" past – it is significant that what she pinpoints as particularly susceptible to being forgotten is a kind of capital "H" historical event. Regarding contemporary political history, she writes in 1921,

> the Germans have gone back to Germany. People go on being shot & hanged in Ireland . . . The worst of it is the screen between our eyes & these [?] gallows is so thick. So easily one forgets it – or I do. For instance why not set down that the Maids of Honour shop was burnt out the other night? Is it a proof of civilisation to envisage suffering at a distance . . .?[12]

In *Orlando* she writes of the "impervious screen of the present,"[13] insisting once more on the extraordinary difficulties of knowing the present. Yet while major contemporary *historical* events are often threatened with being forgotten, or are even, indeed, forgettable in her work, *memory* – a historicity that has developed a meaningful relation to the subjective – falls decidedly into the category of the unforgettable. If we had to name what Woolf forgets (or claims to forget), we could say that at various important moments in her autobiographical writings she "forgets" the First World War, she "forgets" colonialism, and she "forgets" Freud. Of course she writes out all three of these in various forms as well. Septimus Smith in *Mrs. Dalloway* discloses the unforgettableness of the potent mixture of the Great War and desire through his stuttering inability to heal his psychic war wounds; Percival, the problematic silent "hero" of *The Waves*, dies while serving as a colonial officer in India; and we feel the presence of "the colonies" (especially India and Ceylon) in almost all of Woolf's novels. And, as I have been arguing, Woolf engages with versions of Freudian psychoanalysis everywhere in her novels, from the

Oedipal tensions in *To the Lighthouse* to the critique of the psychiatric profession in *Mrs. Dalloway.*

Thus, while Woolf despaired over the failures of cultural memory about the Great War she also participated in this faltering of memory. On 12 July 1919, two weeks after the Peace Treaty had been signed at Versailles, she writes, "In public affairs, I see I've forgotten to say that peace was signed; perhaps that ceremony was accomplished while we were at Asheham."[14] Circling back to imagine what she may have been doing at the moment of the signing, she seeks out a synchronous temporality as the binding glue to an event that otherwise remains at a remove – even to one who suffered through air raids, and despite Leonard's involvement with the problem of peace, through the League of Nations. In having failed to note the official end of the war by having failed to commemorate it in the pages of her personal diary, she reprimands herself for the bathos the war had come to signify. And though she "forgets" to write about the war, she repeatedly emphasizes this very forgetting.

Following the procession for the signing of the peace, for instance, Woolf relates the event in terms of a certain outsidedness – of deliberately missing the ceremony attached to the closure of war. Her description manifests distance and detachment from the occasion:

> One ought to say something about Peace day, I suppose, though whether its worth taking a new nib for that purpose I dont know. . . . Of course we did not see the procession. We have only marked the rim of refuse on the outskirts. Rain held off till some half hour ago. The servants had a triumphant morning. They stood on Vauxhall Bridge & saw everything. Generals & soldiers & tanks & nurses & bands took 2 hours in passing. It was they said the most splendid sight of their lives. Together with the Zeppelin raid it will play a great part in the history of the Boxall family. But I don't know – it seems to me a servants festival; some thing got up to pacify & placate "the people" – & now the rain's spoiling it; & perhaps some extra treat will have to be devised for them. Thats the reason of my disillusionment I think. There's something calculated & politic & insincere about these peace rejoicings. Moreover they are carried out with no beauty, & not much spontaneity [*sic*].[15]

Part of Woolf's response to the procession centers on its aesthetic failings, as though if it had been beautiful its contrived status would have been more easily forgiven. Still, she claims that people had said it was "the most splendid sight of their lives." Her critique of the celebration is at once classist in its disdain for the working-class element of the nationwide event (the sector of society who lost more numbers than any other), wryly conscious of the government's manipulation of the crowd's emotions, and startlingly removed from the historical moment as it had been officially conceived.

While the servants "saw everything," she claims that "we" (she and Leonard) "did not see." Her description shows, though, that while she may have missed a tedious procession that "took 2 hours in passing," she still participated in the moment at one remove by noting and "seeing" how others responded to it, registering the event with a certain care allied with an alienation from both her fellow Englishmen and the ceremony's historical citation. Her efforts at rendering memorialization are intimately linked with her sense of *writing time*, and of writing her present for future memory. She describes the parade with a paratactic phrase by moving from those high in command ("Generals"), to the bodies who fought the war ("soldiers"), to the technology of machines ("tanks"), the medical aides ("nurses"), and finally to the music that accompanied the moment. And as she records having missed the commemorative ceremony of the "Peace" (with *co*-mmemoration appropriately designating the togetherness and *withness* of such memory) she notes that this event will nevertheless "play a great part in the history of the Boxall family" – a name perhaps chosen for its echoic rhyme with "Vauxhall Bridge" upon which the servants stood. Woolf thus claims that a public display which helps to stake out the end of war – simultaneously to look back to re-member its (dis-membered) end, and to claim a new beginning of peacetime – is already imagined as a future aspect of a specifically familial history. Like the tangible coextensiveness of Sackville-West's aristocratic family lineage with the history of England in *Orlando*, Woolf points to the imbrication of the familial and the historical for the working classes.

This connection between individual bodies, families, and English history was an equation she sometimes felt did not apply to herself, and this might help to explain Woolf's status as something of an outsider in relation to the occasion of the Peace. In 1928, after attending a wedding in "the heart of England," she observes in her diary,

> history I felt; Cromwell; The Osbornes; Dorothy's sheperdesses singing: of all of whom Mr & Mrs Jarrad seem more the descendants than I am: as if they represented the unconscious breathing of England & L.[eonard] & I, leaning over the wall, were detached, unconnected. I suppose our thinking is the cause of this. We dont belong to any "class"; we thinkers: might as well be French or German. Yet I am English in some way [*sic*].[16]

Eight years later, in 1926, from the vantage point of retrospect, she reiterates that the war was productive of nothing but a vast desert, a kind of Eliotian, dry "waste land": "The war is now barren sand after all."[17] Recalling her earlier trope about the "fruits" of victory, implicit in Woolf's reasoning is a desire that the past should retain some remainder of its value for the psyche at the time; that especially the most violent chapter experienced by her generation ought to make something happen for the future. The Great War, though, failed as this marker of productivity, and thus disturbed the notion that had still held sway through the nineteenth century that sacrifices are necessary to noble (and still dreamable) endeavors like "development" or "progress." Rupert Brooke's highly romantic, idealizing, and nationalistic war poetry – "If I shall die, think only this of me: / That there's some corner of a foreign field / That is forever England"[18] – gave way to Wilfred Owen's and Siegfried Sassoon's radical and unforgiving realism as the sign of what the war had meant. It only did so, however, over Brooke's dead body.[19] The war was a staggering temporal disruption, cutting into the ways culture, collective history, and inheritance could be thought. It had been a war that sacrificed more than any had imagined possible, a war of attrition, a war that killed off nearly an entire European generation. Discovering itself as uncognizable, the war announced itself as an unfathomably destructive military and technological sublime that could no longer find a remotely adequate witnessing in the material of written histories.

Woolf actually tended to forget an awful lot about *events*, which might partly explain why she insisted on the necessary supplement of "writing time" by obsessively recording, almost as poetic reportage, thoughts and events in the hope of capturing some aspect of their passing. As we have seen above, she troubles the performance of public and national remembrance and citation, preferring a mode of memorialization that finds a greater authenticity in its unsought, spontaneous return to the past. Her own mode of memorialization works by accident, and Woolf embraces this haphazard nature of memory as one of its felicities. On 5 May 1919 she begins her diary entry: "The day mother died twenty something years ago. The smell of wreaths in the hall is always in the first flowers still; without remembering the day I was thinking of her, as I often do."[20] She then pronounces that such a coincidence of remembering her mother while forgetting the calendar – remembering without being prompted to do so – is "as good a memorial as one could wish."[21] A memorial that does not rely on the insistence of marked time to achieve its homage; an utterly genuine commemoration, and a form of involuntary memory that serendipitously coincides with filial duty. In her lifetime Woolf filled what have now become five large edited volumes of journals, as well as six volumes of letters, and she would frequently lament the passage of unmarked weeks, calling days that are not written about "lost days."[22] As early as 1897, when she was just fifteen, Woolf was already conscious of her reliance on writing to capture memory and time: "this diary has been neglected (owing to the disablement of my pen) & I cannot remember."[23]

In February 1922, she openly asks herself why she persists in keeping a diary. "Why do I trouble to be so particular with facts? I think it is my sense of the flight of time: so soon Towers Place will be no more; & twigs, & I that write. I feel time racing like a film at the Cinema. I try to stop it. I prod it with my pen. I try to pin it down."[24] The entry ends there. Using a simile of the high speed of the recently developed medium of the cinema – an unusual topic for her – Woolf imagines the mode of present "modernist" time as analogous to the rapidity of filmic time; a time that has spun slightly out of control, a time that is no longer "real time," to use a film studies term that puns marvelously on what is *real* about time. Her pen is her best tool for arresting the momentum of time's acceleration, catching actuality as narration to enunciate the truth of her day. Indeed, we might say, as Stanislaus Joyce said of his brother James Joyce, that Woolf was obsessed with the "steady flow of the past through the present."[25] We inhabit the present temporal location at all times, and yet Woolf keenly felt that she did not possess the facticity of her experience until it was narrated in the ledger of words that is her diary, or her letters, or novels. In a journal entry from 1921 she figures the words of her diary as small tokens gathered against the onslaught of time. Language as such becomes another materiality that jostles with the materiality of memory. Paradoxically, through the abstraction of language, semiotics, and symbol – what Jacques Lacan has termed the "defiles of the signifier," as I explore in chapter 3[26] – she believes she can make events more concrete and discrete. One of the reasons the present is more fragile for Woolf than the past is because it has not yet met the signifying system of an anterior representation. Once the present makes its way into narration she is able to operate on the (perhaps illusory) premise that she has made her present more secure by chronicling it as personal history. Words help trace, gather, and even capture time, while simultaneously broadening both temporality and the domain of experience by opening their emerging legibility to the play and remaking of textuality and fiction. Marking events helps to guard against forgetting them in the future, while writing and memory both enable a transformation of past events into a domain that approaches an ideation of permanence. Woolf's drive to record the past thus forms part of an ethics of memory; we might also say that she is centrally concerned with what Cathy Caruth has called "the unremitting problem of *how not to betray the past.*"[27] For Woolf, writing performs the labor of elegy while acceding to the responsibility of transforming one's present. Narration thus touches the events of history – whether personal or cultural – while such transliteration is responsible for creating a newly understandable symbolic order that the future will be able to receive. As Lynn Hunt suggests, history in this guise is an "ethical and political practice," and not only "an epistemology with a clear ontological status."[28]

WOOLF AS HISTORIAN

The effects of recollection and the remembered historical on the familial, the individual, and the communal are central subjects of almost every one of Woolf's novels, from *Jacob's Room* (1922), to *Mrs. Dalloway* (1925; originally titled "The Hours" in her drafts), *To the Lighthouse* (1927), *Orlando* (1928), *The Waves* (1931), *The Years* (1937), and *Between the Acts* (1941). Gillian Beer reads Woolf as having "a strong interest in history," proposing that " 'History,' almost in a textbook sense, is a recurrent theme in her work. *Orlando* jubilantly fantasizes the possibility of the self surviving history, looking different, gendered differently, but not much changed from century to century."[29] Beer continues with a rather odd formulation, arguing that in Woolf "History is stationary, inhabited by replaceable figures whose individuality is less than their community with other lives already lived."[30] Here I have to disagree, for history is hardly stationary in Woolf. On the contrary, Woolf presents the historical as the always-moving and always-changing temporal medium that human beings move through which demands a deliberate inscription. The contact between the dynamic poles of the cultural-historical, and the individual-in-and-as-history means history can never simply be summed up. For Beer to imagine that Woolf considered history as merely "a series of tableaux, a pageant"[31] is not to heed the fluid interpenetration of time and history, agency and narration, along with Woolf's sense that even the most trivial thoughts and movements make up the human and the historical.

Indeed, despite Woolf's occasional amnesia, on several occasions she expressed some desire to be a historian of sorts herself and she frequently complained that "History" is radically misrepresented in traditional modes of writing the past. After her self-conscious confessions about her own amnesiac failings vis-à-vis the public sphere, she goes on to outline an anti-amnesiac commitment to registering the *life* of history. In late 1919 she laments, "No one who has taken stock of his own impressions since 4 August 1914, can possibly believe that history as it is written closely resembles history as it is lived," asserting that unless we take a more active role in forming our historical self-understanding, "we have no right to complain if we are fobbed off once more with historians' histories."[32] Two years later, in 1921, she begins a diary entry with a sense of obligation to writing the current historical moment:

> I have been long meaning to write a historical disquisition on the return of peace; for old Virginia will be ashamed to think what a chatterbox she was, always talking about people, never about politics. Moreover, she will say, the times you lived through were so extraordinary. They must have appeared so, even to quiet women living in the suburbs. But indeed nothing happens at one moment rather than another. The history books will make it much more definite than it is. The most significant sign of peace this year is the sales.[33]

Woolf suggests here that in the "nothing happens" there is something to be told, and that there are other "sign[s]" to be read beyond the "event" as the privileged site of decipherability. Even the daily economic is part of the historically effaced, and she implicitly protests, as she will again in *A Room of One's Own*, that writing history ought to be more inclusive than it has (historically) been. A few months later she transcribes a conversation with Lytton Strachey, during which he had proposed that "History must be written all over again. Its all morality – & battles, I added" [*sic*].[34] In *A Room of One's Own* she rephrases this once again: "history is too much about wars; biography too much about great men."[35] Elena Gualtieri points out that

> for some time before she started writing *Melymbrosia* in 1908, her declared ambition was to write history rather than fiction, but a kind of history which she was striving to infuse . . . with the breath of living life rather than with the hard contours of facts . . . Traces of this unrealised project can be found scattered throughout Woolf's critical work.[36]

This idea remained with Woolf to the very end of her life, and in the autumn of 1940 she notes that while "blackberrying, I conceived, or remoulded, an idea for a Common History book – to read from one end of lit. including biog; & range at will, consecutively [*sic*]."[37]

When Woolf delivered her lectures to the women of Newnham and Girton Colleges, Cambridge, on "women and fiction" – lectures that are the blueprint for *A Room of One's Own* – she lamented the absence of women from history, and even from memory, deploring the fact that for women there was, in effect, no history of themselves. In *A Room of One's Own* she appeals to her audience to "re-write history, though I own that it often seems a little queer as it is, unreal, lop-sided; but why should they not add a supplement to history? calling it, of course, by some inconspicuous name so that women might figure there without impropriety?"[38] Aware of contemporary cultural prejudices, Woolf knew that even the act or the fact of women appearing in history might be construed as a sexual misdemeanor, as though to inscribe oneself in the eros of the past would be tantamount to subjecting women to an erotic narration, that would be "ambitious beyond my daring."[39] She imagines that history's "supplement" might just be the invaluable surplus of gender difference. Rather than seeking an idea of lost presence, this "supplement" would itself be the origin of a history that still would always be lacking, but which would labor to take notice of moments other than "battles" and "morality."

Woolf then points out that if one were to ask an elderly "respectably booted" woman on the street about her own personal past that extends to the "battle of Baclava" and "the birth of King Edward the Seventh," she would be able to give you little information:[40]

> And if one asked her, longing to pin down the moment with date and season, but what were you doing on the fifth of April 1868, or the second of November 1875, she would look vague and say that she could remember nothing. For all the dinners are cooked; the plates and cups washed; the children set to school and gone out into the world. Nothing remains of it all. All has vanished. No biography or history has a word to say about it. And the novels, without meaning to, inevitably lie.[41]

What is at stake in this vision of history is an early feminist lament for the effaced and the invisible that precedes 1970s, 1980s, and still-ongoing gestures of retrieval and valorization by half a century and more. Woolf's arguments depend on a positive relation between history and textuality, where the ontology of history requires the "supplement" of translation to become historically knowable. To capture time, to know time at all, it needs to be written; one needs to *write time*. This premise is repeated in different guises everywhere in Woolf's oeuvre. Her desires to plumb a different shade of meaning in syntactical, literary, and emotional repetitions, to relive (and relieve) her own past through rendering it as fiction, and to render such a mnemonics as intrinsic to the authenticity of desire, are all indivisible from her feminist politics. The yearning to make an inscription where there has formerly been only a blank, and to demand a space for the unwritten, therefore stand at the root of both her feminism and her impulses to think historiographically. As Merry Pawlowski proposes, we might even begin to think of Woolf as an early and groundbreaking "feminist historian."[42] Her frantic desires to write her time parallel her appeals to write a history replete with contradiction, difference (and *différance*), and obscurity.

It is time, then, that we think of Virginia Woolf not only as an author and feminist polemicist, but also as an important modernist thinker of time, memory, and history whose refusal to privilege the status of public event and moments of national or cultural display anticipates postmodernist revisionist histories. Mary Jacobus describes "Woolf's post-Impressionist experiments with time and memory" by comparing her to Berthe Morisot, arguing that Morisot, too, had the "ambition" to "*to capture something that passes.*"[43] Woolf's urge to write in a historical vein asserts, along with Walter Benjamin that "nothing that has ever happened should be regarded as lost for history."[44] She is, it turns out, pursuing a model of historical investigation that is remarkably akin to Michel Foucault's proposal in "Nietzsche, Genealogy, History," that we replace traditional historiographic paradigms with a genealogical method. Genealogy, he argues,

> must record the singularity of events outside of any monotonous finality; it must seek them in the most unpromising places, in what we tend to feel is without history – in sentiments, love, conscience, instincts; it must be sensitive to their recurrence, not in order to trace the gradual curve of their evolution, but to isolate the different scenes where they engaged in different roles. Finally, genealogy must define even those instances where they are absent, the moment when they remain unrealized.[45]

Woolf enunciated a similar commitment to writing and thinking the overlooked history of the senses in conjunction with desire and remembrance. Perhaps, following Foucault, we might do well to name her method *genealogical history.*

TOPOGRAPHY AND MEMORY IN *BETWEEN THE ACTS*

> Landscapes are culture before they are nature; constructs of the imagination projected onto wood and water and rock . . . But it should also be acknowledged that once a certain idea of landscape, a myth, a vision, establishes itself in an actual place, it has a peculiar way of muddling categories, of making metaphors more real than their referents; of becoming, in fact, part of the scenery. (Simon Schama, *Landscape and Memory*[46])

In his discussion of Borges's list from a "'certain Chinese encyclopedia'" that divides animals into categories ranging from "'(a) belonging to the Emperor,'" to "'(b) embalmed,'" to "'(f) fabulous,'" and to (perhaps the most delightful) "'(n) that from a long way off look like flies,'" Michel Foucault marvels at the incongruous juxtapositions in Borges's criteria for cataloguing animals. "In the wonderment of this taxonomy, the thing we apprehend in one great leap, the thing that, by means of the fable, is demonstrated as the exotic charm of another system of thought, is the limitation of our own, the stark impossibility of thinking *that*."[47] A little later Foucault proposes that "Borges adds no figure to the atlas of the impossible; nowhere does he strike the spark of poetic confrontation; he simply dispenses with the least obvious, but most compelling of necessities; he does away with the *site*, the mute ground upon which it is possible for entities to be juxtaposed."[48] We might say that in Woolf's 1941 novel, *Between the Acts*, we find an opposite gesture: Woolf turns to the "site" of the "Pointz Hall" estate and its views as a major topographical grounding that contains, speaks, and presents the disparate moments in history under the guise of materiality – offering a different register to the textual and spoken fragments from the past evoked through the village pageant.[49] And the grand historical bearing of the Elizabethan "Pointz Hall" influences the inhabitants and guests, urging them to consider an array of former temporalities and types of memory (personal and cultural). Woolf uses place as a palpable concretization of the past that coheres multiple temporal locations because it operates as both the locus for the action of the present and, through its own legibility as a historical monument, as a visible arrangement that carries the marks of past time. As T. S. Eliot does in "Tradition and the Individual Talent" when he argues "that the past should be altered by the present as much as the present is directed by the past,"[50] Woolf here proposes that experiencing the past and present together on a single day elicits and deepens a crucial awareness of the plurality and layering of time. The substance of remembrance allows a fuller consciousness to both the past and the present. In Eliot's terms, "the difference between the past and the present is that the conscious present is an awareness of the past in a way and to an extent which the past's awareness of itself cannot show."[51]

The ways in which memory and history will score *Between the Acts* are inaugurated on its first page. Here, Mr. Oliver – the elderly, benign, patriarch of the novel, a former civil servant in colonial India, and the owner of Pointz Hall, the estate on which all of the action takes place – muses aloud: "the site they had chosen for the cesspool was, if he had heard aright, on the Roman road. From an aeroplane, he said, you could still see, plainly marked, the scars made by the Britons; by the Romans; by the Elizabethan manor house; and by the plough, when they ploughed the hill to grow wheat in the Napoleonic wars."[52] The text thus opens with a meditation on the memory of the land, the topography of memory, and the marks the land receives from the course of human habitation and event. Is the mind like the land? Does the mind receive "plough" marks in the terrain of memory? Woolf seems to be imagining a visual analogue to the workings of recollection that is not unlike Freud's attempts to render memory "pictorial" in *Civilization and Its Discontents.* Here, as I have shown, Freud draws parallels between the palimpsestic architectural "history of the Eternal City" with mnemonic layers of the psyche as he hypothesizes that memory traces are only very rarely destroyed.[53] Walter Benjamin writes about "the topographical tradition representing the connection with the dead of this ground,"[54] while Claude Lévi-Strauss claims affinities between geology, history, and psychoanalysis: "unlike the history of the historians, that of the geologist is similar to that of the psychoanalyst, in that it tries to project in time – rather in the manner of a *tableau vivant* – certain basic characteristics of the physical or mental universe."[55] Throughout *Between the Acts* the landscape conspicuously contains evidence of what other generations intended – in their architecture, in their roads, and in their agriculture – as Woolf articulates a theory of reading the past that proposes not only a corporeality of memory, but affirms that this bodiliness of memory may be traced through ancient marks of pain and desire in stone, mortar, pavement, and even plantation. She writes in her journal in 1920, "I'm often overcome by London; even think of the dead who have walked in the city."[56] In a letter twenty years later while London is under aerial bombardment by the Germans, she writes to Ethel Smyth of her visceral and even erotic attachment to the cityscape: "the passion of my life, that is the City of London – to see London all blasted, that too raked my heart. Have you that feeling for certain alleys and little courts, between Chancery Lane and the City? I walked to the Tower the other day by way of caressing my love of all that."[57]

In *Between the Acts* the narrator informs us quite early that for this particular rural spot in England a nineteenth-century guide is still accurate:

The Guide Book still told the truth. 1833 was true in 1939. No house had been built; no town had sprung up. Hogben's Folly was still eminent; the very flat, field-parcelled land had changed only in this – the tractor had to some extent superseded the plough. The horse had gone; but the cow remained. If Figgis [the author of the Guide Book] were here now, Figgis would have said the same. (34)

A remarkable fixity thus holds sway in the English landscape. Indeed, one might imagine that this stability – this preservation of the past as architectural and topographic effect – would be cause for celebration in a writer who persistently valorizes past time. Instead, Mrs. Swithin, the elderly matriarch of the novel, quickly jumps in to proclaim, "'That's what makes a view so sad . . . And so beautiful. It'll be there,' she nodded at the strip of gauze laid upon the distant fields, 'when we're not'" (34). Her turn to elegy happens by moving dizzyingly forward and backward through centuries of time. We are taken from a rumination on the distant past that endures in landscape to a perplexing sadness at an anticipated future anterior of mourning about the inevitability of mortality in relation to such uninterrupted duration.[58] In her proleptic imagination, "we" will be absent from a scene that remains. Causing a reflection on the impermanence of human lives, the landscape thus again offers a correlative to memory's workings, even as it outdoes the scale of individual remembrance. A melancholy of impermanence sits juxtaposed with the beautiful and sublime of permanence.

This topographical containment of the past through its scars is a version of writing the body, while the "proper name" of the family (the *pater* of the name in contrast to the *mater* of memory's materiality) simultaneously notates identity as rife with the genealogy of signification and address. Continuing the fascination with the nineteenth-century writer of the guidebook, Woolf's narrator proposes, "had Figgis been there in person and called a roll call, half the ladies and gentlemen present would have said '*Adsum*; I'm here, in place of my grandfather or great-grandfather,' as the case may be" (47). The proper name thus stands as a fixed but exchangeable currency of past time that even has the power to instigate a linguistic shift from English to Latin under the compulsion of an address. Such a response also, importantly, conveys a blending of temporality and spatiality, signifying in numerous old Latin texts – from Cicero through Lucretius and Ovid's *Metamorphoses* – "Of time, *to be present, be at hand*."[59] While the stamp of previous technologies has inscribed the land, the human is overwritten by the repetition of a prior, but still viable, nomenclature. If names do not change, then on the level of pure signification these 1939 descendants can truthfully claim that Figgis's *figures* are "here," in the present, present as themselves. Only, a substitution has been made; new identities and bodies inhabit the old names and spaces. In acknowledging these characters' affiliations to the past through the proper name, Woolf opens the question of what exactly it is about the substitution that is different. Where does individual subjectivity supervene to displace the historical valence of a repeated appellation?

In the sentence immediately following the section I cite above, the narrator shifts to the present time to insist still further on these characters' interchangeability with their ancestors:

> At this very moment, half-past three on a June day in 1939 they greeted each other, and as they took their seats, finding if possible a seat next one another, they said: "That hideous new house at Pyes Corner! What an eyesore! And those bungalows! – have you seen 'em?"
>
> Again, had Figgis called the names of the villagers, they too would have answered. (47)

The abrupt shift means that, for an instant, Woolf achieves a doubling of temporality and identity: "they" refers to both the people present in 1939, and to their ancestors whom they replace. Contradicting her earlier comment that "No house had been built; no town had sprung up" – perhaps simply because the panorama from this point is slightly different – the villagers and their ghostly other selves object to the small changes that have, after all, emerged. Woolf thus blurs past and present time while she mixes past and present subjectivities, proposing for an instant that the audience members assembling for Miss La Trobe's pageant experience their predecessors' horizon of sight and expectation.[60]

Homi Bhabha makes a useful remark for our reading of the way in which the lay of the land, its physicality, and its "bodiliness" bring back the past. In "DissemiNation" he argues, "For Bakhtin, it is Goethe's vision of the microscopic, elementary, perhaps random, tolling of everyday life in Italy that reveals the profound history of its locality (*Lokalität*), the spatialization of historical time, 'a creative humanization of this locality, which transforms a part of terrestrial space into a place of historical life for people.'"[61] If we think of this reasoning in terms of T. S. Eliot's pornotropic poetry, there is a way in which the land, topography, and architecture of the "New World" – of a place like Eliot's Cuba, where "King Bolo and his Big Black Kween" hold court – lack this ability to carry cultural time as a decipherable marker of space. Cuba and the rest of the New World stood for its European colonial explorer-invaders as a fantasized tabula rasa. The structures the native populations had erected, the pathways they had beaten, and the histories they had etched, were apparently not imposing or permanent enough to mark the land with a history the Europeans were capable of comprehending. By contrast, the topography in *Between the Acts* is criss-crossed with History's stamp. This topography – this *graphein* of *topos*, this writing of place – is always at least partially legible to the people who inhabit the land, and produces a consciousness of themselves as linked to a past through physical structures that still cover the land, and which they still use. And the desire to read the signification of past event, and to know the "pastness of the past," as Eliot phrases it,[62] subtly begins to possess the villagers at the pageant, as the leisure to contemplate the physicality of the land promotes an interrogation and interpolation of their own location in history and cultural memory.

At the same time, as Mrs. Swithin observes, the permanence of the land, and the ways in which topography and architectonics hold memory, run the risk of outstripping the human. Walter Benjamin worried about just this kind of imbalance in memories associated with and lodged in the cityscape, where personal and human stimuli to memory are threatened by the overpowering impressions of architectural space. In this way the *site* that corresponds with memory's encoding can threaten to dis-*place* the human. That is, whereas Benjamin's writings are compelled and enchanted by the modernist cityscape, he supplements this positivity with an anxiety about what the supremacy of *place* and *space* do to the presence of actual "people." While reminiscing about his childhood in Berlin he notes the sway that *topos* holds over the imagination:

> The more frequently I return to these memories, the less fortuitous it seems to me how slight a role is played in them by people: I think of an afternoon in Paris to which I owe insights into my life that came in a flash, with the force of an illumination . . . I tell myself it had to be in Paris, where the walls and quays, the places to pause, the collections and the rubbish, the railings and the squares, the arcades and the kiosks, teach a language so singular that our relations to people attain, in the solitude encompassing us in our immersion in that world of things, the depths of a sleep in which the dream image waits to show the people their true faces. I wish to write of this afternoon because it made so apparent what kind of regimen cities keep over imagination, and why the city . . . indemnifies itself in memory, and why the veil it has covertly woven out of our lives shows the images of people less than those of the sites of our encounters with others or ourselves.[63]

We might say that the dialectic Benjamin describes between the commemorative quality of the land, its restorative potential (to give us what we had already had, but had forgotten), and the landscape's obliteration of the face of the human is at work in *Between the Acts*, even while

Woolf's novel displaces the overdetermined "cityscape" of the modernist venture by making the city marginal rather than central to its setting.[64]

Buildings, the Roman road, the barn, and even centuries-old plough rifts betray permanent scars that reveal the traces of the long-term historical. And these physical manifestations exist in such disproportion to the fleetingness of individual human existence that the imbalance threatens to disrupt the commerce between remembrance as a vivifying excess for the imagination and as a historical plenitude that cannot be thought. This is the meaning of Mrs. Swithin's melancholic reading of the "view" and the relative evanescence of the human. The narrator even muses wittily on the barn as a still-functioning relic that stimulates each observer diversely: "The Barn, the Noble Barn, the barn that had been built over seven hundred years ago and reminded some people of a Greek temple, others of the middle ages, most people of an age before their own, scarcely anybody of the present moment, was empty" (61). What remains and reminds of past time is, here, a shell, and operates – even in its cascade of not-quite-identical names, from "The Barn" to "the Noble Barn," to, simply, "the barn" – much as do the human bodies that retain the signs of history through their barely varying names, criss-crossed by multiple ideations of the past.

Family and audience members inhabit this spatiality that encroaches on the fourth dimension of time on a day contemporaneous with Woolf's writing of the novel in June 1939. Together with the land itself, the words of the pageant entreat them to do the work of thinking of their place in the history of the nation (as place). While the lay of the land is coextensive with history in *Between the Acts* – evincing a material facticity of past culture in the present time – we also discover this kind of coextensivity of the material with the temporal in the novel's treatment of objects. Even a teacup holds history. When William Dodge catches a teacup that Isa "half purposely, knocked over," he examines it in his hands, and notes the date, "about 1760" (38).

The topography of this moment in England's history, just two months before England entered the Second World War, is, however, far from standing as an irreproachable marker of stability. As Gillian Beer points out in one of her excellent footnotes to the novel, details about place only *seem* to have "the ring of 'fact' (which Woolf wished to include) though the geography of the house's position is shifty."[65] We are told that the house is fairly far north in England (possibly in Lincolnshire or Yorkshire, Beer speculates), but, as Beer asserts, one has the impression that the action is taking place in Sussex. It feels as though Woolf is writing out her wartime experience of inhabiting Monk's House, near the South Downs at Rodmell, when southern England was susceptible to raids from German war planes – a situation of constant danger that seriously unsettled Woolf's nerves, and likely contributed to her final breakdown and decision to kill herself. The locale is never definite, and the specificity of place is frequently reason for confusion. Likewise, details about foreign geography are hazy, as place bears the task of credibility and historical stability, while it shudders under this weight. Isa Oliver, one of the novel's principal women protagonists, and the daughter of the owner of the estate, overhears members of the audience mistaking Canada and India: "'I must say,' the voice said behind her, 'it's brave of the King and Queen. They're said to be going to India'"; a few lines later the voices continue, "'I thought they said Canada, not India'" (64). In both instances, geography is as indeterminate as speculation. Canada, part of the British Commonwealth, is confused with India – perhaps because both may be reduced to signifying "the colonies." Yet despite the lack of specificity about location and the confusion about territories, Woolf positions topography through the text as evidence for the signs of the past.

On the first page of the novel, while several characters are discussing the history of the location of the proposed "cesspool," Mrs. Haines, "the wife of the gentleman farmer," insists to the proprietor of Pointz Hall, Mr. Oliver, "'But you don't remember . . . '" (5). These are Woolf's ellipses, and Mrs. Haine's sentence trails off here, leaving her phrasing ambiguous – both in the ways it refers to memory, and in its rhetorical status. Is she asking a question, wanting Mr. Oliver to elaborate on what he *does* remember, or is she making an accusation, chastising him for his forgetfulness? If the latter is the case, is she accusing him of forgetting whether the "site chosen for the cesspool" is on the old Roman road, or implying that he forgets history's past ages (the "Britons . . . the Romans . . . the Elizabethans") (5)? Through free-indirect discourse we are given access to Mr. Oliver's thoughts, as he ponders, "No, not that. Still he did remember – and he was about to tell them what, when there was a sound outside" (5). He is interrupted by the entrance of his daughter-in-law, Isa, and he informs her they had been "'Discussing the cesspool'" (6); after a short tangential diversion in the narration Mr. Oliver then offers yet another interruptive to turn the discussion back to memory. What he *does* remember, he tells his interlocutors, is his mother:

"I remember," the old man interrupted, "my mother . . ." Of his mother he remembered that she was very stout; kept her teacaddy locked; yet had given him in that very room a copy of Byron. It was over sixty years ago, he told them, that his mother had given him the works of Byron in that very room. He paused.

"She walks in beauty like the night," he quoted.

Then again:

"So we'll go no more a-roving by the light of the moon." (6)

As with the first reminiscence Woolf records in "A Sketch of the Past" – which is, she tells us, her "first memory," so that her account is set in motion with an effort to approximate, mimetically, memory's temporal order – and, as with the opening of *Orlando*, when remembrance is called upon it inevitably speaks of the maternal. And Mr. Oliver is prompted to recollect his mother, at least in part, through a spatialized analogy: they are in the "very room" in which his mother gave him Byron. This choice of beginnings shows the economies between intertextual fragments and the spatialization of memory that will provide the backbone and background to the novel and to Miss La Trobe's pageant. Because the older Mr. Oliver has retained the passage from Byron almost perfectly – he misses a comma, a line break, and replaces "Yet" with "So" to begin the second quotation – we understand, too, that poetry and language are commensurate vehicles with location for containing and storing memory. Mr. Oliver's mother, in the middle of the Victorian period, had also, then, given him her immediate cultural and literary antecedent of Romanticism. In having "given him" Byron she, in effect, gave him her past. His memory of her gift is thus a very private remembrance of the gift of literary history that further emphasizes and extends the immediate horizon of the novel's time frame. Writing and *reading* the marks of time preserve the past, with intertextual echoes providing metonymic and synecdochic referents for the momentous repositories of both memory and history.

Marcel Proust also perceives a link between memory, landscape, and literature. In his marvelous essay, "On Reading," he writes of the experience of reading a good book in childhood, proposing that "On no days of our childhood did we live so fully [*si pleinement vécus*] perhaps as those we thought we had left behind without living them, those that we spent with a favourite book."[66] On such days games, friends, rays of sunshine, mealtimes all are secondary and "vulgar" to the utmost "divine pleasure [*plaisir divin*]" of reading – a pleasure, Proust conveys, that brings us into the nearest proximity with the essential *fullness* of our existence. Remembering the time of reading – or, the instance of literary experience – turns out to be one of the greatest stimuli to memory for Proust:

> so sweet is the memory it engraved in us [*elle en gravait*] (and so much more precious in our present estimation than what we then read so lovingly) that if still, today, we chance to leaf [*de feuilleter*] through these books from the past, it is simply as the only calendars we have preserved of the days that have fled, and in the hope of finding reflected on their pages the homes and the ponds that no longer exist.[67]

Proust finds a tonic for memory in the textuality of a good book, whose pages in the present are capable of taking us back to the beloved "preserved" topographies ("homes" and "ponds") that have otherwise disappeared. Like Eliot, Woolf, and Benjamin, Proust moves through the word – even via the physicality of leaves and pages – to find a suddenly rediscoverable calendar of desire and landscape, which in turn stand as pointers to the larger reality of the past. Memory has been "engraved in us," we only need promptings from language and from the page to shed light on what has already been tattooed on us and waits to be rediscovered.

THE SPECTACLE OF MEMORY

As we move further into *Between the Acts*, Woolf takes up the question she had mused on in her diary in 1918 at the end of the Great War that I consider above, which obtains between a history that demands to be situated and a population's tendency to forget: "people will soon forget all about the war, & the fruits of our victory will grow as dusty as ornaments under glass cases in lodging house drawing rooms."[68] Importantly, this novel is Woolf's last, and she was still proofreading it when she committed suicide in 1941. The novel therefore stands as a potent comment on contemporary history in relation to the possibility of historical legacy. Woolf was quite literally unable to make it through another war: the escalation of atrocities on the continent and Hitler's attack on European Jewry were historical developments she would finally not be able to write about as "the past." While *Orlando* traces a single body and consciousness that move through historical ages, *Between the Acts* concerns the responses of multiple bodies and consciousnesses to a single, staged spectacle of the historical past. We might even say that the novel is written as a historical score: on every page characters inflect their own speech with intertextual language from past literature, they recall their childhood, past generations, and "history" more generally as they prepare to watch and then encounter a version of English literary history enacted as theater before them.

In *Between the Acts*, the director and author of the village pageant, Miss La Trobe, takes her audience to task for the labor of remembering English history as the sign of their particular inheritance. As in *Orlando*, Woolf indexes a subtle cross-over between "history" and "memory," striking at the boundary between the two and laying bare their interpenetration. The pageant that Miss La Trobe offers the crowd at Pointz Hall literally "plays" out and performs what it means to narrate and give *body* to the history of England as a nation. The first character who appears on the stage is "a small girl, like a rosebud in pink" (48) who offers the opening lines of the play, but whose exact function is at first illegible:

> *Gentles and simples, I address you all . . .*
>
> So it was the play then. Or was it the prologue?
>
> *Come hither for our festival* (she continued)
> *This is a pageant, all may see*
> *Drawn from our island history.*
> *England am I . . .*
>
> 'She's England,' they whispered. 'It's begun.' 'The prologue,' they added, looking down at the programme.
>
> '*England am I*,' she piped again; and stopped.
>
> She had forgotten her lines. (48)

Although this takes place within England's sovereign boundaries – in a well-to-do country setting no less – the nation-as-character is initially unrecognizable. Her audience is unsure whether this little girl is part of the play, or merely of the prologue. What role might she be playing? In order for her significance to become plain she must pronounce herself, through language, as a substitutive emblem of the nation-state. But, immediately upon entering a legible domain, "England," dressed as a virginal English rose, immediately forgets what she is meant to say. While dozens of intertextual citations (language-as-history) fill the air through the afternoon, England's historical presence, identity, and self-expression are at first unsayable: not only does "England" forget her lines, but the syntax in her utterance of *being* England is inverted and antiquated. The girl does not say "I am England," but "*England am I*." Later in the pageant the audience is again confused about England's identity, wondering about Mabel Hopkins's role: "Who was she? What did she represent? . . . England was she? Queen Anne was she?" (75). The inscrutability of the nation-as-character may attest to Woolf's unease with the state of England's iterability as it was entering another international war. The nation-state was, in a very real sense to Woolf during her last months, an England incapable of speaking itself.

Choosing to privilege Western *literary* history and a symbolics of sovereignty as the best representatives of England's past ages, Miss La Trobe then has the village children act out allusions and segments from canonical literature ranging from Chaucer to Shakespeare (with heavy stress on *King Lear*), Milton, Dryden, and T. S. Eliot. Fragments and snippets of major literary texts evoke entire ages, with the play's intertextuality operating as a kind of humorous mock pastiche, as Woolf pastes together suggestions of different styles – in similar fashion to Joyce's "Oxen of the Sun" section of *Ulysses* – in addition to having the actors perform segments from actual plays. Julia Briggs suggests that "The pageant reduces English history to a sequence of familiar, and therefore essentially comic, plots,"[69] while Gillian Beer points out that "Woolf skeins together words and phrases recognizable from a wide, and multiple, range of poetic contexts."[70] Miss La Trobe's audience is subjected to sometimes agonizingly dull renditions, and are then at the end asked to confront the unsettling fact of themselves as the present history of the nation and its literature.

In Beer's interpretation, "none of these events matter, Miss La Trobe suggests, save to produce emotion."[71] I would argue, though, that Woolf frames the novel's preoccupations with the events of history (especially the events of history-as-literature) as immensely important, precisely because Miss La Trobe's exhausting and didactic effort is to interpellate her audience, challenging them to recognize their own coextensiveness with history and their temporal position as the culmination of past ages. Miss La Trobe, signaled as a lesbian through the text, with no children of her own, stages history with a cast of small children, locals, and the village idiot. She is the presiding mother over all of them, giving birth to both history and art through her great effort of establishing and maintaining a spectacularly allusive "illusion" that would hold them in history's thrall (84). For Woolf, Miss La Trobe's labor of retrieving history from oblivion at the start of another international war even prompts an analogy to racialized oppression: "Down among the bushes she worked like a nigger" (90). Miss La Trobe's hard labor of questioning history's registers of thinkability and performativity is very nearly thankless, though it will intensify as the novel proceeds as she persistently confronts the bankruptcy of her audience's historical imagination.

After the long pageant has carefully moved through England's historical eras, Miss La Trobe announces on the programme that the last act will be "The present time. Ourselves" (106). Instead of offering a performance from the stage, though, or a tissue from contemporary literature, which would continue the logic of dramatizing time as theatrical and literary event, Miss La Trobe directs the actors to jump suddenly from behind trees and bushes into the audience with multiple kinds of mirrors:

> hand glasses, tin cans, scraps of scullery glass, harness room glass, and heavily embossed silver mirrors – all stopped. And the audience saw themselves, not whole by any means, but at any rate sitting still.
>
> The hands of the clock had stopped at the present moment. It was now. Ourselves.
>
> So that was her little game! To show us up, as we are, here and now. All shifted, preened, minced; hands were raised, legs shifted. Even Bart, even Lucy, turned away. All evaded or shaded themselves – save Mrs. Manresa who, facing herself in the glass, used it as a glass; had out her mirror; powdered her nose; and moved one curl, disturbed by the breeze, to its place.
>
> "Magnificent!" cried old Bartholomew. Alone she preserved unashamed her identity, and faced without blinking herself. Calmly she reddened her lips. (110)

Miss La Trobe's experiment with the spectrality of now-time deeply unsettles the audience. Even the narrator protests, identifying with the audience by borrowing the language of photography: "Ourselves? But that's cruel. To snap us as we are, before we've had time to assume . . . And only, too, in parts. That's what's so distorting and upsetting and utterly unfair"(109). The disaster the mirrors produce is one of *méconnaissance*, of sudden unease, of the terrible absence of illusion, and of the pressure of fragmentation. In Eliot's words from "The Love Song of J. Alfred Prufrock," there has not been "time / To prepare a face to meet the faces that you meet."[72] The alienated half-identification and boredom the audience has already experienced during the pageant's staging of history suddenly faces a logic of similitude: *we*, in this moment, in being asked to gaze at ourselves, embody the march of history. If the present is not told for them, if they themselves must embody a time, the burden of obligation exceeds the scope of their courage, and the audience members suffer. They are not quite ready to read themselves as part of history, or to think that one day their present will be transformed into the material of memory.

Miss La Trobe's act is perceived as coercive and unethical. In compelling them by surprise to consider themselves *as event*, and as a moment in the history of the nation, she induces a moment of ontological self-reflection about what one *is* within the history of a culture and a country. Her effort is to stimulate a kind of historical consciousness akin to what Eliot writes about in "Little Gidding:"

> A people without history
> Is not redeemed from time, for history is a pattern
> Of timeless moments. So, while the light fails
> On a winter's afternoon, in a secluded chapel
> History is now and England.[73]

History does not "redeem" us from time because history itself is "timeless," and history repeats infinitely, even in its most unique moments. In "Little Gidding" Eliot embraces the ineluctable experience of finding history *via* location, as his speaker discovers history's presence during World War Two in the specific site of a small chapel in Cambridgeshire. Similarly, the mirror scene of *Between the Acts* marks the point where we realize that one of the primary desires of the text is Miss La Trobe's wish to cause an affective reaction in the audience in relation to historical and mnemonic consciousness. She wants to assert, as does the narrator in *Jacob's Room*, that "All history backs our pane of glass. To escape is vain."[74] But the audience resents the trick of specularity and time, self-consciously and awkwardly refusing to look at themselves in the mirrors upheld by the characters of history, and insisting on *méconnaissance*. Only Mrs. Manresa overcomes the inanity of the sudden ontological query as to their place in history. She quite unselfconsciously powders her face in the mirror, treating it simply as an object of practical utility, insisting that the burden of epistemological self-reflection and the vanity of self-presentation and composure show no incompatibility. Devoid of Nietzsche's "debilitating historical fever" that Miss La Trobe is, in some senses, laboring to re-ignite,[75] Mrs. Manresa chooses to play a most ordinary part within the moment. She will not admit to the humiliating didacticism of Miss La Trobe's play, and will only live *within* a historical moment, without expressly conceding that Miss La Trobe has made her conscious of her dislocated place in time. Nevertheless, she is moved; as the scene continues we find, parenthetically, "(Mrs. Manresa's [eyes] were wet; for an instant tears ravaged her powder)" (112). Perhaps she is living the most genuine historical present of any of them.

While the intertextuality of the pageant is so conspicuous that it, like Miss La Trobe with her mirrors, literally forces us to consider the function of citation, Woolf also structures the rest of the novel around dozens of other, more subtle, intertextual fragments – so much so that Woolf generates a text shimmering with the words of others in ways analogous to Eliot's intertextual achievement of *The Waste Land.* Walter Benjamin has proposed that a modernist historiography "must raise the art of quoting without quotation marks to the very highest level. Its theory is intimately linked to that of montage."[76] In *Between the Acts* quoted phrases grace conversations, repeat themselves in the voice of the narrator, and form the substance of the spectacle. The audience members are tacitly aware of this intertextual contract: "'Another scene from another play, I suppose,' said Mrs. Elmhurst, referring to her programme" (76). Other writers like Yeats, Kipling, and Sappho are not cited directly, but Woolf alludes to them through paraphrase. As such, intertextual tissues constitute a major part of each person's subjectivity, as Woolf writes a novel in which citation is intrinsic to thinking, being, and speaking, suggesting that language and history together make who we are and give us identity.

In conjunction with the history of the nation and its literature that the audience is prompted to recall in viewing the pageant, personal memory is everywhere recollected in *Between the Acts.* Childhood memories are frequently summoned, even by the very old, as the characters conjure up favorite childhood meals of "Lobsters" and "salmon" "when we were children, living in a house by the sea" (20) – reminiscent of Eliot's, "when we were children, staying at the arch-duke's, / My cousin's."[77] They also remember a "play" acted in the nursery (60), and sing or hum lullabies and songs from infancy and early youth (86). During one of the intervals several members of the audience extrapolate from the historical context of the play to turn suddenly to their own memories; in one instance phrases about personal remembrance – "'I remember,'" "'You remember,'" and "'They remembered'" – are repeated eleven times on a single page (95). Part of the labor that the pageant performs, therefore, is that of eliciting a necessary repetition and reiteration of both public and private recollection. Woolf in this way blends history and memory by juxtaposing the expressly historical content of Miss La Trobe's spectacle with the very private, personal memories of childhood. When Mrs. Manresa tells Giles and Mrs. Swithin that she had taken her nephew "to *Pop Goes the Weasel*" the other day, Giles responds by humming one of its songs, "'Up and down the City Road'" (86). In a novel where the new technology of the gramophone contributes to the machine-like unity (and failure of this comm-unity) of an ambivalently entranced and committed audience, breath and voice further flesh out the corporeal architecture of memory's notation.[78] This popular song from the Victorian era was still being staged in contemporary productions, but it carries with it a whole cultural milieu. Woolf was well aware that we are steeped in the cultural histories of the nation from earliest childhood. National history becomes deeply personal to one's singular identity in part because we nostalgically recollect instances of childhood song. Through this accrual of language and history, the nation gradually becomes an indistinguishable facet of Woolf's version of the human.

While the pageant performs England's history, the most elderly woman of the text, Mrs. Swithin, happens to be fascinated by "pre-history." Her "favourite reading" is a book called an "Outline of History" (8),[79] which describes an England with "rhododendron forests in Piccadilly; when the entire continent, not then, she understood, divided by a channel, was all one; populated, she understood, by elephant-bodied, seal-necked, heaving, surging, slowly writhing, and, she supposed, barking monsters; the iguanodon, the mammoth, and the mastodon; from whom presumably, she thought, jerking the window open, we descend" (8). This reading stays with Mrs. Swithin in a way Harold Bloom might call a slight misprisioning.[80] Despite her pride in her "book" learning she (slightly) misremembers specific details, and in a later conversation she muses on what she has learned from this post-Darwinian natural history: "'Once there was no sea,' said Mrs. Swithin. 'No sea at all between us and the continent. I was reading that in a book this morning. There were rhododendrons in the Strand; and mammoths in Piccadilly'" (20). The moment also comes close to repeating an instance in *Mrs. Dalloway*, written sixteen years earlier, when Peter Walsh reflects on the potent durability of passion:

> Through all ages – when the pavement was grass, when it was swamp, through the age of tusk and mammoth, through the age of silent sunrise – the battered woman – for she wore a skirt – with her right hand exposed, her left clutching at her side, stood singing of love – love which has lasted a million years, she sang, love which prevails, and millions of years ago, her lover, who had been dead these centuries, had walked, she crooned, with her in May; but in the course of ages, long as summer days, and flaming, she remembered, with nothing but red asters, he had gone; death's enormous sickle had swept those tremendous hills.[81]

Nestled in a "modernist" contemplation of the epochal changes and erosions of natural history, Woolf again depicts memory and desire as unassailably permanent; the recollection and potency of enduring human love will even outstrip the architectural palimpsests of ruins that come and go in time. In Mrs. Swithin's favorite reading she is called to map and understand a different historical era contained within the same spatiality of twentieth-century urban London. This is nothing less than history-made-evident, reminding us that other ages once shared our location. To understand history in this way means to know that the past is always present *spatially* – in relics, artifacts, and bodies – if not temporally; that is, temporality can be known, in part, through spatiality. In *Orlando* the narrator asserts that "things remain much as they are for two or three hundred years or so, except for a little dust and a few cobwebs which one old woman can sweep up in half an hour."[82] This passage echoes the "Time Passes" section of *To the Lighthouse* – published just one year before *Orlando* – in which Mrs. McNab and Mrs. Bast fend off the ruin and decay impinging on the Ramsay family house. These representatives of the working classes, Woolf suggests, achieve a small triumph over Time itself: they "stayed the corruption and the rot; rescued from the pool of Time that was fast closing over them now a basin, now a cupboard."[83]

In an interesting play on mixing memory and desire, Woolf locates the imagined "rhododendron forests" of prehistory in "Piccadilly," a public space that was dominated by a statue of eros from about 1890 onward, and associated with prostitution. Woolf was well aware of this connotation, and in a letter to her nephew Quentin Bell she describes Piccadilly as a sexual cure-all: Sydney Waterlow was "impotent for years; and Clive heard his miracle, how he found a woman in Piccadilly and brought it off there and then."[84] Mark Hussey also points out that the young heroine of *The Voyage Out*, Rachel Vinrace, learns to affiliate the location with prostitution.[85] In the contemporary London that Mrs. Swithin conjures, a sculpted emblem designating the erotic (eros) is thus palimpsestically, ideologically overlaid with the same space as primeval and natural history.

Mrs. Swithin's reading of an "Outline of History" also acts as a frame for the cultural and personal histories that the novel requests its characters to revive. Her musings on prehistory telescope us away from the present just when we, as readers, are also interpellated by Miss La Trobe's play to hold up our own mirrors to ourselves and our historical and readerly positions. The pre-textual, archaeological history of London that enchants Mrs. Swithin thus brackets the time-frame of the very literary, written, human histories that are central to the intertextual opus of the play-within-the-novel. Textuality is not quite all, as Woolf again renders history and memory as always overshadowed with a materiality and corporeality that sits on the boundaries of the semiotic. Further, the novel draws analogies between Mrs. Swithin's ancient body and the ancientness of prehistory. Toward the end of the pageant, after Miss La Trobe has dramatized the Victorian era in part by parodying its observance of norms, and its frightening colonial logic of "*the white man's burden*" (97), Isa "looked at Mrs. Swithin as if she had been a dinosaur or a very diminutive mammoth. Extinct she must be, since she had lived in the reign of Queen Victoria" (104). Evincing an intrapersonal, intratextual, and uncanny omniscient narrative access to Mrs. Swithin's musings, such a rendition conflates Mrs. Swithin with the material (and materiality) of her reading. Then, as if privy to Isa's thoughts, Mrs. Swithin offers a quick and clever retort: "'The Victorians,' Mrs. Swithin mused. 'I don't believe,' she said with her odd smile, 'that there ever were such people. Only you and me and William dressed differently'" (104). There were, of course, "rhododendron forests in Piccadilly," but a people overwritten with the name of Queen Victoria is an imaginative figment. *We* are simultaneously the Victorians and these mid twentieth-century English villagers.

William Dodge misses the cleverness of Mrs. Swithin's response to an age that only predates the novel's setting by thirty-eight years – a span that would have been well within the memory of most people in the audience – exclaiming, "'You don't believe in history'" (104). In the terms of the book, this stands as a real accusation. He implies that historical understanding is a kind of credo, involving a faith and belief that might not be available to the uninitiated. Mrs. Swithin, though, does not need this admonishment. She is one of the few who assents to Miss La Trobe's appeal to know herself as both an object and a subject of history, finding access (and dynamic axes) to the immediacy of the past in both her reading and in the lived continuity of her many years. Her sphere of influence is threatened with extinction, though, and the narrator later reports, "The old lady, the indigenous, the prehistoric, was being wheeled away by a footman" (121). The old woman as the living genealogical link to a Victorianism that already seems as remote as prehistory – in a flattening of time that conflates ancient and modern, natural and cultural, symbolic and repressed – is passively led away by a servant who is himself a vestige of past time. Mrs. Swithin persists, however, in her reading of an "Outline of History": the quiet seer of the novel keeping scraps of time imaginatively alive.

At the very close of the novel the potency of this prehistory arises again with sufficient force to infect and overtake the narrative voice. In an abrupt shift from a unifying, filmic survey of several key characters retreating to bed after the pageant, Woolf again collapses space together with time, moving backward and then forward at breathtaking speed. This is how her last book ends: "The house had lost its shelter. It was night before roads were made, or houses. It was the night that dwellers in caves had watched from some high place among rocks. Then the curtain rose. They spoke" (129-30). The play has not, in fact, ended, and it goes on still, with the curtain having *risen*, not fallen, inviting a new speaking in common. As she does in *Orlando*, Woolf pushes the temporal confines of the novel past its borders, through a certain physicality (the curtain, Sackville-West's body, and Woolf's gift of the manuscript to Sackville-West), to the commensurate present and future tenses of desire. In "East Coker" (1940) of the *Four Quartets*, Eliot conveys a similar vision of being that would announce (and exist through) the creative element of speech in relation to time. The poem was published just a year before *Between the Acts*, and in it we find what approximates an incantation that would overcome time as we know it: "In my beginning is my end," and "In my end is my beginning" (lines 1 and 211). Origins and teleologies are no mere means to ends, but are inseparable ends in themselves. Ethical and achronological, his circular logic promises to break past its variegated repetitions to a new illumination. Both Eliot and Woolf are thus also gesturing to a kind of *logos*, a beginning-again through the word, that would startingly supervene beyond temporality and text. Memory and history have already moved into their futures, but that anticipated time remains embedded in the eros of the past.

Epilogue

> Here is the past and all its inhabitants miraculously sealed as in a magic tank; all we have to do is to look and to listen and to listen and to look and soon the little figures – for they are rather under life size – will begin to move and speak, and as they move we shall arrange them in all sorts of patterns of which they were ignorant, for they thought when they were alive that they could go where they liked.
>
> Virginia Woolf, "I am Christina Rossetti"[1]

I have been diagnosing the ways in which two exemplary modernist writers thought about time, memory, and desire in their fictional, poetic, and autobiographical writings, making the case that in writing the present of the avant-garde both Woolf and Eliot obsessively turned to history and memory, and when they did so they found themselves called upon to articulate a poetics of desire. Differing from a number of critics who have emphasized a sense of disconnection, discontinuity, breach, and rupture in modernist postures toward the past, I have been arguing that modernism's looking to the past denotes *both* a return and a departure. Intrinsic to the modernist project was a new, widely shared awareness that their relation to the past could only ever be belated, self-conscious, and palimpsestic – a building on and among ruins whose vitality remains. Such structures of return, where revisitation means a perpetual *reopening* to the demands and plentitude of the final Otherness of time (rather than just a compulsion to repeat), tell us a great deal about the workings of desire. In Lacan's terms desire indicates an anxious approach to the responsivity of an Other that one can never fully know, but the approach and the Other nonetheless incite the wish to try again to understand the erotogenesis of alterity: "desire becomes bound up with the desire of the Other, but . . . in this loop lies the desire to know."[2]

The tropological turn involved in Eliot and Woolf's recurring inclinations to approach the becoming of the past also takes us into questions about the nature of textuality vis-à-vis time, remembrance, and desire.

So many of Eliot and Woolf's writings affirm that knowing the past and discovering a kind of cubist, poly-temporality (where one is simultaneously within, outside of, beyond, and present to time as we know it), occurs in a privileged relation to literary expression. Both writers announce a kinship between the mysteries of poetic creation and past time, immersed as each was in the practical and metaphysical reasoning of the bind to histories, presents, and futures that they finally did not want to lose. As Woolf asks, "Was not writing poetry a secret transaction, a voice answering a voice?"[3] Writing as such involves a response to the speech of both the living and the dead, and an answering to an abiding call where the stakes are almost theological. Neither writer was after a holistic apprehension of *chronos* and *kairos* that would make final, manageable sense. But they did wrestle consistently with the perplexities of being in time as they rendered the interpenetrating truths of the corporeal, the libidinal, and the mnemonic.

We might say that Eliot and Woolf's perspective on the past is fundamentally incorporative. Both are solicitous to *incorporate* (with all of its punning on the corpus/body) prior time into the present, and in so doing to recognize the substantial durability and even materiality of its still-potent architecture of desire. The past (as event, idea, text, tissue, fragment of culture, and even as place) functions in their writing as a never-fully-lost object that can always be revived in and for the present. Its archive is undestroyed, and the passageways to what has been can thus be counted on for illuminations the present cannot show. Each acknowledges (and often embraces) the animation and plenitude of indestructible marks of psychic time, while enacting historiographic gestures that refuse what Paul Ricoeur calls the "objectivity of history."[4] They favor instead a delightfully unpredictable *subjectivity* of history. Ricoeur proposes that "history's ambition . . . is not to bring the past back to life but to recompose and reconstruct, that is to say, to compose and construct a retrospective sequence. The objectivity of history consists precisely in repudiating the attempt to relive and coincide with the past; it consists in the ambition to elaborate factual sequences."[5] In contradistinction, Woolf and Eliot's fiction and poetry repeatedly insist that the backward glance re-affiliates the present with the past, bringing the past, bodily, into the spectrum of contemporary experience. As such, it would be incorrect to say merely that the past is granted new life in their reflections. We would also have to say the reverse: knowing the past grants life to the present.

For Eliot in "Little Gidding" (1942), "History is now and England,"[6] while for Woolf in *Orlando* (1928), history is the undying trace of embodied and androgynous desire embedded in an aristocratic national past. Eliot insists in "Tradition and the Individual Talent" that "the past should be altered by the present as much as the present is directed by the past. And the poet who is aware of this will be aware of great difficulties and responsibilities."[7] When Woolf pairs her remembrances with the task of their inscription during World War Two, she discovers the fullest experience of the "real" through a present that makes sense and is sensually available only through an impressionistic shading from the past. This "vision" of anterior experience then acts as a restorative supplement to the present's always consequential absences:

> I say to L[eonard]: "What's there real about this? Shall we ever live a real life again?" "At Monks house," he says. So I write this [memoir], taking a morning off from the word filing and fitting that my life of Roger means – I write this partly in order to recover my sense of the present by getting the past to shadow this broken surface. Let me then, like a child advancing with bare feet into a cold river, descend again into that stream.[8]

The present is a "broken surface," a wounded temporality, that begs for the healing of word, text, narration, and the intransigency of poetic language that are not yet available to it because it has not yet become the past.

Part of what Woolf and Eliot are addressing is the notion of time as a clear and delineated temporal "order" – a belief that had been called into question in part by an early twentieth-century, post-Nietzschean and Freudian insistence on the fragmentation of the subject. Experience, time, and event were acknowledged as rent open to psychic instability. Writing in juxtaposition to the new language of psychoanalysis, which sought to make sense of the stuttering histories of the commonest psychopathologies of everyday life, Eliot famously writes of "these fragments I have shored against my ruins,"[9] while Woolf notes that her diary is "written, as 'this' is so often written, to fill up a little jagged piece of time."[10] With the fantastic image of (historical) progress having crumbled, it was left to writers like Eliot and Woolf to compose the in-betweens of time, text, and being, through mosaic-like patchworks, in chance fits and starts, all the while submitting themselves to an emerging, eminent, self-consciousness about such an endeavor. Meanwhile, a "new" articulateness about the work of personal memory in relation to aesthetic expression and cultural and historical circumstance was arising. E. M. Forster urges his reader in his epigraph to *Howard's End* (1910), "Only connect" – as if to protest *and* remedy the perceived alienations at the heart of modernist subjectivities. To find connection – in interpersonal relations, or, with what we might say is the *différance* of the past – may be the lost grail of a modernist sensibility that was always already aware of the brokenness and extratemporality of time itself.

In both Eliot and Woolf the sense of a crucial – even if frangible – continuity with anteriority manifests itself as a wish to touch the past through (re)discovering the history of physical and corporeal traces whose enigmatic imprints remain legible long into the future. In each writer we find post-Freudian explorations that read epistemology and ontology as archaeologically stratified, where past desire and time crave restoration to a purified instantiation whose perfection might exist in the remembering. In his introduction to a study of Proust, Harold Bloom suggests that Proust's "only recourse is to search for lost time, in the hopeless hope that the aesthetic recovery of illusion and experience alike, will deceive him in a higher mode than he fears to have been deceived in already."[11] In Eliot and Woolf's schema, past time provides a less masochistic pleasure. In Eliot the past is almost always threatened with its own death (or it is already buried), but he demands its unearthing to promote the flowering of a new unknown from "roots that clutch . . . / Out of this stony rubbish."[12] He challenges the typology of both mourning and melancholia, exposing a plenitude of the past that needs and wants a positive reconnection and reconstruction rather than a total letting go or a hopeless attachment to some scene of loss. In Woolf's terms, memory and personal history run as generative currents alongside the present; the past is envisioned as a still-living continuity *and* contiguity whose sensation touches the subject in every instant and without which perceptions and an ontogeny of the present cannot be.

As Bergson contends, layers of anterior experience condition future time, accruing material meaning in the body and the psyche: "the memory of the sensation is the sensation itself beginning to be."[13] The threat of ruin always hangs over memory and the body of the past, but such a ruin only occurs when the subject fails to undertake the labor of facing the past's vitality as part of the never-to-be-effaced Real. Paul Veyne calls this enduring aspect of the Real the "truth" of history, arguing that "There is no method of history because history makes no demands; so long as one relates true things, it is satisfied. It seeks only truth."[14] Woolf also suggests that the material of history is the Real of psychic experience – which we later arrange by way of somewhat bewildered and enchanted narrations – in order to tell ourselves understandable and assimilable stories of what the past most authentically means. As Michel de Certeau reminds us, history "vacillates between two poles. On the one hand, it refers to a practice, hence to a reality; on the other, it is a closed discourse, a text that organizes and concludes a mode of intelligibility."[15] History and memory are all at once event and word, fact and discourse. "We attach ourselves to the breath of life by our pens," Woolf declares.[16]

By sketching a poetics of memory and history in Eliot and Woolf I have also wanted to explore how modernist writers *wrote time*, wrote an epoch, and in the process of writing, *created* that time. In tracing my responses, I have proposed that Woolf and Eliot's understanding of temporality acknowledges that time itself is the ungraspable medium in which we exist, while their work discloses a yearning to know and narrate time within the frame of their unique historical and cultural locations. Both writers suggest that language and experience are most replete when they evince a discernible remembrance of the presence of the past. Each seeks a language that might begin to speak presence by taking on the task and the risk of conveying the sublime Otherness *and* familiar intimacy of memory within its experiment. That is, despite its literal irretrievability *in time*, the past offers itself as responsive to knowing the present of both being and the drive to inscription. Time is animated and preserved by eros, and encodings of attachment thus preserve its immanence. Another way of saying this would be to affirm that love opens up the indestructibility of event and the infinity of time: "a lifetime burning in every moment / And not the lifetime of one man only / But of old stones that cannot be deciphered," Eliot writes in "East Coker."[17] For both Eliot and Woolf, then, the past exists as a deepening and much-needed "shadow" that shores up the "broken surface" of the present.[18]

Notes

INTRODUCTION

1 Virginia Woolf, *The Diary of Virginia Woolf*, 5 vols., ed. Anne Olivier Bell (New York: Harcourt, 1980), vol. III, 118.
2 Marcel Proust, *Remembrance of Things Past: The Captive, The Fugitive, and Time Regained*, trans. C. K. Scott Moncrieff and Terence Kilmartin (New York: Vintage, 1982), 1105.
3 Lines 1-4, in *T. S. Eliot: The Complete Poems and Plays* (London: Faber and Faber, 1990).
4 Animated debates about the chronology of modernism(s) continue, and these parameters could certainly be extended. Susan Stanford Friedman, Brian Richardson, Molly Hite, and Melba-Cuddy Keane brilliantly took up these questions at the 2005 Modernist Studies Association (MSA) conference in Chicago in a panel entitled "Re-Figuring the Boundaries of Modernism," in which they argued that the temporal boundaries of modernism(s) can only be thought of as flexible.
5 Virginia Woolf, 22 July 1936, *The Letters of Virginia Woolf*, 6 vols., ed. Nigel Nicolson and Joanne Trautmann (New York: Harcourt, 1980), vol. VI, 59.
6 Djuna Barnes, *Nightwood*, 1937 (New York: New Directions, 1961), 39.
7 Hayden White, *Tropics of Discourse: Essays in Cultural Criticism* (Baltimore: Johns Hopkins University Press, 1978), 31 and 37.
8 Leo Bersani, *The Culture of Redemption* (Cambridge, MA: Harvard University Press, 1990), 47–8.
9 Gregory Jay, "Postmodernism in *The Waste Land*: Women, Mass Culture, and Others," in *Rereading the New: A Backward Glance at Modernism*, ed. Kevin J. H. Dettman (Ann Arbor: University of Michigan Press, 1992), 221.
10 Charles Altieri, "Can We Be Historical Ever? Some Hopes for a Dialectical Model of Historical Self-Consciousness," in *The Uses of Literary Theory*, ed. Marshall Brown (Durham, NC: Duke University Press, 1995), 229.
11 Nicholas Andrew Miller, *Modernism, Ireland and the Erotics of Memory* (Cambridge: Cambridge University Press, 2002), 6.
12 James Longenbach, *Modernist Poetics of History: Pound, Eliot, and the Sense of the Past* (Princeton: Princeton University Press, 1987), ix.
13 *Ibid.*

14 Susan Stanford Friedman (ed.), *Joyce: The Return of the Repressed* (Ithaca, NY: Cornell University Press, 1993), 7. See also Ronald Bush (ed.), *T. S. Eliot: The Modernist in History* (Cambridge: Cambridge University Press, 1991); Peter Fritzsche, "The Case of Modern Memory," *The Journal of Modern History* 73 (2001), 87–117; Elena Gualtieri, *Virginia Woolf's Essays: Sketching the Past* (Basingstoke: Macmillan, 2000); Lawrence Rainey, *Revisiting The Waste Land* (New Haven: Yale University Press, 2005), 71; John Whittier-Ferguson, "Stein in Time: History, Manuscripts, and Memory," *Modernism/Modernity* 6.1 (1999), 115–51; and Longenbach, *Modernist Poetics of History.*

15 Lawrence Rainey, *Revisiting*, 71.

16 Eliot attended weekly lectures by the French philosopher, Henri Bergson, at the Sorbonne in the fall of 1910, around the time when he was composing "The Love Song of J. Alfred Prufrock," and it is generally agreed that versions (and critiques) of Bergson's ideas appear in poetic guise within Eliot's verse. Woolf's writings also have major resonances with Bergson's thinking on memory, as I will go on to explore. Henri Bergson, *La perception du changement* (Conferences Given at the University of Oxford, 26 and 27 May 1911), Bibliothèque Nationale, Paris, my translations.

17 Eliot, "Ash Wednesday," lines 135–8, in *The Complete Poems and Plays.*

18 Sigmund Freud, "Mourning and Melancholia," 1917 [1915], in *The Standard Edition of the Complete Psychological Works of Sigmund Freud*, trans. James Strachey, 24 vols. (London: Hogarth Press, 1978), vol. XIV, 246.

19 David Chinitz, *T. S. Eliot and the Cultural Divide* (Chicago: University of Chicago Press, 2003).

20 T. S. Eliot, "Tradition and the Individual Talent," 1919, in *T. S. Eliot: Selected Essays* (London: Faber and Faber, 1999), 14. After decades during which Eliot reigned as *the* asexual exemplar of modernism, several important studies of sexuality in his work have emerged. See especially Cassandra Laity and Nancy K. Gish, *Gender, Desire, and Sexuality in T. S. Eliot* (Cambridge: Cambridge University Press, 2004); Richard Kaye, "'A Splendid Readiness for Death': T. S. Eliot, the Homosexual Cult of St. Sebastian, and World War I," *Modernism/Modernity*, 6.2 (1999), 107–34; Colleen Lamos, *Deviant Modernism: Sexual and Textual Errancy in T. S. Eliot, James Joyce, and Marcel Proust* (Cambridge: Cambridge University Press, 1998); and Wayne Koestenbaum's groundbreaking *Double Talk: The Erotics of Male Literary Collaboration* (New York: Routledge, 1989). Gregory Jay also paved the way for much of this work in his penetrating book, *T. S. Eliot and the Poetics of Literary History* (Baton Rouge: Louisiana State University Press, 1983), where he argues presciently that "Eliot's fragments cohere chiefly in their physicality, in the music of their borrowed sounds and in the kinds of sensual experiences they represent" (149).

21 Sandra Gilbert deems Woolf "almost neurasthenically intellectual and unworldly" in her important "Introduction" to *Orlando*, and such a view often still persists. *Orlando: A Biography*, 1928, ed. Brenda Lyons, Introduction and notes by Sandra M. Gilbert (New York: Penguin, 1993), xvi.

Meanwhile, critics have placed significant stress on Woolf's early sexual abuse following the lead of Louise de Salvo's influential study, *Virginia Woolf: The Impact of Childhood Sexual Abuse on Her Life and Work* (New York: Ballantine, 1989); but see also retorts to this kind of psychobiographical study, including Thomas C. Caramagno's "The Lure of Reductionism in Psychological Treatments of Woolf's Life," in *Virginia Woolf and the Arts: Selected Papers from the Sixth Annual Conference on Virginia Woolf*, eds. Diane F. Gillespie and Leslie K. Hankins (New York: Pace University Press, 1997), 320–6. Significant attention has also been paid to Woolf's lesbianism and/or bisexuality, but a great deal of work remains to be done. For some important recent studies that incisively address the issue of sexuality in Woolf's texts see Christine Froula, *Virginia Woolf and the Bloomsbury Avant-Garde: War, Civilization, Modernity* (New York: Columbia, 2005); Daryl Ogden, *The Language of the Eyes: Science, Sexuality, and Female Vision in English Literature and Culture 1690–1927* (Albany, New York: SUNY Press, 2005); Dennis Denisoff, *Sexual Visuality from Literature to Film, 1850–1950* (New York: Palgrave, 2004); and Alison Booth, "The Scent of a Narrative: Rank Discourse in *Flush* and *Written on the Body*," *Narrative* 8.1 (2000), 3–22.

22 Julia Kristeva, *Proust and the Sense of Time*, trans. Stephen Bann (London: Faber and Faber, 1993), 3–4.

CHAPTER 1
AN UNEXPECTED BEGINNING: SEX, RACE, AND HISTORY IN T. S. ELIOT'S COLUMBO AND BOLO POEMS

1 Lines 77-83, in *T. S. Eliot: The Complete Poems and Plays* (London: Faber and Faber, 1990).

2 T. S. Eliot, *Inventions of the March Hare: Poems 1909–1917*, ed. Christopher Ricks (London: Faber and Faber 1996), 318.

3 I designate Eliot's poems as "pornotropic" because I want to emphasize the *tropological* nature of Eliot's very self-conscious use of pornography: he is both *turning* from the *graphein* of sexual availability and writing from within its midst. I use the term in a very different sense from that employed by Anne McClintock in *Imperial Leather*, where "porno-tropics" puns on the "tropical" aspect of European colonial territory while emphasizing the prevalence of tropes of titillation in colonial writing. Anne McClintock, *Imperial Leather: Race, Gender and Sexuality in the Colonial Contest* (New York: Routledge, 1995), 21–4.

4 Eliot, *Inventions*, 315.

5 *Ibid.* Eliot's relation to Jewishness is deeply complex, convoluted, and riddled. My sense is that Eliot alternated between outright anti-Semitic prejudices and a philosemitism bordering on fetishism. I cannot begin to do justice to the extensive debates on this topic, but see especially Anthony Julius, *T. S. Eliot, Anti-Semitism and Literary Form*, new edn. (New York:

Thames and Hudson, 2003); "Special Section: Eliot and Anti-Semitism: The Ongoing Debate," *Modernism/Modernity* 10.1 (2003), 1–67; "*Special Issue:* Eliot and anti-Semitism: the Ongoing Debate II," *Modernism/Modernity* 10.3 (2003), 417–54; and Melvin Wilk, *Jewish Presence in T. S. Eliot and Franz Kafka* (Atlanta, GA: Scholars Press, 1986).

6 Eliot, *Inventions*, 316.

7 I am grateful to Ella Shohat and Robert Stam for permission to quote this phrase from a lecture they gave at the School of Criticism and Theory at Cornell University, "Tupi or not Tupi: A Tupi Theorist," 17 July 2006.

8 Ricks chose his title from the provisional one that Eliot gave his poetry notebook from 1909 to 1917. Interestingly, Eliot at some point scratched through his title with single solid strokes, effectively placing his title under erasure. He makes only one other known reference to the notebook in a letter to Conrad Aiken in 1914, when he jokes, "Do you think it possible, if I brought out the 'Inventions of the March Hare,' and gave a few lectures, at 5 P.M. with wax candles, that I could become a sentimental Tommy." T. S. Eliot, 30 September 1914, *The Letters of T. S. Eliot*, ed. Valerie Eliot (New York: Harcourt, 1988), vol. 1, 59.

9 In his 1996 collection of Eliot's verse, *Inventions of the March Hare: Poems 1909–1917*, in which many of Eliot's Columbo and Bolo stanzas first appeared, Christopher Ricks implicitly frames these poems as juvenilia by placing the dates 1909–17 in his title – a period when Eliot was between twenty-one and twenty-nine. We know from certain jocular letters of Bonamy Dobrée and Conrad Aiken, however, that Eliot was still composing the Bolo poems at least until 1928, and most likely until as late as 1964. Aiken writes to Eliot on 3 January 1928: "I had somehow supposed, ever since that day, some years ago, when I recommended a diet of Götterdämmaroids for the King, that Bolo was gone to his reward. Perhaps he had merely enlisted, incog, in the tank corps. Anyway, I rejoice to hear that he still lives. And I will do him homage at the earliest opportunity." *Selected Letters of Conrad Aiken*, ed. Joseph Killorin (New Haven: Yale University Press, 1978), 140. References to the poems also appear regularly in Eliot's unpublished correspondence with Bonamy Dobrée through 1930, Brotherton Collection. Brotherton Library, University of Leeds. And, as I will show, Aiken comments decades later on Eliot's continued output of Bolo verses less than a month before Eliot's death.

10 I have been able to examine approximately seventy-five stanzas in total, and although I am not permitted to cite directly from the bulk of these, all of the stanzas I have seen inform my analysis.

11 Eliot, *Letters*, vol. 1, 206.

12 Until more becomes known about the details of Eliot's life, there is no way of checking dates with absolute certainty. At present there is still a great deal of personal material that is under copyright, or being held by his wife, Valerie Eliot.

13 Aiken, December 1964, *Selected Letters*, 318.

14 Personal communication.

15 T. S. Eliot, 19 July 1914, *The Letters of T. S. Eliot*, ed. Valerie Eliot (New York: Harcourt, 1988), vol. 1, 40.

16 *Ibid.*, 43.
17 *Ibid.*, 48.
18 David Chinitz, "T. S. Eliot's Blue Verses and Their Sources in the Folk Tradition," *Journal of Modern Literature* 23 (1999–2000), 332.
19 B. C. Southam, *A Student's Guide to the Selected Poems of T. S. Eliot*, 6th edn. (London: Faber and Faber, 1994), 103. In a rather fascinating historical coincidence of which Eliot may or may not have been aware, Matteo Realdo Columbo designates the name of the first (known) person to depict the female clitoris as "the seat of women's delight" in his *De re anatomica* (1559). Valerie Traub writes that, "Columbo's influential treatise, repeated verbatim by medical writers for two centuries, reports that without sufficient attention paid to this organ, a woman neither conceives nor desires to conceive, for it alone governs the expulsion of female seed." Valerie Traub, *Desire and Anxiety: Circulations of Sexuality in Shakespearean Drama* (New York: Routledge, 1992), 91. I want to thank Jodie Medd for drawing my attention to this reference.
20 Southam, *Student's Guide*, 103.
21 Eliot, 10 January 1916, *Letters*, 126.
22 Eliot, Ezra Pound Papers, Beinecke Library, Yale University.
23 Eliot, 19 July 1914, *Letters*, 42.
24 Eliot, 31 October 1917, *Letters*, 205.
25 bell hooks, "Selling Hot Pussy: Representations of Black Female Sexuality in the Cultural Marketplace," in *Writing on the Body: Female Embodiment and Feminist Theory*, eds. Katie Conboy, Nadia Medina, and Sarah Stanbury (New York: Columbia, 1997), 114.
26 Jonathan Goldberg, *Sodometries: Renaissance Texts, Modern Sexualities* (Stanford: Stanford University Press, 1992), 193.
27 Hayden White, *Metahistory* (Baltimore: Johns Hopkins University Press, 1973), 4.
28 Frantz Fanon, *Black Skin, White Masks* (New York: Grove Press, 1967), 151.
29 Eliot, letter to Bonamy Dobrée of 27 September 1927, Brotherton Collection, University of Leeds.
30 McClintock, *Imperial Leather*, 47.
31 Wyndham Lewis, *The Letters of Wyndham Lewis*, ed. W. K. Rose (Norfolk, CT: New Directions, 1963), 68.
32 Ezra Pound, 27? January 1922, *Letters of T. S. Eliot*, 505.
33 Eve Kosofsky Sedgwick, *Epistemology of the Closet* (Berkeley: University of California Press, 1990), 72.
34 Eliot, *Inventions*, 317.
35 Eliot, in *The Faber Book of Blue Verse*, ed. John Whitworth (London: Faber and Faber, 1990), 24.
36 Wendy Wall, *The Imprint of Gender: Authorship and Publication in the English Renaissance* (Ithaca, NY: Cornell University Press, 1993), 14.
37 *Ibid.*, 13.
38 Koestenbaum's essay on Eliot and Pound's collaborative effort on *The Waste Land* in *Double Talk: The Erotics of Male Literary Collaboration* (New York:

Routledge, 1989) undertakes one of the very first queer readings of Eliot's poetic practices.

39 Pound, Ezra Pound papers, Beinecke Library, Yale University.

40 Michael North, *The Dialect of Modernism: Race, Language, and Twentieth-Century Literature* (Oxford: Oxford University Press, 1994), 77.

41 Herbert Read, "T. S. Eliot – A Memoir," in *T. S. Eliot: The Man and His Work*, ed. Allen Tate (London: Chatto and Windus, 1967), 15.

42 Carole Seymour-Jones, *Painted Shadow: A Life of Vivienne Eliot* (London: Constable, 2001), 422.

43 Eliot, 10 January 1916, *Letters*, 126. Charlie Chaplin is an interesting figure for Eliot to invoke: he played with mask, mime, and gesture along with a gender-bending self-presentation through the new medium of film. Eliot, however, "with his aversion to cinema . . . acknowledged Chaplin's genius only reluctantly," as David Chinitz aptly indicates. *T. S. Eliot and the Cultural Divide* (Chicago: University of Chicago Press, 2003), 210. Michael North also notes that, in a 1932 study of London, Thomas Burke claimed that Chaplin "is the first man in the history of the world of whom it can truly and literally be said that he is world-famous. Kings, prime ministers, and singers may be famous in the civilised world, but Charles is known in regions where Napoleon and Beethoven and Mussolini have never been heard of." Michael North, *Reading 1922: A Return to the Scene of the Modern* (New York: Oxford University Press, 1999), 220.

44 Homi Bhabha, *The Location of Culture* (New York: Routledge, 1994), 88.

45 Eliot was sensitive to intimations of his homosexual predilections, and famously tried to suppress an essay written by John Peter in 1952 that made the case for *The Waste Land* as a homosexual love story about Phlebas.

46 Eliot, *Inventions*, 316.

47 Eliot, 30 September 1914, *Letters*, 59.

48 Eliot, 19 July 1914, *Letters*, 42.

49 Perhaps not realizing that Eliot had initially tried to get some of these poems published, Anthony Lane suggests in a review of Ricks's volume in *The New Yorker* that Eliot may have "held back from publishing houses some of these verses for fear they would turn weak stomachs." Anthony Lane, "Writing Wrongs," *The New Yorker* (10 March 1997), 86.

50 Lewis, *Letters*, 66–7. With an uncanny appropriateness, the *Oxford English Dictionary* cites Lewis's letter to Eliot about Eliot's poems "The Triumph of Bullshit" and "Ballade pour la grosse Lulu" as the first examples of the use of the term "bullshit" in the English language.

51 Ezra Pound, *The Correspondence of Ezra Pound: Pound/Lewis*, ed. Timothy Materer (New York: New Directions, 1934), 9.

52 Eliot, 2 February 1915, *Letters*, 86.

53 "Rhapsody of a Windy Night" was the title under which Eliot's poem first appeared. This was changed to read "Rhapsody on a Windy Night" in later collections.

54 Eliot, 28 July 1922, *Letters*, 553.

55 *The Waste Land: A Facsimile and Transcript of the Original Drafts, Including the Annotations of Ezra Pound*, ed. Valerie Eliot (New York: Harvest, 1971), 39.
56 Eliot, 21 May 1921, *Letters*, 455.
57 *Ibid.*
58 Eliot, 9 July 1919, *Letters*, 314.
59 Eliot, 21 May 1921, *Letters*, 455.
60 Eliot, 10 January 1916, *Letters*, 125.
61 Lines 62-3, in *The Complete Poems and Plays*.
62 Eliot, 10 January 1916, *Letters*, 125.
63 Eliot, 19 July 1914, *Letters*, 41.
64 Eliot, 14 October 1914, *Letters*, 61.
65 Eliot, 13 March 1918, *Letters*, 224.
66 Eliot, 11? July 1919, *Letters*, 318.
67 Eliot, 23 June 1919, *Letters*, 307.
68 Eliot, 26 January 1919, *Letters*, 269.
69 Eliot, 19 July 1922, 21 September 1922, and 27 December 1922, *Letters*, 547–8, 571–4 and 615. See also Christopher Ricks's Preface, *Inventions*, xi–xxi.
70 Virginia Woolf, 20 September 1920, *The Diary of Virginia Woolf*, 5 vols., ed. Anne Olivier Bell (New York: Harcourt, 1980), vol. II, 68.
71 Eliot, 15 February 1920, *Letters*, 363.
72 James Graham, "Brand New Eliot," review of *Inventions of the March Hare, Literary Supplement*, http://www.newmassmedia.com/ls97spring/eliot.html (Spring 1997), 2.
73 Jan Gorak, "Mind in Motion," *Denver Quarterly* 33 (Spring 1998), 32–9.
74 Bonamy Dobrée, quoted in Eliot, *Inventions*, 321.
75 North, *Dialect*, 82.
76 Jonathan Gill, "Protective Coloring: Modernism and Blackface Minstrelsy in the Bolo Poems," in *T. S. Eliot's Orchestra: Critical Essays on Poetry and Music*, ed. John Xiros Cooper (New York: Garland, 2000), 70–1.
77 Entry in Alex Preminger and T. V. F. Brogan, eds., *The New Princeton Encyclopedia of Poetry and Poetics* (Princeton: Princeton University Press, 1993), 219.
78 Alex Zwerdling, "Inventions of the March Hare: Poems," *Modernism/Modernity* 5.2 (1998), 43.
79 *Ibid.*
80 Eliot, *Inventions*, 318 and 319.
81 Colleen Lamos, *Deviant Modernism: Sexual and Textual Errancy in T. S. Eliot, James Joyce, and Marcel Proust* (Cambridge: Cambridge University Press, 1998), 1 and 10.
82 The Krazy Kat comic strip (1913–44), penned by George Herriman (1880–1944), a mixed-race cartoonist born in New Orleans but raised in California, obsessively charts the confrontations between a mouse, a cat named Krazy Kat, and a dog police officer, Bull Pupp. Like Bolo's Kween, "Krazy's gender is explicitly indeterminate," as Eyal Amiran shows

in "George Herriman's Black Sentence: The Legibility of Race in *Krazy Kat*," *Mosaic* 33:3 (September 2000), 59. The cartoon was not especially popular in its day, but it has come to be considered one of the great incarnations of early comics, and now has a rather large following.

83 Conrad Aiken, "King Bolo and Others," in *T. S. Eliot: A Symposium from Conrad Aiken and Others*, eds. Richard March and Thurairajah Tambimuttu (London: London Editions, 1948), 21.

84 I am grateful to Hortense Spillers for these comments, written in response to an early version of this chapter.

85 Aiken, "King Bolo and Others," 22.

86 Jacques Derrida, *The Truth in Painting*, trans. Geoff Bennington and Ian McLeod (Chicago: University of Chicago Press, 1987), 54.

87 *Ibid.*, 56.

88 Aiken, "King Bolo and Others," 22.

CHAPTER 2
MIXING MEMORY AND DESIRE: REREADING ELIOT AND THE BODY OF HISTORY

1 T. S. Eliot, *The Letters of T. S. Eliot*, ed. Valerie Eliot (New York: Harcourt, 1988), vol. I, 172.

2 Dante Alighieri, *Divine Comedy: The Inferno*, trans. Mark Musa (New York: Penguin, 2002), Canto IV, lines 41-2, and *Divina Commedia: Inferno, Purgatorio, Paradiso* (Rome: Newton e Compton, 1993).

3 T. S. Eliot, *The Waste Land. T. S. Eliot: The Complete Poems and Plays* (London: Faber and Faber, 1990), lines 1-4. All subsequent quotations from Eliot's poetry are taken from *The Complete Poems and Plays*, and in each instance I will give line numbers parenthetically within the text.

4 Alexander Pope, *The Rape of the Lock*, ed. Cynthia Wall (Boston: Bedford, 1998), Canto III, line 8.

5 Virginia Woolf, *The Years*, 1937 (New York: Penguin, 1968), 224.

6 Charles Baudelaire, "Correspondences," *Les fleurs du mal/The Flowers of Evil*, ed. Jonathan Culler, trans. James McGowan (Oxford: Oxford University Press, 1993), 18. "Nature is a temple where living pillars / sometimes emit confusing speech" (my translation).

7 T. S. Eliot, *The Selected Prose of T. S. Eliot*, ed. Frank Kermode (New York: Harcourt 1988), 60.

8 Paul Veyne, *Writing History: Essay on Epistemology*, 1971, trans. Mina Moore-Rinvolucri (Middletown, CT: Wesleyan University Press, 1984), 65.

9 Michel de Certeau, *The Writing of History*, 1975, trans. Tom Conley (New York: Columbia University Press, 1988), 80.

10 The feminization of remembering and historicizing that takes place in "Gerontion" is not unique to T. S. Eliot, and we find a similar tendency at work in other major modernist writers. John S. Rickard draws our attention to a key passage in James Joyce's *A Portrait of the Artist as a Young Man* where

Stephen Dedalus, he argues, "imagines those who remember as feminine and weak." Rickard quotes from Stephen's diary entry of "*6 April*" to illustrate his point: "Certainly she remembers the past. Lynch says all women do . . . The past is consumed in the present and the present is living only because it brings forth the future. Statues of women, if Lynch be right, should always be fully draped, one hand of the woman feeling regretfully her own hinder parts." Stephen thus associates historicity with a too provocative, slightly distasteful, feminization and sexualization. In the analogy, female statues (quite literally, ossified emblems of the past's physicality) ought to be veiled, lest the erotic, masturbatory element drawing one to the "hinder parts" (hindsight?) of history proves too much. John S. Rickard, *Joyce's Book of Memory: The Mnemotechnic of* Ulysses (Durham, NC: Duke University Press, 1999), 73, and James Joyce, *A Portrait of the Artist as a Young Man*, ed. R. B. Kershner (New York: Bedford, 1993), 216.

11 This chiasmus fits within a pattern of reversals that dominate the poem's chain of logic. Using Eliot's language, we might call these reversals the poem's "backward devils" (line 53). Our expectations are continually turned around when we encounter conceits such as, "the giving famishes the craving" (line 39), "Unnatural vices / Are fathered by our heroism" (lines 44-5), "Virtues / Are forced upon us by our impudent crimes" (lines 45-6). This counterpointed movement further encodes Eliot's poetics of (queer) inversion.

12 Virginia Woolf, *To the Lighthouse*, 1927, Foreword by Eudora Welty (New York: Harcourt, 1981), 178.

13 Edmund Burke, *A Philosophical Enquiry into the Origin of our Ideas of the Sublime and the Beautiful*, 1757 (Oxford: Oxford University Press, 1990), 136 and 160.

14 Christine Froula, "Eliot's Grail Quest, or, The Lover, the Police, and *The Waste Land*," *Yale Review* 78 (1989), 243.

15 Jacques Lacan, *The Four Fundamental Concepts of Psychoanalysis: The Seminar of Jacques Lacan, Book* XI, ed. Jacques-Alain Miller, trans. Alan Sheridan (New York: Norton, 1981), 38.

16 Jacques Lacan, *Ecrits: A Selection*, trans. Alan Sheridan (New York: Norton, 1977), 58.

17 Patrick Fuery, *Theories of Desire* (Carlton: Melbourne University Press, 1995), 17.

18 Walter Benjamin, "A Berlin Chronicle," 1932, in *Reflections: Essays, Aphorisms, Autobiographical Writings*, ed. Peter Demetz (New York: Schocken, 1978), 6.

19 This near synonymity of memory and history seems endemic both to modernism and to writings about the period. In a wonderfully comprehensive review article, "The Case of Modern Memory," *The Journal of Modern History* 73 (2001), 87–117, Peter Fritzsche catalogues more than fifteen books on modernism, history, and memory. Quite strikingly, the terms "memory" and "history" are frequently conjoined in the titles he delineates – all of which Fritzsche himself writes about under the rubric of "Modern Memory." Here are a few examples: *Acts of Memory: Cultural Recall in the Present*, eds. Mieke Bal, Jonathan Crewe, and Leo Spitzer (Hanover, NH: University Press

of New England, 1999); Cathy Caruth, *Unclaimed Experience: Trauma, Narrative, and History* (Baltimore: Johns Hopkins University Press, 1996); Adrian Gregory, *The Silence of Memory: Armistice Day 1919–1946* (Oxford: Berg Publishers, 1994); Dominick LaCapra, *History and Memory after Auschwitz* (Ithaca, NY: Cornell University Press, 1998); and Jay Winter, *Sites of Memory, Sites of Mourning: The Great War in European Cultural History* (Cambridge: Cambridge University Press, 1995). In *Literatures of Memory: History, Time, and Space in Postwar Writing* (Manchester: Manchester University Press, 2000), Peter Middleton and Tim Woods point out on the first page that

> Memory, both individual and social, plays such a large part in this cultural poetics that the framing axioms of literary historicism are commonly represented by the texts themselves as forms of memory. We have, therefore, entitled this study *Literatures of Memory*, to describe the intersection between this self-understanding of contemporary literature when it looks backward and a prevalent politics of history in public culture which also relies on memory as the mediator between present and past.

Finally, in a discussion of Nietzsche's proto-modernist historical and mnemonic model, Hayden White makes the boundaries between memory and history purposefully uncertain: "it is not a matter of man's *needing* memory; it is the glory and perdition of man that he irredeemably *has* memory. Therefore, he *has* history, whether he wants it or not." *Metahistory* (Baltimore: Johns Hopkins University Press, 1973), 348.

20 See Veyne, *Writing History*, 12.

21 Frederic Jameson, *The Political Unconscious: Narrative as a Socially Symbolic Act* (Ithaca, NY: Cornell University Press, 1981), 35.

22 Roland Barthes, "The Discourse of History," trans. Stephen Bann, Comparative Criticism 3 (1981), 12.

23 De Certeau, *The Writing of History*, 287.

24 Jan Assman, "Collective Memory and Cultural Identity," *New German Critique* 65 (1995), 132–3.

25 *Ibid.*, 130.

26 Sigmund Freud, "Leonardo da Vinci and a Memory of his Childhood," 1910, in *The Standard Edition of the Complete Psychological Works of Sigmund Freud*, trans. James Strachey, 24 vols. (London: Hogarth Press, 1978), vol. XI, 83.

27 Sigmund Freud, "Screen Memories," 1899*a*, in *The Standard Edition*, vol. III, 315.

28 Veyne, *Writing History*, 26.

29 *Ibid.*, 72.

30 Freud, "Leonardo," in *The Standard Edition*, 84. The parenthetical insertion occurs in James Strachey's English translation. Strachey points out in a note that "Chapter IV of *The Psychotheology of Everyday Life* (1901*b*) deals with childhood memories and screen-memories, and, in an addition made to it in 1907, Freud makes the same comparison with historical writing," 84.

31 Michel Foucault, "Nietzsche, Genealogy, History," in *Language, Counter-Memory, Practice: Selected Essays and Interviews*, trans. and ed. Donald F. Bouchard (Ithaca, NY: Cornell University Press, 1977), 162.

32 Michael Steinberg (ed.), *Walter Benjamin and the Demands of History* (Ithaca, NY: Cornell University Press, 1996).

33 Virginia Woolf, "A Sketch of the Past," 1941, in *Moments of Being*, ed. Jeanne Schulkind (New York: Harcourt, 1985), 142.

34 Homi Bhabha (ed.), *Nation and Narration* (New York: Routledge, 1990), 293.

35 Grover Smith, *T. S. Eliot and the Use of Memory* (Lewisburg, PA: Bucknell University Press, 1996).

36 No trace of Bergson's lectures remains at the Sorbonne, the Bibliothèque Nationale, or the Archives Nationale. He did, though, give a series of talks entitled "The Perception of Change" at Oxford in May 1911 from which I cite. In his wonderfully comprehensive list of Eliot's "Student Papers," Lawrence Rainey points out that the Houghton Library at Harvard University houses twenty-four leaves of *Eliot's* notes on Bergson's lectures. Lawrence Rainey, *Revisiting The Waste Land* (New Haven: Yale University Press, 2005), 194.

37 Henri Bergson, *Matter and Memory*, trans. N. M. Paul and W. S. Palmer (from the 5th edition of 1908) (New York: Zone Books, 1991), 67.

38 *Ibid.*, 65–6.

39 *Ibid.*, 73.

40 Donald Childs, "Eliot's Rhapsody of Matter and Memory," *American Literature* 63 (1991), 475.

41 *Ibid.*

42 Frank Kermode draws our attention to Eliot's repeated use of this remarkable phrase from *The Revenger's Tragedy* (1607): "*Are lordships sold to maintain ladyships / For the poor benefit of a bewildering minute?*" Eliot cites the passage in "Tradition and the Individual Talent," then again in his essay on Tourneur in 1931, as well as in a letter to Stephen Spender in 1935. To Spender he writes, "You don't . . . really criticize any author to whom you have never surrendered yourself . . . Even just the bewildering minute counts." Frank Kermode (ed.), *The Selected Prose of T. S. Eliot* (New York: Harcourt, 1975), 13.

43 Compare this elegiac invocation of the "rose-garden" with one of Eliot's earliest poems, "Song," published in *The Harvard Advocate* in 1907, while Eliot was an undergraduate:

> When we came across the hill
> No leaves were fallen from the trees;
> The gentle fingers of the breeze
> Had torn no quivering cobweb down.
>
> The hedgerow bloomed with flowers still
> No withered petals lay beneath;
> But the wild roses in your wreath
> Were faded, and the leaves were brown.

44 Rather than signaling erotic tribute, Eliot's flowers frequently designate an inaccessibility, a deadness, a desiccation, or even a kind of trickery (we might think of the snow on the hedgerow in "Little Gidding" that momentarily appears as blossoms: "Now the hedgerow / Is blanched for an hour with

transitory blossom / Of snow," lines 14-16). Flowers also point to sensory breakdown, as in the "hyacinth girl" section of *The Waste Land.*

45 Sigmund Freud and Joseph Breuer, "Studies on Hysteria," 1895*d* [1893–5], in *The Standard Edition*, vol. II, 7.

46 *Ibid.*, 17.

47 H. D., *Tribute to Freud*, 1944 (New York: New Directions, 1974), 103.

48 Nancy K. Gish points out that "The hysteria has been read as either the man's or the woman's. I suggest that in terms of then-current views of hysteria, both characters are hysterics. The uncontrollable laughter is, in Janet's terms, one form of 'automatic agitation.'" Cassandra Laity and Nancy K. Gish (eds.), *Gender, Desire, and Sexuality in T. S. Eliot* (Cambridge: Cambridge University Press, 2004), 128. Gish refers her reader here to Pierre Janet, *The Major Symptoms of Hysteria* (New York: Macmillan, 1907), 257–62.

49 John Peter, "A New Interpretation of *The Waste Land*," *Essays in Criticism* 2 (1952), 243.

50 Sandra M. Gilbert and Susan Gubar, *No Man's Land: The Place of the Woman Writer in the Twentieth Century: The War of the Words* (New Haven: Yale University Press, 1988), 235.

51 Wayne Koestenbaum, *Double Talk: The Erotics of Male Literary Collaboration* (New York: Routledge, 1989), 135.

52 *Ibid.*, 137.

53 Harold Bloom (ed.), *T. S. Eliot* (New York: Chelsea House, 1985), 2.

54 See my Introduction for a brief outline of arguments in the past decades that have insisted on modernism's disavowals of historical awareness.

55 John Middleton Murry, review of T. S. Eliot's *Poems*, in *The Times Literary Supplement* (12 June 1919).

56 W. B. Yeats, "Modern Poetry," in *Essays and Introductions* (New York: Macmillan, 1961).

57 W. B. Yeats, "Coole and Ballylee," in *The Collected Poems of W. B. Yeats*, ed. Richard J. Finneran (New York: Scribner, 1996), lines 41-2, my emphasis.

58 T. S. Eliot, *On Poetry and Poets* (London: Faber and Faber, 1957), 262.

59 T. S. Eliot, 23 June 1918, *The Letters of T. S. Eliot*, ed. Valerie Eliot (New York: Harcourt, 1988), vol. I, 235.

60 Eliot, 16 March 1920, *Letters*, 371 and 13 September 1920, *Letters*, 406.

61 Lyndall Gordon, *T. S. Eliot: An Imperfect Life* (London: W. W. Norton, 1998), 503.

62 Walter Benjamin, "A Berlin Chronicle," 26.

63 John Webster, *The White Devil*, 1612, ed. John Russell Brown (Manchester: Manchester University Press, 1996), lines 9-10.

64 When the facsimile and transcript of *The Waste Land* were finally published in 1971, Eliot's widow, Valerie Eliot, included a brief Preface by Ezra Pound written in Venice in 1969, four years after Eliot's death. In an interesting echo of the *topos* of burial in the poem, Pound begins with the statement, "The more we know of Eliot, the better. I am thankful that the lost leaves have been unearthed." *The Waste Land: A Facsimile and Transcript of the Original Drafts,*

Including the Annotations of Ezra Pound, ed. Valerie Eliot (New York: Harvest, 1971), vii.

65 In a poet noted for his "impersonality" – an issue to which I will return – in this section of *The Waste Land* Eliot comes as close to autobiography as at any other point in the poem, naming the exact seaside town where he went to convalesce after his psychological breakdown in October of 1921. Margate was also where he first worked on drafting the poem.

66 Christine Froula, "Eliot's Grail Quest, or, The Lover, the Police, and *The Waste Land*," *Yale Review* 78 (1989), 245.

67 Freud, "Remembering, Repeating, and Working Through," 1914g, in *The Standard Edition*, vol. XII, 147 and ff.

68 Cathy Caruth (ed.), *Trauma: Explorations in Memory* (Baltimore: Johns Hopkins University Press, 1995), 5.

69 Caruth, *Unclaimed Experience*, 11.

70 *Ibid.*, 17 and 58.

71 *Ibid.*, 61.

72 Paul de Man, *Blindness and Insight: Essays in the Rhetoric of Contemporary Criticism*, 2nd edn. (Minneapolis: University of Minnesota Press, 1983), 147.

73 *Ibid.*

74 Friedrich Nietzsche, "On the Utility and Liability of History for Life," in *Unfashionable Observations*, trans. Richard T. Gray (Stanford: Stanford University Press, 1995), 107.

75 *Ibid.*, 87.

76 Richard Macksey, "The Architecture of Time: Dialectics and Structure," in *Marcel Proust's Remembrance of Things Past*, ed. Harold Bloom (New York: Chelsea House, 1987), 91.

77 Walter Jackson Bate, *The Burden of the Past and the English Poet* (Cambridge, MA: Belknap Press, 1970).

78 Eliot, 31 December 1914, *Letters*, 75.

79 Alan Marshall, "England and Nowhere," in *The Cambridge Companion to T. S. Eliot*, ed. A. David Moody (Cambridge: Cambridge University Press, 1994), 100.

80 Eliot, lines 106-9, *The Waste Land: A Facsimile*, 31 and 43, with slight variations in punctuation, as per the facsimile.

81 Pound, Postmark 28 June 1915, *Letters of T. S. Eliot*, 100–1.

82 John Donne, qtd. in T. S. Eliot, "The Metaphysical Poets," in *Selected Prose of T. S. Eliot*, 60.

83 Virginia Woolf, "Modern Fiction," 1925, in *The Common Reader*, ed. Andrew McNeillie (New York: Harcourt, 1984), 150.

84 Yeats, "Sailing to Byzantium," lines 1-3, in *Collected Poems of W. B. Yeats.*

85 Jean-Jacques Rousseau, "Essay on the Origin of Languages," in *On the Origin of Language*, trans. John H. Moran and Alexander Gode (Chicago: University of Chicago Press, 1966), 19.

86 Michel Foucault, "Nietzsche, Genealogy, History," 148.

87 Thirteen years later Eliot revisits this phrase, "heart of light," including distinctly Eastern overtones, through his reference to a "lotos" flower: "the

pool was filled with water out of sunlight, / And the lotos rose, quietly, quietly, / The surface glittered out of heart of light" ("Burnt Norton," lines 37-9). This "heart of light," of course, stands in stark contrast to Joseph Conrad's vision of the "heart of darkness," and we might read Eliot's recurring attention to this image as a way of asserting the possibility of sexual, spiritual, or psychic redemption *contra* Kurtz's world view. Eliot was certainly indebted to Conrad, and he had initially given an epigraph to *The Waste Land* from *Heart of Darkness* but removed it at Pound's request: "Did he live his life again in every detail of desire, temptation, and surrender during that supreme moment of complete knowledge? He cried in a whisper at some image, at some vision, – he cried out twice, a cry that was no more than a breath – 'The horror! the horror!'" *The Waste Land: A Facsimile*, 2-3. The questions here very forcefully draw together key aspects of the relation between memory and desire that Eliot makes central to the poem. Pound, however, wrote to Eliot: "I doubt if Conrad is weighty enough to stand the citation." Pound, 24 Saturnus An I [24 December 1921], *Letters of T. S. Eliot*, 497. In 1925 Eliot returned to Conrad's *Heart of Darkness*, this time without an intervention, for another epigraph: "*Mistah Kurtz – he dead*," "The Hollow Men."

88 In his footnotes to the poem Eliot links line 20 to Ezekiel (II, i) and line 23 to Ecclesiastes (XII, v).

89 Michael Levenson, "Does *The Waste Land* Have a Politics?" *Modernism/Modernity*, 6.3 (1999), 5.

90 Harriet Davidson, "Improper Desire: Reading *The Waste Land*," in *The Cambridge Companion to T. S. Eliot*, 122.

91 Eliot, lines 39-40 and 40-1, *The Waste Land: A Facsimile*, 10-11 and 16-17.

92 Virginia Woolf, 19 April 1925, *The Diary of Virginia Woolf*, ed. Anne Olivier Bell, vol. III (New York: Harcourt, 1980), 10.

93 Eliot, lines 45-6, *The Waste Land: A Facsimile*, 12-13 and 18-19.

94 Nicholas Andrew Miller, *Modernism, Ireland and the Erotics of Memory* (Cambridge: Cambridge University Press, 2002), 176.

95 Ralph Waldo Emerson, *Nature. Emerson's Prose and Poetry*, eds. Joel Porte and Saundra Morris (New York: Norton, 2000), 27.

96 Richard Badenhausen, *T. S. Eliot and the Art of Collaboration* (Cambridge: Cambridge University Press, 2004), 25.

97 John Davy Hayward Bequest, King's College Library, Cambridge University.

98 Eliot, "The Metaphysical Poets," 66.

CHAPTER 3
ELIOT, EROS, AND DESIRE: "OH, DO NOT ASK, 'WHAT IS IT?'"

1 T. S. Eliot, *The Complete Poems and Plays* (London: Faber and Faber, 1990). All subsequent quotations from Eliot's poetry are taken from this source and in each instance I will give line numbers parenthetically within the text.

2 T. S. Eliot, 30 September 1914, *The Letters of T. S. Eliot*, ed. Valerie Eliot (New York: Harcourt, 1988), vol. I, 58.

3 *Ibid.*
4 I am grateful to Tim Conley for pointing out the attribution to Wellington, and to alerting me to the frequency with which the phrase appears in Joyce's novel.
5 Eliot, 30 September 1914, *Letters*, 59.
6 *Ibid.*
7 Wayne Koestenbaum, *Double Talk: The Erotics of Male Literary Collaboration* (New York: Routledge, 1989).
8 Ezra Pound, 24 Saturnus An 1 [24 December 1921], *Letters of T. S. Eliot*, 497.
9 Eliot, 24? January 1922, *Letters*, 504.
10 Pound, 27? January 1922, *Letters of T. S. Eliot*, 505.
11 Pound, 24 Saturnus An 1 [24 December 1921], *Letters of T. S. Eliot*, 497, and Eliot, 24? January 1922, *Letters*, 504.
12 Pound, 27? January 1922, *Letters of T. S. Eliot*, 505.
13 Eliot, 9 July 1922, *Letters*, 539.
14 Eliot, 19 July 1922, *Letters*, 550.
15 In the published correspondence we have of Eliot's, most of his letters are signed, even if with only an initial or a nickname. Eliot, though, also happens to leave unsigned the early January 1922 letter to Pound in which he notes, "Wish to use Caesarean operation in italics in front." *Letters*, 504.
16 Eliot, 6 September 1916, *Letters*, 151.
17 Jewel Spears Brooker, "The Great War at Home and Abroad: Violence and Sexuality in Eliot's 'Sweeney Erect,'" *Modernism/Modernity* 9.3 (2002), 426.
18 Jacques Lacan, "Of the Subject of Certainty," *The Seminar of Jacques Lacan, Book XI*, ed. Jacques-Alain Miller, trans. Alan Sheridan (New York: Norton, 1998), 31 and 30.
19 *Ibid.*, 31.
20 T. S. Eliot, "Baudelaire," in *T. S. Eliot: Selected Essays* (London: Faber and Faber, 1999), 235. My emphasis.
21 B. C. Southam, *A Student's Guide to the Selected Poems of T. S. Eliot*, 6th edn. (London: Faber and Faber, 1994), 48.
22 Marja Palmer, *Men and Women in T. S. Eliot's Early Poetry* (Lund, Sweden: Lund University Press, 1996), 23.
23 Paul Fussell, *The Great War and Modern Memory* (New York: Oxford University Press, 1975), 13.
24 *Ibid.*, 17.
25 *Ibid.*, 41.
26 Lyndall Gordon, *T. S. Eliot: An Imperfect Life* (London: W. W. Norton, 1998), 137.
27 Although the Great War stands as a major historical and mnemonic experience in Eliot's mind, Eliot did not see it as *the* watershed point that so many critics have claimed initiated our particular modernity. Paul Fussell, for instance, claims that the First World War brought about a total shift in the ethos of the modern world. With notably anti-Foucauldian interests in tracing specific historical origins, Fussell suggests that when the Military

Service Act (establishing conscription) was passed in England early in 1916, the event "could be said to mark the beginning of the modern world." Fussell, *The Great War*, 11. Certainly there was a strong sense among modernist writers that the early twentieth century marked a decisive break from the past. Woolf herself famously asserts that "on or about December 1910 human character changed." Virginia Woolf, "Character in Fiction," 1924, in *The Essays of Virginia Woolf: 1919–1924*, 6 vols., ed. Andrew McNeillie (London: Hogarth Press, 1967), vol. III, 421. Her statement reveals a playful wish to seek out originary moments, even if, as Rachel Bowlby argues, Woolf here "takes the line of historical determination as far as it will go, to a point where chronological precision practically becomes a caricature of this type of explanation." Rachel Bowlby, *Virginia Woolf: Feminist Destinations* (Oxford: Blackwell, 1988), 4. In a short essay from 1939, "Last Words," with which Eliot "terminate[d]" his "editorship of *The Criterion*," he looked back on the First World War and its aftermath as the last gasp of an *old* order rather than the birth of a new: "Only from about the year 1926 did the features of the post-war world begin clearly to emerge – and not only in the sphere of politics. From about that date one began slowly to realize that the intellectual and artistic output of the previous seven years had been rather the last efforts of an old world, than the first struggles of a new." T. S. Eliot, "Last Words," *The Criterion* 71 (January 1939), 271.

28 Eliot, 18 November 1915, *Letters*, 121.

29 Eliot, 10 January 1916, *Letters*, 125.

30 I. A. Richards, *Principles of Literary Criticism*, 1926 (New York: Harcourt, 1926), 292.

31 T. S. Eliot, "The Three Provincialities," 1922, *Essays in Criticism* 1 (1951), 40.

32 Virginia Woolf, 15 November 1918, *The Diary of Virginia Woolf*, 5 vols., ed. Anne Olivier Bell (New York: Harcourt, 1980), vol. I, 219.

33 *Ibid.*, 217.

34 *Ibid.*, 218–19.

35 Joseph Conrad, *The Nigger of the Narcissus*, 1897 (London: Penguin, 1988), xlix.

36 Roland Barthes, "The Death of the Author," in *Image, Music, Text*, ed. and trans. Stephen Heath (New York: Hill, 1977), 148.

37 Julia Kristeva, *Desire in Language: A Semiotic Approach to Literature and Art*, ed. Leon S. Roudiez, trans. Thomas Gora, Alice Jardine, and Leon S. Roudiez (New York: Columbia University Press, 1980), 117.

38 Walter Benjamin, "The Task of the Translator," in *Illuminations: Essays and Reflections*, ed. Hannah Arendt, trans. Harry Zohn (New York: Schocken, 1968), 79.

39 T. S. Eliot, "Dante," in *The Selected Prose of T. S. Eliot*, ed. Frank Kermode (New York: Harcourt, 1988), 206 and 207.

40 *Ibid.*, 206.

41 Jacques Lacan, "The Subversion of the Subject and the Dialectic of Desire in the Freudian Unconscious," *Écrits: A Selection*, trans. Alan Sheridan (New York: Norton, 1977), 309.

42 Lyndall Gordon, "Eliot and Women," in *T. S. Eliot: The Modernist in History*, ed. Ronald Bush (Cambridge: Cambridge University Press, 1991), 16.
43 Slavoj Žižek, *The Ticklish Subject* (London: Verso, 1999), 267.
44 Françoise Meltzer, *Hot Property: The Stakes and Claims of Literary Originality* (Chicago: University of Chicago Press, 1994), 159.
45 I take this suggestion about colonizing the feminine from Judith Butler, *Gender Trouble: Feminism and the Subversion of Identity* (New York: Routledge, 1990), 122.
46 Sigmund Freud, "The 'Uncanny,'" 1919*h*, in *The Standard Edition of the Complete Psychological Works of Sigmund Freud*, trans. James Strachey, 24 vols. (London: Hogarth Press, 1978), vol. XVII, 224.
47 *Ibid.*, 241.
48 I want to thank Jonathan Culler for insisting, in a discussion on the topic of Eliot and sexuality, on the erotic dimension of Prufrock's corporeal discovery.
49 Eliot, 31 December 1914, *Letters*, 75.
50 Eliot, "Philip Massinger," in *Selected Essays*, 206.
51 Valerie Eliot, footnote 2, Eliot, 27 March 1916, *Letters*, 135.
52 Eliot, 27 March 1916, *Letters*, 135. Jodie Medd has examined at length a tendency to blame female editors of little magazines for ostensible plagiarism and indecencies of male writers. She argues that the important modernist patron, John Quinn, held the lesbian editors of *The Little Review*, Margaret Anderson and Jane Heap, responsible for the editorial decisions that allowed sexually explicit phrases such as "scrotumtightening sea" into the serialized version of Joyce's *Ulysses*. In Medd's argument, Quinn's criticism stems from a homophobic panic about the content of scandalous sexual material – a panic that was then displaced and projected onto Anderson and Heap, who then became guilty for the "dirty" content of the novel. Jodie Medd, "Extraordinary Allegations: Scandalous Female Homosexuality and the Culture of Modernism," PhD dissertation, Cornell University, 2001.
53 Françoise Meltzer, *Hot Property*, 48.
54 Eliot, "Philip Massinger," 206.
55 Richard Aldington, "Epigrams," in *Images of Desire* (London: Elkin Mathews, 1919), 10.
56 Richard Aldington, "Reserve," in *Images of Desire*, 20.
57 Eliot, "Tradition and the Individual Talent," 1919, in *Selected Essays*, 15.

CHAPTER 4
T. S. ELIOT: WRITING TIME AND BLASTING MEMORY

1 Lines 126-30, in T. S. Eliot, *The Complete Poems and Plays* (London: Faber and Faber, 1990). All subsequent quotations from Eliot's poetry are taken from this source, and in each instance I will give line numbers parenthetically within the text.

2 This is the opening octet from what Eliot calls "the original draft of the first poem I ever wrote to be shown to other eyes." T. S. Eliot, "If Time and Space as Sages Say," John Davy Hayward Collection, V2/F2, King's College Library, Cambridge University.
3 Virginia Woolf, "A Sketch of the Past," 1941, in *Moments of Being*, ed. Jeanne Schulkind (New York: Harcourt, 1985), 147.
4 Jacques Lacan, *The Four Fundamental Concepts of Psychoanalysis: The Seminar of Jacques Lacan, Book* XI, ed. Jacques-Alain Miller, trans. Alan Sheridan (New York: Norton, 1981), 61.
5 Lyndall Gordon, *Virginia Woolf: A Writer's Life* (London: Oxford University Press, 1984).
6 Lyndall Gordon, *T. S. Eliot: An Imperfect Life* (London: W. W. Norton, 1998), 511–12.
7 Friedrich Nietzsche, "On the Utility and Liability of History for Life," in *Unfashionable Observations*, trans. Richard T. Gray (Stanford: Stanford University Press, 1995), 130.
8 Edwin Muir, "What is Modern," qtd. in *Modernism: An Anthology of Sources and Documents*, ed. Vassiliki Kolocotroni, Jane Goldman, and Olga Taxidou (Chicago: University of Chicago Press, 1998), 355.
9 John Middleton Murry, editorial, *Rhythm* 1.36 (Summer 1911), 27.
10 Muir, "What is Modern," 357.
11 *Ibid.*
12 Michael Levenson, "Does *The Waste Land* Have a Politics?" *Modernism/Modernity* 6.3 (1999), 1.
13 T. S. Eliot, communication to Henry Ware Eliot, Jr., epigraph, *The Waste Land: A Facsimile and Transcript*, ed. Valerie Eliot (New York: Harcourt, 1971), 1.
14 Frank Kermode, *The Selected Prose of T. S. Eliot*, ed. Frank Kermode (New York: Harcourt, 1988), 17.
15 Kermode draws an important analogy between Eliot's notion of impersonality and his preoccupation with what I am calling "writing time," noting that in Eliot's essay on Seneca, Eliot, in effect, claims that the "great poet" " 'writes his time,' not himself." Kermode, *Selected Prose*, 17. Kermode also alludes to Eliot's remarks in "Thoughts After Lambeth," where Eliot writes, "some of the more approving critics said I had expressed the 'disillusionment of a generation,' which is nonsense. I may have expressed for them their own illusion of being disillusioned, but that did not form part of my intention." T. S. Eliot, *T. S. Eliot: Selected Essays* (London: Faber and Faber, 1999), 368.
16 T. S. Eliot, 28 April 1918, *The Letters of T. S. Eliot*, ed. Valerie Eliot (New York: Harcourt, 1988), vol. 1, 230.
17 Samuel Hynes, *The Auden Generation: Literature and Politics in England in the 1930s* (New York: Viking, 1972), 27.
18 Ezra Pound, in Wyndham Lewis, *Blast* (London: J. Lane, 1914), 153.
19 William Carlos Williams later emphasizes the *making* of poetry as a kind of *making* time via history in a comment on Ezra Pound's *Cantos*, when he

suggests that the collection "discloses history by its odor, by the feel of it – in the words; fuses it with the words, present and past, to MAKE his *Cantos. Make* them." Cited on the back cover of *The Cantos of Ezra Pound*, 1934 (New York: New Directions, 1993).

20 Wyndham Lewis, *Blast*, 7.

21 *Ibid.*, 5.

22 Advertisement, *The Little Review* 3.2 (1 March 1915).

23 Eliot, 17 November 1921, *Letters*, 487.

24 Eliot, "Tradition and the Individual Talent," 1919, in *Selected Essays*, 14. Hereafter I will cite page numbers from the essay parenthetically within the text.

25 Michel de Certeau, *The Writing of History*, 1975, trans. Tom Conley (New York: Columbia University Press, 1988), 36. James Longenbach draws some fascinating comparisons between Eliot and nineteenth- and twentieth-century philosophers of history – ranging from Wilhelm Dilthey (1833–1911) to F. H. Bradley (1846–1924, on whom Eliot wrote his PhD dissertation at Harvard), Benedetto Croce (1866–1952), and R. G. Collingwood (1889–1943) – that confirm Eliot's perspective on the vitality of the past within the present that I am trying to elaborate. Longenbach points out that for Collingwood in 1946, "history arises from the act of thinking about the past: it is 'a living past, kept alive by the act of historical thinking itself.'" James Longenbach, *Modernist Poetics of History: Pound, Eliot, and the Sense of the Past* (Princeton: Princeton University Press, 1987), 168.

26 Eduardo Cadava, "Lapsus Imaginus: The Image in Ruins," *October* 96 (2001), 53.

27 Woolf, "Sketch," 67.

28 Douglas Mao, *Solid Objects* (Princeton: Princeton University Press, 1999), 38.

29 Elisa K. Sparks, "Old Father Nile: T. S. Eliot and Harold Bloom on the Creative Process as Spontaneous Generation," in *Engendering the Word: Feminist Essays in Psychosexual Politics*, ed. Temma F. Berg (Chicago: University of Illinois Press, 1989), 62 and 71.

30 Elizabeth Beaumont Bissell, "'Something Still More Exact': T. S. Eliot's 'Traditional Claims,'" in *Angelaki: Authorizing Culture*, eds. Gary Hall and Simon Wortham (London: Antony Rowe, 1996), 117.

31 Sandra M. Gilbert and Susan Gubar, *No Man's Land: The Place of the Woman Writer in the Twentieth Century: The War of the Words* (New Haven: Yale University Press, 1988), 154.

32 Eliot, "The Metaphysical Poets," *Selected Prose*, 63.

33 I. A. Richards, *Principles of Literary Criticism*, 1926 (New York: Harcourt, 1926), 292.

34 Cassandra Laity points out that James E. Miller "suggested that Eliot's evocation of poetry as 'an escape from emotion' 'seems not shaped by the 'impersonal theory' but by a personal anguish (and the possible need for concealment)' caused by obsessive homoerotic desires." Cassandra Laity and Nancy K. Gish (eds.), *Gender, Desire, and Sexuality in T. S. Eliot* (Cambridge: Cambridge University Press, 2004), 9.

35 Eliot, "In Memoriam," in *Selected Essays*, 332.

36 Eliot, "Reflections on Contemporary Poetry," *The Egoist* (1919), 39. Hereafter I will cite page numbers from the essay parenthetically within the text.

37 Eliot, Preface to Simone Weil, *The Need for Roots: Prelude to a Declaration of Duties Towards Mankind* (London: Routledge, 1952), 2.

38 Michele Tepper gives a welcome treatment of this piece in "'Cells in One Body': Nation and Eros in the Early Work of T. S. Eliot," which I came across after writing this chapter. There she points out that "Critics have long stumbled over, or refused to see, the workings of desire in this essay," noting that only Colleen Lamos and Cassandra Laity have treated it in terms of its erotic metaphoricity. *Gender, Desire, and Sexuality in T. S. Eliot*, 68.

39 Homi Bhabha, *The Location of Culture* (London: Routledge, 1994), 85–92.

40 Paul Ricoeur, *History and Truth*, trans. Charles A. Kelbley (Evanston, IL: Northwestern University Press, 1965), 37.

41 Eliot, *Selected Prose*, 216.

42 Linda Hutcheon, *A Poetics of Postmodernism: History, Theory, Fiction* (New York: Routledge, 1988), 97.

43 Sigmund Freud, "Mourning and Melancholia," 1917 [1915], in *The Standard Edition of the Complete Psychological Works of Sigmund Freud*, trans. James Strachey, 24 vols. (London: Hogarth Press, 1978), vol. XIV, 243.

CHAPTER 5
VIRGINIA WOOLF, (AUTO)BIOGRAPHY, AND THE EROS OF MEMORY: READING *ORLANDO*

1 Virginia Woolf, 21 April 1928, *The Diary of Virginia Woolf*, 5 vols., ed. Anne Olivier Bell (New York: Harcourt, 1980), vol. III, 180–1.

2 Virginia Woolf, *The Waves*, 1931, ed. Molly Hite (New York: Harcourt, 2006), 88.

3 Virginia Woolf, *Orlando: A Biography*, 1928, ed. Brenda Lyons, Introduction and notes by Sandra M. Gilbert (New York: Penguin, 1993), 12. Hereafter I will cite page numbers from the novel parenthetically within the text.

4 This fact is nowhere explicitly announced in the text, and most readers at the time would have had no knowledge of Woolf and Sackville-West's affair, unless they were aware of Bloomsbury gossip. The link to the "real life" Sackville-West as the "origin" for Orlando thus functioned as a kind of open secret. More recent readers have the privilege of knowing a good deal more about Woolf's biography, and the Woolf/Sackville-West liaison is often mentioned in introductions to *Orlando*. See, for example, Sandra M. Gilbert's Introduction to the 1993 Penguin edition of *Orlando*, xi–xxxviii.

5 I take this from a letter Virginia Woolf wrote to Jacques Raverat on 26 December 1924. *The Letters of Virginia Woolf*, 6 vols., ed. Nigel Nicolson and Joanne Trautmann (New York: Harcourt, 1980), vol. VI, 150. Of a visit to Sackville-West's ancestral home at Knole early in 1927, before she had

conceived of *Orlando*, Woolf observes that Sackville-West there seemed entirely continuous with the history of English nobility:

> All the centuries seemed lit up, the past expressive, articulate; not dumb & forgotten; but a crowd of people stood behind, not dead at all; not remarkable; fair faced, long limbed; affable; & so we reach the days of Elizabeth quite easily. After tea, looking for letters of Dryden's to show me, she tumbled out a love letter of Ld Dorset's (17th century) with a lock of his soft gold tinted hair which I held in my hand a moment. One had a sense of links fished up into the light which are usually submerged.
>
> (Woolf, 23 January 1927, *Diary* vol. III, 125.)

6 Keats's letters are filled with both a desire to appreciate "the Beautiful," and a quasi-erotic captivation by the mystery and sublimity of death. In a letter to his fiancée, Fanny Brawne, he claims,

> I have two luxuries to brood over in my walks, your Loveliness and the hour of my death. O that I could have possession of them both in the same minute. I hate the world: it batters too much the wings of my self-will, and would I could take a sweet poison from your lips to send me out of it.
>
> (John Keats, 25 July 1819, *The Letters of John Keats*, two vols., ed. Hyder Edward Rollins (Cambridge: Cambridge University Press, 1958), vol. II, 133.)

In a romantic blending of eros and thanatos, invoking the mythical mixing of love and poison from *Romeo and Juliet*, Keats's letter resonates deeply with *Orlando*, which is (playfully) hyper-romantic, and obsessed with the inscrutable specter of mortality in relation to the vitality of desire.

7 Woolf, 21 December 1925, *Diary*, vol. III, 52.

8 Vita Sackville-West, 17 August 1926, in *Vita and Harold: The Letters of Vita Sackville-West and Harold Nicolson*, ed. Nigel Nicolson (New York: Putnam, 1992). Woolf experienced a number of breakdowns during her lifetime, several of which led to suicide attempts, culminating in her death by drowning in 1941. Woolf herself, as well as friends and acquaintances, occasionally referred to her emotional instability as "madness," although I think we need to resist the too-easy route of assuming a diagnosable pathology. The still-persistent and rather ubiquitous references to Woolf's "madness" in public fora, biographies, and film are astonishingly gendered. We do not, by contrast, automatically highlight the various emotional instabilities of male writers such as Joyce, Eliot, Pound, Faulkner, Proust, Fitzgerald, or Hemingway.

9 *Ibid.*, 27 September 1928.

10 In Sandra Gilbert's notes to the novel she points out, "Vita had two sons, Ben and Nigel; when they asked which of them this was supposed to be, Woolf replied, 'Both of you' . . . Neither was born on 20 March, though this date is suggestively close to 17 March (1928), when Woolf completed *Orlando*" (262). In this way Woolf again draws a parallel between writing and birthing a life. Although she had no offspring herself, *Orlando* in many senses involves a corporeal generation of textuality.

11 He is referring to Violet Keppel Trefusis, with whom Sackville-West had a long and intense love affair, dating back to early adolescence, which reached its apex

during the first years of her sons' lives. Nigel Nicolson, *Portrait of a Marriage: Vita Sackville-West and Harold Nicolson* (New York: Atheneum, 1980), 144.

12 Mark Hussey, *Virginia Woolf A to Z: A Comprehensive Reference for Students, Teachers, and Common Readers to Her Life, Work and Critical Reception* (New York: Facts on File, 1995), 59.

13 Alex Zwerdling, "Mastering the Memoir: Woolf and the Family Legacy," *Modernism/Modernity* 10.1 (2003), 176.

14 Daniel Albright, "Virginia Woolf as Autobiographer," *Kenyon Review* 6 (1984), 1.

15 Virginia Woolf, "I am Christina Rossetti," 1930, in *The Second Common Reader*, ed. Andrew McNeillie (New York: Harcourt, 1986), 237.

16 Virginia Woolf, "A Sketch of the Past," 1941, in *Moments of Being*, ed. Jeanne Schulkind (New York: Harcourt, 1985), 65.

17 Virginia Woolf, "The Memoirs of Sarah Bernhardt," 1908, in *The Essays of Virginia Woolf: 1904–1912*, ed. Andrew McNeillie (London: Hogarth Press, 1967), vol. 1, 164.

18 Roland Barthes, "Réponses" (interview), *Tel Quel* 47 (Autumn 1971), 89.

19 Virginia Woolf, "The Art of Biography," in *The Death of the Moth and Other Essays*, 1942 (London: Hogarth Press, 1947), 121.

20 Pierre Bourdieu, *The Logic of Practice*, trans. Richard Nice (Cambridge: Polity Press, 1990), 72–3.

21 Virginia Woolf, *Jacob's Room*, 1922, ed. Kate Flint (Oxford: Oxford University Press, 1992), 37.

22 Virginia Woolf, *The Years*, 1937 (New York: Penguin, 1968), 269.

23 Woolf is here intratextually (mis)quoting and inverting a phrase from her recent essay, "The New Biography," where she describes the biographic "art" as a "queer amalgamation of dream and reality, that perpetual marriage of granite and rainbow." Virginia Woolf, "The New Biography," 1927, in *Granite and Rainbow* (London: Hogarth Press, 1960), 155.

24 *Ibid.*, 150.

25 *Ibid.*, 151.

26 *Ibid.*, 149–50.

27 *Ibid.*, 150.

28 Virginia Woolf, *A Room of One's Own*, 1928 (New York: Harcourt, 1981), 4–5.

29 Michel de Certeau, *The Writing of History*, 1975, trans. Tom Conley (New York: Columbia University Press, 1988), 43.

30 Claude Lévi-Strauss, *La pensée sauvage* (Paris: Plon, 1962), 344.

31 *Ibid.*

32 Woolf, "The New Biography," 153–4.

33 Henry James, in "The Art of Fiction," in *The Art of Criticism: Henry James on the Theory and the Practice of Fiction*, ed. William Veeder and Susan M. Griffin (Chicago: University of Chicago Press, 1986), 166–7, my emphasis.

34 Woolf, "The New Biography," 155.

35 In a writer who is endlessly preoccupied with the workings of memory, it is not too surprising a coincidence (or confluence of preoccupations) that

biographies on Virginia Woolf have proliferated over the last decades, to the point of creating and self-perpetuating a cult of personality around the auratic figure of "Virginia Woolf." These biographies have in part exploited and in part criticized the popular image of Woolf as a half-crazed, brilliant woman author, whose sapphic or bisexual leanings lend fascination to a major figure who was significant not only for her contribution to twentieth-century letters, but also for her part in the Bloomsbury group. There is not space here for a full discussion of the biographies of Virginia Woolf, but two of the most influential studies remain Quentin Bell's *Virginia Woolf: A Biography* (London: Random House, 1972), and Hermione Lee's *Virginia Woolf* (New York: Vintage, 1997).

36 Woolf, 8 August 1926, *Letters*, vol. III, 285.

37 Nicolson, *Portrait of a Marriage*, 202–3.

38 Lines 99-102, in *T. S. Eliot: The Complete Poems and Plays* (London: Faber and Faber, 1990). All subsequent quotations from Eliot's poetry are taken from this source and in each instance I will give line numbers parenthetically in the text.

39 Woolf uses rather irregular punctuation in her diaries, letters, and drafts. Instead of marking every single instance with "sic," if a section of her prose contains more than one irregularity I will signify that it was written thus at the end of the passage.

40 Woolf, 20 September 1927, *Diary*, vol. III, 157.

41 Woolf, 9 October 1927, *Letters*, vol. III, 428–9. The parenthetical insertions, apart from "sic," are as they appear in the edited letters.

42 Woolf, 31 January 1928, *Letters*, vol. III, 454, my emphasis.

43 Woolf, 20 September 1927, *Diary*, vol. III, 157.

44 Woolf, 24 January 1933, *Letters*, vol. V, 153.

45 Virginia Woolf, "Professions for Women," in *The Death of the Moth*, 1931 (New York: Harcourt, 1970), 241.

46 Elena Gualtieri, *Virginia Woolf's Essays: Sketching the Past* (Basingstoke: Macmillan, 2000), 32.

47 "Byron and Mr. Briggs," 1922, in *The Essays of Virginia Woolf: 1919–1924*, ed. Andrew McNeillie (London: Hogarth Press, 1967), vol. III, 477–80.

48 Woolf, *A Room of One's Own*, 78.

49 Virginia Woolf, *Between the Acts*, ed. Stella McNichol, Introduction and notes by Gillian Beer (New York: Penguin, 1992), 106.

50 Woolf, "Sketch," 72.

51 Virginia Woolf, *To the Lighthouse*, 1927, Foreword by Eudora Welty (New York: Harcourt, 1981), 172.

52 Henri Bergson, *Matter and Memory*, trans. N. M. Paul and W. S. Palmer, from 5th edn. of 1908 (New York: Zone Books, 1991), 33. Despite their resonant philosophical overlaps, Woolf may not have read Bergson – a point that Jörg Hasler argues in his article, "Virginia Woolf and the Chimes of Big Ben," *English Studies: A Journal of English Language and Literature* 63 (1982), 146. Nevertheless, Bergson's ideas had been sufficiently popularized during

the first decades of the century that Woolf would almost certainly have come across his major premises.

53 Virginia Woolf, "Phases of Fiction," in *The Essays of Virginia Woolf: 1912–1918*, ed. Andrew McNeillie (London: Hogarth Press, 1967), vol. II, 56; my emphasis.

54 *Ibid.*, 55.

55 Virginia Woolf, "Modern Fiction," 1925, in *The Common Reader*, ed. Andrew McNeillie (New York: Harcourt, 1984), 150.

56 The temptation to turn "memory" out of the house recalls Woolf's slightly later polemical attempts to be rid of another feminized cultural figure: in her 1931 essay "Professions for Women," Woolf seeks to banish the "angel of the house" – a do-good woman trained and conditioned to please the men around her above all else. The home in each of these examples signifies the starting place, and it is striking to see how often Woolf takes recourse to metaphors of expunging, banishing, or cleaning the unwanted from the domestic sphere. We might also think of the "Time Passes" section of *To the Lighthouse* where, as I explore below, hired female help take on the task of clearing the domestic space of years of debris and the damage of time to create a tabula rasa on whose stage and environs the upper-middle-class Ramsay family will undertake a belated journey of psychic healing.

57 Woolf, 15 September 1921, *Diary*, vol. II, 138.

58 We might compare Orlando's wish for posterity with those of Mr. Ramsay in *To the Lighthouse*, who exhorts, "The very stone one kicks with one's boot will outlast Shakespeare." Woolf, *To the Lighthouse*, 35.

59 *Ibid.*, 7.

60 *Ibid.*, 139.

61 *Ibid.*, 136.

62 *Ibid.*, 140, my emphasis.

63 Adam Phillips, *On Flirtation* (London: Faber and Faber, 1994), 22.

64 Freud, *Civilization and Its Discontents*, 1930*a* [1929], in *The Standard Edition of the Complete Psychological Works of Sigmund Freud*, trans. James Strachey, 24 vols. (London: Hogarth Press, 1978), vol. XXI, 69.

65 Henri Bergson, *Creative Evolution*, 1907, trans. Arthur Mitchell (New York: Modern Library, 1944), 7.

66 Phillips, *On Flirtation*, 24.

67 *Ibid.*, 29.

68 Freud, "Remembering, Repeating, and Working Through," 1914*g*, in *The Standard Edition*, vol. XII, 147 and ff.

69 Freud, *Civilization*, 71.

70 *Ibid.*, 72.

71 Phillips, *On Flirtation*, 23.

72 Friedrich Nietzsche, "On the Utility and Liability of History for Life," in *Unfashionable Observations*, trans. Richard T. Gray (Stanford: Stanford University Press, 1995), 86–7, and 96.

73 Marcel Proust, *Remembrance of Things Past: The Captive, The Fugitive, and Time Regained*, trans. C. K. Scott Moncrieff and Terence Kilmartin (New York: Vintage, 1982), 47–8.
74 For an especially good discussion of the widely debated issue of time in relation to "involuntary" and "voluntary" memory in Proust, see Richard Duràn's "Fourth-Dimensional Time and Proust's *A la recherche du temps perdu*," *South Atlantic Quarterly* 56.2 (1991), 73–90.
75 Freud, *Civilization*, 69.
76 Woolf, 11 September 1923, *Diary*, vol. II, 268.
77 Proust, *Remembrance*, 51.
78 Virginia Woolf, *Mrs. Dalloway*, 1925, ed. Mark Hussey, annotated and Introduction by Bonnie Kime Scott (New York: Harcourt, 2005), 149.
79 Woolf, *The Waves*, 96.
80 Woolf, *To the Lighthouse*, 135. Woolf frequently turns to the trope of "ruins" in her writing. In *To the Lighthouse* it is Mrs. Ramsay's task to stave off the "ruin" Mr. Ramsay constantly threatens to bring down upon their domestic peace – "she was relieved to find that the ruin was veiled; domesticity triumphed" (31); and it is Lily Briscoe's task to stay the "ruin" and the "chaos" that "approached" every time Mr. Ramsay comes near her painting in progress (148).
81 Freud, *Civilization*, 69–70.
82 *Ibid.*, 71.
83 Woolf, "Sketch," 67.
84 Woolf, *The Waves*, 129.

CHAPTER 6
OTHER KINDS OF AUTOBIOGRAPHIES: SKETCHING THE PAST, FORGETTING FREUD, AND REACHING THE LIGHTHOUSE

1 Virginia Woolf, *A Passionate Apprentice: The Early Journals, 1897–1909*, ed. Mitchel A. Leaska (New York: Harcourt, 1990), 178–9.
2 Virginia Woolf, *The Years*, 1937 (New York: Penguin, 1968), 344.
3 Virginia Woolf, "A Sketch of the Past," 1941, in *Moments of Being*, ed. Jeanne Schulkind (New York: Harcourt, 1985), 70 and ff. Hereafter I will cite page numbers from the memoir parenthetically within the text.
4 Sigmund Freud, "Beyond the Pleasure Principle," 1920g, in *The Standard Edition of the Complete Psychological Works of Sigmund Freud*, trans. James Strachey, 24 vols. (London: Hogarth Press, 1978), vol. XVIII, 52.
5 See, for example, Virginia Woolf, 1 and 9 November 1939, in *The Diary of Virginia Woolf*, 6 vols., ed. Anne Olivier Bell (New York: Harcourt, 1980), vol. V, 244, 245.
6 Woolf, 6 December 1936, *Diary*, vol. VI, 90.
7 Anne Olivier Bell, footnote, Woolf, 6 March 1920, *Diary*, vol. II, 23.
8 S. P. Rosenbaum, ed., *The Bloomsbury Group: A Collection of Memoirs and Commentary* (Toronto: University of Toronto Press, 1995), xi.

9 Woolf, 18 March 1920, *Diary*, vol. II, 26.
10 Woolf, 5 December 1920, *Diary*, vol. II, 77.
11 Woolf, "Old Bloomsbury," in *Moments of Being*, 181.
12 See, for example, Woolf, 20 January 1919, *Diary*, vol. I, 234; 15 September 1924, *Diary*, vol. II, 314; 8 February 1926, *Diary*, vol. III, 58; and 3 February 1927, *Diary*, vol. III, 125.
13 Alex Zwerdling, "Mastering the Memoir: Woolf and the Family Legacy," *Modernism/Modernity* 10.1 (2003), 168.
14 Virginia Woolf, 26 December 1924, *The Letters of Virginia Woolf*, 6 vols., ed. Nigel Nicolson and Joanne Trautmann (New York: Harcourt, 1980), vol. VI, 150. In Zwerdling's article he traces Woolf's proclivity to life writing through several generations to Woolf's great-grandfather, James Stephen, who wrote his memoirs between 1819 and 1825. In addition to listing other relatives who composed autobiographies, he reminds us that besides acting in his capacity as editor of *The Dictionary of National Biography*, Woolf's father, Sir Leslie Stephen, wrote an "official biography of his distinguished brother Sir James Fitzjames Stephen" when Woolf was thirteen, and a "private memoir of his wife Julia for the audience of their children." *Ibid.*, 168.
15 Woolf, 15 September 1924, *Diary*, vol. II, 314.
16 Virginia Woolf, *Jacob's Room*, 1922, ed. Kate Flint (Oxford: Oxford University Press, 1992), 48.
17 Kate Flint, note to *ibid.*, 249.
18 Virginia Woolf, *A Room of One's Own*, 1928 (New York: Harcourt, 1981), 53.
19 *Ibid.*, 86.
20 *Ibid.*, 89.
21 Virginia Woolf, *Women and Fiction: The Manuscript Versions of A Room of One's Own*, 1929, ed. S. P. Rosenbaum (Oxford: Blackwell, 1992), 44.
22 Virginia Woolf, *Three Guineas*, 1938 (New York: Harcourt, 1966), 63.
23 Virginia Woolf, *Roger Fry: A Biography*, 1940 (London: Harcourt, 1968), 11.
24 Virginia Woolf, "The Art of Biography," in *The Death of the Moth and Other Essays*, 1942 (London: Hogarth Press, 1947), 120.
25 Cathy Caruth, *Unclaimed Experience: Trauma, Narrative, and History* (Baltimore: Johns Hopkins University Press, 1996), 61.
26 *Ibid.*, 62.
27 Woolf, 12 October 1940, *Diary*, vol. V, 329.
28 Hermione Lee, *Virginia Woolf* (New York: Vintage, 1997), 83.
29 Virginia Woolf, *To the Lighthouse*, 1927, Foreword by Eudora Welty (New York: Harcourt, 1981), 209.
30 I am indebted here to Eric Santner, whose brilliant work in *On Creaturely Life* (Chicago: University of Chicago Press, 2006) helped me to see this connection to Barthes's notion of the *punctum*. For my understanding of Benjamin and shock, I also want to thank Eduardo Cadava for his compelling work on Benjamin and photography in *Words of Light: Theses on the Photography of History* (Princeton: Princeton University Press, 1997).

31 T. S. Eliot, "The Metaphysical Poets," 1921, in *The Selected Prose of T. S. Eliot*, ed. Frank Kermode (New York: Harcourt, 1988), 64.

32 This is not the only time that Woolf claims a greater realness of the past. Among other instances, we might consider a letter she writes to Ethel Smyth: "Did I tell you Bertie Russell has sent us, to publish, his fathers and mothers old letters – sweepings of old desks – 2,000 pages: so fascinating and tragic, I live almost as much with the Amberleys in the 80[ties] as here and now." Woolf, 18 September 1936, *Letters*, 73.

33 Henri Bergson, *The Perception of Change: Conferences Given at the University of Oxford the 26 and 27 May 1911* (Oxford: Clarendon Press, 1911), 28.

34 *Ibid.*, 35.

35 Virginia Woolf, *Orlando: A Biography*, 1928, ed. Brenda Lyons, Introduction and notes by Sandra M. Gilbert (New York: Penguin, 1993), 200.

36 Woolf, *A Room of One's Own*, 14.

37 Virginia Woolf, 11 and 13 May 1936, *The Letters of Virginia Woolf*, 6 vols., ed. Nigel Nicolson and Joanne Trautmann (New York: Harcourt, 1980), vol. VI, 39.

38 For an insightful article that resists this paradigm, see Molly Hite's "Virginia Woolf's Two Bodies," *Genders* 31 (2000): 1–23, which posits that Woolf constructed two types of bodies, one that is "cast in social roles and bound by the laws of social interaction," and another "visionary body" that is extra-social and beyond "the societal consequences of female eroticism that had shaped the romance plot" (1).

39 See Louise de Salvo's *Virginia Woolf: The Impact of Childhood Sexual Abuse on Her Life and Work* (New York: Ballantine, 1989) on the topic of Woolf's early sexual traumas.

40 Woolf, 9 October 1927, *Letters*, vol. III, 428.

41 Decades later, when writing his own autobiography, Leonard Woolf touchingly mirrors and repeats this chain of mnemonic effects when he recalls Woolf's ecstatic delight in revisiting her childhood memories: Cornwall "remained in her memory as summer days of immaculate happiness. *To the Lighthouse* is bathed in the light of this happiness and, whenever she returned to Cornwall, she recaptured some of it." Leonard Woolf, *Sowing: An Autobiography of the Years 1880–1904* (New York: Harcourt, 1988), 166.

42 Avrom Fleishman, *Figures of Autobiography: The Language of Self-Writing in Victorian and Modern England* (Berkeley: University of California Press, 1983).

43 Woolf, 11 February 1928, *Diary*, vol. III, 174.

44 Roland Barthes, *Barthes par Barthes* (Paris: Éditions du Seuil, 1975), 103 and 107; this translation is taken from Barthes, *The Rustle of Language*, trans. Richard Howard (New York: Hill and Wang, 1986).

45 Virginia Woolf, *Mrs. Dalloway*, 1925, ed. Mark Hussey, annotations and Introduction by Bonnie Kime Scott (New York: Harcourt, 2005), 167.

46 Freud, "Screen Memories," 1899*a*, in *The Standard Edition*, vol. III, 317. James Strachey's note gives us the translation from Virgil's *Aeneid*, I, 203.

47 Freud, "Screen Memories," in *The Standard Edition*, vol. III, 321 and 305.

48 *Ibid.*, 305.

49 *Ibid.*, 322.
50 Freud, "Leonardo da Vinci and a Memory of his Childhood," 1910, in *The Standard Edition*, vol. XI, 83.
51 Woolf, *To the Lighthouse*, 4.
52 Woolf, *A Room of One's Own*, 11, 31.
53 Woolf, *Mrs. Dalloway*, 103.
54 Woolf, 29 January 1939, *Diary*, vol. v, 202.
55 Woolf, 2 December 1939, *Diary*, vol. v, 248.
56 Elizabeth Abel, *Virginia Woolf and the Fictions of Psychoanalysis* (Chicago: University of Chicago Press, 1989), 13.
57 Woolf, 11 November 1936, *Diary*, vol. v, 32.
58 Virginia Woolf, "Freudian Fiction," 1920, in *The Essays of Virginia Woolf: 1919–1924*, ed. Andrew McNeillie (London: Hogarth Press, 1967), vol. III, 196–7.
59 *Ibid.*, 197.
60 Woolf, 2 October 1924, *Letters*, vol. III, 134–5.
61 Freud, "Obsessive Actions and Religious Practices," 1907*b*, in *The Standard Edition*, vol. IX, 120. I am most grateful to Eva Badowska for pointing this reference out to me.
62 Woolf, 8 December 1939, *Diary*, vol. v, 249.
63 Woolf, 28 November 1928, *Diary*, vol. III, 208.
64 William Wordsworth, *The Prelude*, in *William Wordsworth*, ed. Stephen Gill (Oxford: Oxford University Press, 1984), Book Second, lines 346–52.
65 *Ibid.*, line 311.
66 James Joyce, *Stephen Hero*, ed. Theodore Spencer, rev. edn. John J. Slocum and Herbert Cahoon (London: Jonathan Cape, 1960), 216.
67 *Ibid.*
68 *Ibid.*
69 James Joyce, *A Portrait of the Artist as a Young Man*, ed. R. B. Kershner (New York: Bedford Books, 1993), 152.
70 William Wordsworth, "Lines Written a Few Miles Above Tintern Abbey," in *Selected Poetry*, eds. Stephen Gill and Duncan Wu (Oxford: Oxford University Press, 1997), line 49. Slavoj Žižek offers a compelling reading of Kant that might help us understand the *necessary* brevity of such "moments of being." He suggests that this temporal limitation is in fact fundamental to human being and "moral freedom," since overcoming the abyss that separates us from noumena, or, as he phrases it, "Things in themselves," would lead to "catastrophic consequences": "men would *lose* their moral freedom and/or transcendental spontaneity; they would turn into lifeless puppets." *The Ticklish Subject: The Absent Centre of Political Ontology* (London: Verso, 1999), 25. In Woolf's case we might say that the mystery of the space of separation between being and an ideation of ontology animates and charges her with the ethical responsibility and turn to writing.
71 Jacques Lacan, *The Language of the Self: The Function of Language in Psychoanalysis*, trans. Anthony Wilden (Baltimore: Johns Hopkins University Press, 1968), 161.

72 Woolf, 4 September 1927, *Diary*, vol. III, 154.
73 Woolf, *Orlando*, 124.
74 Ann Banfield, *The Phantom Table: Woolf, Fry, Russell and the Epistemology of Modernism* (Cambridge: Cambridge University Press, 2000).
75 Fleishman, *Figures of Autobiography*, 467.
76 Paul Veyne, *Writing History: Essay on Epistemology*, 1971, trans. Mina Moore-Rinvolucri (Middletown, CT: Wesleyan University Press, 1984), 11.
77 Henri Bergson, *Matter and Memory*, trans. N. M. Paul and W. S. Palmer (New York: Zone Books, 1991), 13 and 22.
78 *Ibid.*, 24.
79 *Ibid.*, 67.
80 Lines 240-3, in *T. S. Eliot: The Complete Poems and Plays* (London: Faber and Faber, 1990).
81 Woolf, 24 February 1926, *Diary*, vol. III, 61.
82 Lee, *Virginia Woolf*, 436.
83 Woolf, 20 May 1938, *Diary*, vol. V, 141.
84 *Ibid.*
85 Woolf, 27 June 1925, *Diary*, vol. III, 34.
86 Woolf, 18 February 1928, *Diary*, vol. III, 176.
87 Woolf, 28 May 1929, *Diary*, vol. III, 229.
88 Woolf, 9 October 1927, *Letters*, vol. III, 429.
89 Woolf, *To the Lighthouse*, 3. All subsequent references will be given parenthetically in the text.
90 For a wonderful discussion of temporality in *To the Lighthouse*, see Dominick LaCapra's chapter, "History, Time, and the Novel: Reading Woolf's *To the Lighthouse*," in LaCapra, *History, Politics, and the Novel* (Ithaca, NY: Cornell University Press, 1987).
91 Eliot, "The Dry Salvages," lines 57-62, in *The Complete Poems and Plays.*
92 Slavoj Žižek, "Melancholy and the Act," *Critical Inquiry* 26 (2000), 658.
93 Woolf, 15 September 1924, *Diary*, vol. II, 314.
94 Abel, *Virginia Woolf*, 49.

CHAPTER 7
REMEMBERING WHAT HAS "ALMOST ALREADY BEEN FORGOTTEN": WHERE MEMORY TOUCHES HISTORY

1 Henri Bergson, "Introduction to Metaphysics," in *Creative Evolution*, trans. Mabelle L. Andison (New York: The Philosophical Library, 1946), 192–3.
2 Virginia Woolf, *The Diary of Virginia Woolf*, 5 vols., ed. Anne Olivier Bell (New York: Harcourt, 1980), vol. III, 5.
3 H. D., *Tribute to Freud*, 1944 (New York: New Directions, 1974), v.
4 Woolf, 30 October 1918, *Diary*, vol. I, 211.
5 In England and Canada, 11 November, the anniversary of the Armistice, is celebrated each year as "Remembrance Day," offering a different cultural valence from the American "Veterans' Day" that marks the same event. In

the English and Canadian versions one is asked to "remember," although the object of remembrance is not specified: its metaphoric reach recalls both the dead and the general tragedy of war. The American version specifically invites one to think of the actual soldiers (the veterans) – both returned and killed in action – who served. The latter relies on representation, naming, and synecdoche; the former on a more generalized appeal to recollection.

6 Virginia Woolf, "The Art of Biography," in *The Death of the Moth and Other Essays*, 1942 (London: Hogarth Press, 1947), 121.

7 Woolf, 16 December 1918, *Diary*, vol. I, 227. We find, too, on 11 November 1936, a diary entry that begins, "Armistice day – completely forgotten. by us" [*sic*]. *Diary*, vol. V, 32.

8 Virginia Woolf, *Mrs. Dalloway*, 1925, ed. Mark Hussey, annotated and Introduction by Bonnie Kime Scott (New York: Harcourt, 2005), 126.

9 Woolf, 9 November 1918, *Diary*, vol. I, 215.

10 Jean-François Lyotard, *The Postmodern Condition: A Report on Knowledge*, trans. Geoff Bennington and Brian Massumi (Minneapolis: University of Minnesota Press, 1984).

11 Paul Fussell, *The Great War and Modern Memory* (New York: Oxford University Press, 1975), 316.

12 Woolf, 13 March 1921, *Diary*, vol. II, 100. The parenthetical question mark appears in the edited diary.

13 Virginia Woolf, *Orlando: A Biography*, 1928, ed. Brenda Lyons, Introduction and notes by Sandra M. Gilbert (New York: Penguin, 1993), 210.

14 Woolf, 12 July 1919, *Diary*, vol. I, 291.

15 Woolf, 19 July 1919, *Diary*, vol. I, 292. Again, instead of marking every instance of irregular punctuation etc. in a particular extract, I will mark "*sic*" at the end of the extract.

16 Woolf, 22 September 1928, *Diary*, vol. III, 197–8.

17 Woolf, 11 May 1926, *Diary*, vol. III, 83.

18 Rupert Brooke, "The Soldier," lines 1-3, in *The Poetical Works of Rupert Brooke*, 2nd edn. (London: Faber and Faber, 1970).

19 In an odd twist of circumstance, Brooke died not in battle, but of blood poisoning on a troopship en route to the ill-fated Gallipoli conflict on the northern shore of the Dardanelles.

20 Woolf, 5 May 1919, *Diary*, vol. I, 269.

21 *Ibid.*

22 Woolf, 9 July 1918, *Diary*, vol. I, 164.

23 Virginia Woolf, 30 June 1897, in *A Passionate Apprentice: The Early Journals 1897–1909 Virginia Woolf*, ed. Mitchell Leaska (London: Hogarth Press, 1990), 108.

24 Woolf, 22 January 1922, *Diary*, vol. II, 158.

25 Cited in James Joyce, *Ulysses*, 1922 (New York: Penguin, 1992), 981.

26 Jacques Lacan, "The Subversion of the Subject and the Dialectic of Desire in the Freudian Unconscious," in *Ecrits*, trans. Alan Sheridan (New York: Norton, 1977), 309.

27 Cathy Caruth, *Unclaimed Experience: Trauma, Narrative, and History* (Baltimore: Johns Hopkins University Press, 1996), 27.

28 Lynn Hunt, "History as Gesture; or, the Scandal of History," in *Consequences of Theory*, eds. Jonathan Arac and Barbara Johnson (Baltimore: Johns Hopkins University Press, 1991), 103.

29 Gillian Beer, *Virginia Woolf: The Common Ground* (Ann Arbor: University of Michigan Press, 1996), 7.

30 *Ibid.*, 8.

31 *Ibid.*

32 Virginia Woolf, "The War from the Street," 1919, in *The Essays of Virginia Woolf*, ed. Andrew McNeillie (London: Hogarth Press, 1967), vol. III, 3.

33 Woolf, 18 February 1921, *Diary*, vol. II, 92.

34 Woolf, 29 April 1921, *Diary*, vol. II, 115.

35 Virginia Woolf, *A Room of One's Own*, 1928 (New York: Harcourt, 1981), 108–9.

36 Elena Gualtieri, *Virginia Woolf's Essays: Sketching the Past* (Basingstoke: Macmillan, 2000), 32. For a period of many months in 1936–7, Woolf was entranced with the historian Edward Gibbon, contributing a centenary piece on him to the *Times Literary Supplement*, planning visits to both his former home and his grave site, and expressing admiration for his prose: "I'm off to see Gibbons [*sic*] grave in a Sussex Churchyard . . . Now I think and dream and live in the august shade. If only I could write like that too!" Woolf, "Christmas Eve" 1936, in *The Letters of Virginia Woolf*, 6 vols., eds. Nigel Nicolson and Joanne Trautmann (New York: Harcourt, 1980), vol. VI, 93. Her delight in Gibbon was sustained, and she writes to Lady Ottoline Morrell nearly six months later, "I've been reading Gibbon: the Autobiography, the history, with the greatest joy. And his letters." 6 May 1937, *Letters*, vol. VI, 127.

37 Woolf, 12 September 1940, *Diary*, vol. V, 318.

38 Woolf, *A Room of One's Own*, 45.

39 *Ibid.*

40 *Ibid.*, 89.

41 *Ibid.*

42 Merry M. Pawlowski (ed.), *Virginia Woolf and Fascism: Resisting the Dictator's Seduction* (New York: Palgrave, 2001), 4.

43 Mary Jacobus, *First Things: The Maternal Imaginary in Literature, Art, and Psychoanalysis* (New York: Routledge, 1995), 279.

44 Walter Benjamin, "Theses on the Philosophy of History," in *Illuminations: Essays and Reflections*, ed. Hannah Arendt, trans. Harry Zohn (New York: Schocken, 1968), 254.

45 Michel Foucault, "Nietzsche, Genealogy, History," in *Language, Counter-Memory, Practice: Selected Essays and Interviews*, trans. and ed. Donald F. Bouchard (Ithaca, NY: Cornell University Press, 1977), 139–40.

46 Simon Schama, *Landscape and Memory* (Toronto: Vintage, 1995), 61.

47 Michel Foucault, *The Order of Things: An Archaeology of the Human Sciences*, 1970 (New York: Vintage, 1994), xv.

48 *Ibid.*, xvii.
49 For an excellent discussion of *Between the Acts* in relation to historicity and the pageant, see Joshua D. Esty, "Amnesia in the Fields: Late Modernism, Late Imperialism, and the English Pageant-Play," *ELH* 69.1 (2002), 245–76.
50 T. S. Eliot, "Tradition and the Individual Talent," 1919, in *T. S. Eliot: Selected Essays* (London: Faber and Faber, 1999), 15.
51 *Ibid.*, 16.
52 Virginia Woolf, *Between the Acts*, 1941, ed. Stella McNichol, Introduction and notes by Gillian Beer (New York: Penguin, 1992), 5. Hereafter I will cite page numbers from the novel parenthetically within the text.
53 Sigmund Freud, *Civilization and Its Discontents*, 1930*a* [1929], in *The Standard Edition of the Complete Psychological Works of Sigmund Freud*, trans. James Strachey, 24 vols. (London: Hogarth Press, 1978), vol. XXI, 69–70.
54 Walter Benjamin, *Reflections: Essays, Aphorisms, Autobiographical Writings*, ed. Peter Demetz, trans. Edmund Jephcott (New York: Schocken, 1978), 28–9.
55 Claude Lévi-Strauss, *Tristes tropiques* (Paris: Union générale d'éditions, 1962), 44.
56 Woolf, 8 June 1920, *Diary*, vol. II, 47.
57 Woolf, Post Script, 12 September 1940, *Letters*, vol. VI, 431.
58 My thinking on the matter of a future anterior of mourning emerged partly out of a conversation with Eric Santner.
59 Charlton T. Lewis and Charles Short, eds., *Latin Dictionary Founded on Andrew's Edition of Freund's Latin Dictionary*, 1879 (Oxford: Clarendon Press, 2002).
60 Woolf here is blurring fiction with details from her life, as she often did. In her letters while she was drafting *Between the Acts*, she makes frequent references to a "village play" being staged in Rodmell, Sussex – the hamlet in Sussex where Virginia and Leonard lived when they were not in London. The Woolfs spent a great deal of time there in the last two years of Woolf's life, after the outbreak of the Second World War, even though they were subject to frequent German air raids. Woolf writes to Ethel Smyth, "We had a fête: also a village play. The sirens sounded in the middle. All the mothers sat stolid. I also admired that very much." Woolf, 11 September 1940, *Letters*, vol. VI, 430.
61 Homi Bhabha, ed., *Nation and Narration* (New York: Routledge, 1990), 143.
62 T. S. Eliot, "Tradition and the Individual Talent," 1919, in *T. S. Eliot: Selected Essays* (London: Faber and Faber, 1999), 14.
63 Benjamin, *Reflections*, 30.
64 This writing outside the city is a gesture that several of Woolf's novels share, including *The Voyage Out*, *To the Lighthouse*, *Orlando*, *The Waves*, and for much of it, *Jacob's Room*. In *Between the Acts*, only one character, Giles Oliver, works "in the city," but "Given his choice, he would have chosen to farm" (30).
65 *Between the Acts*, 135, note 40.
66 Marcel Proust, *On Reading*, 1905 (London: Penguin, 1995), 3. See also Marcel Proust, *Sur la lecture* (Marseilles: Actes Sud, 1988), 9.

67 Proust, *On Reading*, 4 and *Sur la lecture*, 9–10.
68 Woolf, 30 October 1918, *Diary*, vol. I, 211.
69 Julia Briggs, "The Novels of the 1930s and the Impact of History," in *The Cambridge Companion to Virginia Woolf*, ed. Sue Roe and Susan Sellers (Cambridge: Cambridge University Press, 2000), 85.
70 *Between the Acts*, 140, note 94.
71 Beer, *Ibid.*, xxix.
72 Lines 26-7, in *T. S. Eliot: The Complete Poems and Plays* (London: Faber and Faber, 1990).
73 Lines 234-8, in *ibid.*
74 Virginia Woolf, *Jacob's Room*, 1922, ed. Kate Flint (Oxford: Oxford University Press, 1992), 63.
75 Friedrich Nietzsche, "On the Utility and Liability of History for Life," in *Unfashionable Observations*, trans. Richard T. Gray (Stanford: Stanford University Press, 1995), 86.
76 Walter Benjamin, *The Arcades Project*, trans. Howard Eiland and Kevin McLaughlin (Cambridge, MA: Harvard University Press, 1999), 45.
77 Eliot, *The Waste Land*, lines 13-14, in *The Complete Poems and Plays.*
78 For a highly original study of the voice – including its linguistics, metaphysics, physics, ethics, and politics – see Mladen Dolar's *A Voice and Nothing More* (Cambridge, MA: Massachusetts Institute of Technology Press, 2006).
79 In her note to the text, Gillian Beer posits that this text is a combination of H. G. Wells's *The Outline of History: Being a Plain History of Life and Mankind* (1920) and G. M. Trevelyan's *History of England* (1926).
80 Harold Bloom, *The Anxiety of Influence: A Theory of Poetry* (Oxford: Oxford University Press, 1973).
81 Woolf, *Mrs. Dalloway*, 89.
82 Woolf, *Orlando*, 67–8.
83 Virginia Woolf, *To the Lighthouse*, 1927, Foreword by Eudora Welty (New York: Harcourt, 1981), 139.
84 Woolf, 11 May 1929, *Letters*, vol. IV, 56.
85 Mark Hussey, *Virginia Woolf A to Z: A Comprehensive Reference for Students, Teachers, and Common Readers to Her Life, Work and Critical Reception* (New York: Facts on File, 1995), 215.

EPILOGUE

1 Virginia Woolf, "I am Christina Rossetti," 1930, in *The Second Common Reader*, ed. Andrew McNeillie (London: Harcourt, 1986), 237.
2 Jacques Lacan, "The Subversion of the Subject and the Dialectic of Desire in the Freudian Unconscious," *Ecrits*, trans. Alan Sheridan (New York: Norton, 1977), 301.
3 Virginia Woolf, *Orlando: A Biography*, 1928, ed. Brenda Lyons, Introduction and notes by Sandra M. Gilbert (New York: Penguin, 1993), 225.

4 Paul Ricoeur, *History and Truth*, trans. Charles A. Kelbley (Evanston, IL: Northwestern University Press, 1965), 24.
5 *Ibid.*
6 Line 238, in *T. S. Eliot: The Complete Poems and Plays* (London: Faber and Faber, 1990).
7 T. S. Eliot, "Tradition and the Individual Talent," 1919, in *T. S. Eliot: Selected Essays*, (London: Faber and Faber, 1999), 15.
8 Virginia Woolf, "A Sketch of the Past," 1941, in *Moments of Being*, ed. Jeanne Schulkind (New York: Harcourt, 1985), 98.
9 Eliot, *The Waste Land*, line 430, in *The Complete Poems and Plays.*
10 Virginia Woolf, 10 September 1928, *The Diary of Virginia Woolf*, 5 vols., ed. Anne Olivier Bell (New York: Harcourt, 1980), vol. III, 195.
11 Harold Bloom, *Marcel Proust's Remembrance of Things Past* (New York: Chelsea House, 1987), 17.
12 Eliot, *The Waste Land*, lines 19-20, in *The Complete Poems and Plays.*
13 Henri Bergson, *Matter and Memory*, trans. N. M. Paul and W. S. Palmer (New York: Zone Books, 1991), 136.
14 Paul Veyne, *Writing History: Essay on Epistemology*, 1971, trans. Mina Moore Rinvolucri (Middletown, CT: Wesleyan University Press, 1984), 12.
15 Michel de Certeau, *The Writing of History*, 1975, trans. Tom Conley (New York: Columbia University Press, 1988), 21.
16 Woolf, 10 September 1921, *Diary*, vol. II, 135.
17 Eliot, "East Coker," lines 196-8, in *The Complete Poems and Plays.*
18 Woolf, "A Sketch of the Past," 98.

Index

19797803R00162

Printed in Great Britain
by Amazon